W9-BKY-923

Franco Moretti, born in 1950, is professor of English Literature at the University of Salerno. He has edited and intro-
duced an anthology of criticism on T. S. Eliot (Rome 1975),
and written a study of English left-wing intellectuals in the
thirties (*Letteratura e ideologie negli anni Trenta inglesi*, Bari
1976). He is an editor of the journals *calibano* and *Quaderni
Piacentini*, and is at present working on a study of the European *Bildungsroman* from Goethe to Flaubert.

Franco Moretti

NLB

Signs Taken For Wonders

**Essays in the Sociology of
Literary Forms**

WITHDRAWN
FROM
UNIVERSITY OF PENNSYLVANIA
LIBRARIES

*Translated by
Susan Fischer
David Forgacs
David Miller*

UNIVERSITY
OF
PENNSYLVANIA
LIBRARIES

PN
51
M67
1983

The fourth, fifth, seventh and last of the essays collected
here were translated by Susan Fischer; the first, third and
sixth by David Forgacs; the second by David Miller.

First published 1983
© Franco Moretti 1983

Verso Editions and NLB
15 Greek Street, London W1

Filmset in Times Roman by
Preface Ltd
Salisbury, Wilts

Printed in Great Britain by
The Thetford Press Ltd
Thetford, Norfolk

UNIVERSITY
OF
PENNSYLVANIA
LIBRARIES

Contents

83-B319491

Acknowledgements

'The Soul and the Harpy' was written specifically for this volume; a somewhat shorter version hs been published in *Quaderni Piacentini*, 5, 1982. 'The Long Goodbye' appeared in *Studi Inglesi*, 3–4, 1976–77; 'Dialectics of Fear' in *calibano*, 2, 1978; 'Clues' as the introduction to the volume *Polizieschi Classici*, Rome 1978; 'The Great Eclipse' in *calibano*, 4, 1979 (and, in partial translation, in *Genre*, fall, 1982); 'From the Waste Land to the Artificial Paradise' in *calibano*, 5, 1980; 'Kindergarten' in *calibano*, 6, 1981; 'Homo Palpitans' in *Quaderni Piacentini*, 3, 1981. I wish to thank Agostino Lombardo, editor of *Studi Inglesi*, the editorial boards of *calibano*, *Quaderni Piacentini*, and *Genre*, and Savelli Editore for their permission to reprint these essays here.

In the course of time, many friends have offered suggestions and objections, and some of them have been patient enough to discuss with me virtually all of my work: they are Perry Anderson, Pierluigi Battista, Paola Colaiacomo, David A. Miller, Francis Mulhern, Fernando Vianello, and Niccolò Zapponi. I feel greatly indebted to all of them, the more so because my stubbornness in rejecting good advice must have been quite trying.

Finally, a special thanks to David Forgacs, Susan A. Fischer, and David A. Miller. My Italian is very idiomatic and colloquial: I like it that way, but have realized how much this fact complicates things for translation. Yet the English text has turned out to be excellent: if the general tone is slightly more 'highbrow' than that of the Italian, more than once Forgac's, Fischer's, and Miller's choices have helped me to clarify and, I hope, improve local points of the original draft.

The Soul and the Harpy

Reflections on the Aims
and Methods of Literary
Historiography

> Forme is power.
> (Hobbes, *Leviathan*)

Introductions always get written last, perhaps years after some of the work they are supposed to 'introduce'. Rereading one's own work, one immediately notices mistakes and gaps, the ideas that seem so obvious now but which then – God knows why – seemed impossible to grasp. One would like to discard everything and start afresh – or at least look forward, not back, and pursue what has not yet been done, without worrying about making presentable what has long since been left behind.

In short, immediately one starts writing an introduction, one wants to write the exact opposite of an introduction. I have tried to resist this impulse, then to subdue it, then to disguise it. But I might as well admit to feeling that this introduction has rather run away from me. I do not even know whether it is a good idea to read it before the other essays. Not that it has nothing to do with them: on the contrary it tackles precisely those theoretical problems that continually recur in the book. But there are two differences of some substance in the way it deals with them.

For one thing, this is my first attempt at a systematic and abstract discussion of issues that I have always approached in an occasional, intuitive and concrete way: in relation to a specific text or literary genre. And while I am convinced that empirical research is impossible without a guiding theoretical framework, I am by no means sure that I am personally cut out for this sort of work. I feel more at home examining, correcting or falsifying already existing theories in the light of concrete examples than when I have to put forward an alternative theory. Ideally, of course, the two operations ought to coincide: but in reality one finds oneself 'specializing' in one or other of them, and I must say that the operation I find more congenial is the one found in the essays that follow, not the one attempted in this introduction. On the other hand, in the rather frenetic world of literary criticism, theoretical speculation enjoys the same symbolic status as cocaine: one *has to* try it. Readers will judge for themselves whether in my case it has been worthwhile or whether they have simply had dust thrown in their eyes.

The second difference is much simpler and much more important. Over the past few years I have changed my opinion on various questions. In a couple of cases, which I shall mention explicitly, I now think that I was wrong. Overall, though, I would say that I have mainly radicalized and generalized a number of intuitions scattered here and there in my earlier work. It may be that they have thereby gained in clarity and explanatory power, or it may be that they have lost what was good in their original formulation. I (predictably) lean towards the former view, but it is, as always, other people's judgements that count. I simply wanted to state at the outset that the discrepancies between one essay and the next, and between essays and introduction, derive at least in part from the fact that I am unable to consider my work as something complete; that no methodological or historiographic framework wholly convinces me; and that every change I have made has been prompted by the unfashionable and banal conviction that the main task of criticism is to provide the best possible explanation of the phenomena it discusses. That is all; now we can get on with the real problems.

1. Rhetoric and History

'Rhetoric is like a branch ... of the science dealing with behaviour, which it is right to call political.' Aristotle's words (*Rhetoric* 1356a) prefigure those researches of the last few decades aimed at demonstrating that rhetorical conventions exist in order to satisfy specifically *social* requirements. Thus Kenneth Burke in 1950: 'The *Rhetoric* must lead us through the Scramble,

the Wrangle of the Market Place, the flurries and flare-ups of the
Human Barnyard, the Give and Take, the wavering line of pressure and counter-pressure, the logomachy, the onus of ownership,
the Wars of Nerves, the War . . . . Its ideal culminations are more
often beset by strife as the condition of their organized expression,
or material embodiment. Their very universality becomes transformed into a partisan weapon. For one need not scrutinize the
concept of "identification" very sharply to see, implied in it at
every turn, its ironic counterpart: division. Rhetoric is concerned
with the state of Babel after the Fall. Its contribution to a "sociology of knowledge" must often carry us far into the lugubrious
regions of malice and lie.'[1] Thus also, to cite someone who is
intellectually at the opposite pole from Burke, Giulio Preti in
1968: 'Rhetorical discourse is a discourse addressed to a *particular*
(I prefer to call it a "determinate") audience . . . . In other words,
rhetorical argument starts from presuppositions as well as from
feelings, emotions, evaluations – in a word, "opinions" (*doxai*) –
which it supposes to be present and at work in its audience.' And
further on, commenting on some passages from the *Logique du
Port-Royal*: 'Two things stand out in particular here: the first is the
emotional character underlying these kinds of non-rational persuasion, an emotional character indicated a little crudely by terms like
"amour propre", "interest", "utility", "passion", but which is
nonetheless quite definite . . . . The second is the typically *social*
character of these forms of sophism: they are linked to man's
relations to other men within the nation, the social group or the
institution. This social character is contrasted with the universality
of rational conviction.'[2]

Rhetoric has a social, emotive, partisan character, in short, an
evaluative character. To persuade is the opposite of to convince.
The aim is not to ascertain an intersubjective truth but to enlist
support for a *particular* system of values. In the seventeenth century – which witnessed the first great flowering of empirical science, and *at the same time* the collapse of all social 'organicity' in
the fight to the death between opposing faiths and interest – the
perception of this contrast was extremely acute. According to *La
Logique du Port-Royal*: 'Si l'on examine avec soin ce qui attache
ordinairement les hommes plûtot à une opinion qu'à une autre, on

trouvera que ce n'est pas la pénétration de la vérité & la force des raisons; mais quelque lien d'amour propre, d'interêt, ou de passion. C'est le poids qui emporte la balance, & qui nous détermine dans la plupart de nos doutes; c'est ce qui donne le plus grand branle à nos jugements, & qui nous y arrête le plus fortement. Nous jugeons des choses, non par ce qu'elles sont en elles-mêmes; mais par ce qu'elles sont à notre égard: & la vérité & l'utilité ne sont pour nous qu'une même chose.'[3]

So far we have discussed the social character of rhetorical conventions. But the argument applies also to literary conventions. Rhetoric is concerned with so many and such different activities (law, politics, ethics, advertising . . .) that it would be mistaken to restrict it just to literature, yet literary discourse is entirely contained within the rhetorical domain. As Preti puts it in a flawless passage: 'Epideictic discourse, which was the least valued in antiquity (precisely because it is the most . . . "rhetorical" in a derogatory sense) is nowadays however the one which takes on the greatest importance. It can even be said that in present-day philosophy of culture it is the only one with any interest, precisely because it does not have narrow practical ends, but a cultural, "paedeutic" aim. And above all because it provides the *genus* of literary discourse in prose. It bears on moral values, and in general on the values of a civilization. It aims at reinforcing or arousing attitudes (feelings) not just as regards a contingent (legal or political) decision, but as regards the great values that make up a civilization. Precisely because of its non-practical character, it is unlikely to degenerate from a discourse of persuasion to one of propaganda. It is above all the structures and rules of this kind of discourse which are the object of the new Rhetoric.'[4]

The evaluative and persuasive character of literary discourse emerges sharply in that area of the rhetorical tradition with which literary criticism is most familiar, namely 'figures', and particularly in the 'queen of poetry' – metaphor. Far from being 'aesthetic' ornaments of discourse, places where the strategy of persuasion is attenuated or disappears, figures show themselves to be unrivalled mechanisms for welding into an indivisible whole description and evaluation, 'judgements of fact' and 'judgements of value'. To quote once again *La Logique du Port-Royal*: 'Les expressions figurées signifient, outre la chose principale, le mouvement & la passion de celui qui parle, & impriment ainsi l'une & l'autre idée dans l'esprit, au lieu que l'expression simple ne marque que la vérité toute nue.'[5]

'Passion', the 'emotions', 'feeling': these indicate that uncertain object that literary criticism can choose to ignore but which does not thereby disappear from its field of operation. As Pascal said, feeling 'acts in a flash, and is always ready to act'. He traced it back to 'habit', to that 'spontaneous' cultural reaction ('we are automatism as well as spirit . . . ') which tells us with ruthless clarity just how profoundly our psychical apparatus is determined by the socio-historical context.

Rhetoric, then, addresses itself to 'feeling' precisely because it is concerned with evoking and disciplining the most purely *social* parts of us. The most 'automatically' social, we should say, with Pascal in mind, but also recalling the theory of metaphor put forward by Max Black. Metaphor for Black appears as simply unthinkable outside a whole system of moral and cognitive commonplaces (rhetoric, as Aristotle had said, is the art of using commonplaces well) which are used and accepted without any longer being subjected to any control: 'Consider the statement "man is a wolf" . . . . The metaphorical sentence in question will not convey its intended meaning to a reader sufficiently ignorant about wolves. What is needed is not so much that the reader shall know the standard dictionary meaning of "wolf" – or be able to use that word in literal senses – as that he shall know what I will call the *system of associated commonplaces*. . . . From the expert's standpoint, the system of commonplaces may include half-truths or downright mistakes (as when a whale is classified as a fish); but the important thing for the metaphor's effectiveness is not that the commonplaces shall be true, but that they should be readily and freely evoked. (Because this is so, a metaphor that works in one society may seem preposterous in another).'[6]

Seen in this light, the more a rhetorical formulation is turned into a commonplace (or rather – but it is the same thing – the more it has become 'implicit', unnoticeable to us) the more persuasive it will be: 'To us it seems that the value of "dead" metaphors in argument is above all prominent because of the great force of persuasion they possess when, with the aid of one technique or another, they are put back into action. This force results from the fact that they draw their effects from an analogic material which is easily admitted because it is not only known, but integrated, by means of language, into the cultural tradition.'[7] 'Someone who uses a form from the rhetorical system does not have to think, or be consciously aware at that moment, that he is using that form, just as someone driving a car does not have to think, or be consciously aware at that moment, how many cylinders the engine has or how it works . . . the knowledge of rhetorical forms by the listener can in fact jeopardize the effect the speaker hopes to arouse with those forms, in that the effect is subjected to the listener's control.'[8]

Rhetorical figures, and the larger combinations which organize long narratives, are thus of a piece with the deep, buried, invisible presuppositions of every world view. This is why one duly turns to them every time one has to put into focus a particularly complex experience (one can practically speak about time only in metaphors) or to express a judgement that possesses particular importance (almost all emotional language – from 'honey' to 'scum' and beyond – is a long chain of metaphors). I said just now that rhetorical forms are 'of a piece' with the deepest presuppositions of every *Weltanschauung*. The examples just adduced invite us to go further, to suggest that they are the *most widespread* form, and in certain cases the *only* form, in which those presuppositions continue to manifest themselves. Their lasting and undetected effectiveness points to the wide field of study of the *unconscious* culture, the implicit knowledge, of every civilization. It has indeed become difficult to imagine an adequate social history of 'consensus' that does not understand the techniques of persuasion. Reciprocally, literary criticism – as a sociology of rhetorical forms – would have everything to gain from contact with the history of mentalities outlined by the *Annales* school:'Inertia, a fundamental historical force, . . . is more a fact of minds than one of matter, since the latter is often quicker to act than the former. Men make use of the machines they invent while retaining the mentality of prior technical stages. Drivers of motor-cars have a horse-rider's vocabulary, nineteenth-century factory workers have the mentality of their peasant fathers and grandfathers. Mentality is what changes most slowly. The history of mentalities is the history of slowness in history.'[9] Yet it would of course be wrong to say that literature is limited to 'bringing back to life' the rhetorico-ideological forms already deposited in tradition. Literature is traversed by continuous, at times traumatic, innovation: 'daring' figures, works that on their appearance were rejected as 'incomprehensible' or 'absurd' are the most visible evidence of this second side of the question. Yet this does not in the least 'prove' – as is often believed, for the most varied reasons – that 'real' literature is by its nature anti-conventional, and that its interpretation will therefore impel us 'beyond' rhetorical analysis.

Let us begin with the second point. Rhetorical theory is by no means unable to account for the evolutionary character or even the ruptures of literary history. Harald Weinrich's analysis of metaphor in text-linguistic terms aims precisely at explaining the culturally innovative function that it can, if necessary, come to exercise. Indeed when Weinrich notes that metaphor is a 'contradictory predication', he shows that the relation between 'topic' and 'comment', or subject and predicate, established by metaphorical combination is never, orginally, a 'peaceful' one but always implies a 'risky' transition between the two terms.[10] The predication proposed by metaphor – in its interweaving of description and evaluation – can just as well be repulsed. The inert, counter-determinant context can prove too rigid and thus make the predication seem incomprehensible. Literary history, after all, abounds in rhetorical experiments that seem relegated for ever to the limbo of absurdity. But it also abounds – and this is the point – in experiments that seemed absurd and yet now appear not only entirely acceptable but actually indispensable – experiments that have become established as 'commonplaces'. 'Créer un poncif': was not this Baudelaire's – *Baudelaire's* – ideal? When faced with a text that violates the conventions of its time, therefore, critical analysis cannot remain content with the half-truth that tells us how it did so. It cannot look, as it usually does, only at the *past*, at the dislodged convention or the deconstructed *Weltanschauung*. The *future* of a text – the conventions and the world views it will help to form and consolidate – is just as much a part of its history and its contribution to history. This consideration is taken for granted in other kinds of historical studies. Only literary criticism – prey to superstitions specific to itself, as we shall see shortly – has claimed exemption. There is no good reason for this, not only with respect to historiography, but also in the light of rhetorical theory itself. Because rhetoric – remember Kenneth Burke's words – is the daughter of division and strife. By the mere fact of its existence, it bears witness to a society divided, in conflict. It is an entity that continually transforms itself, historical in its essence. Rhetorical 'daring' testifies to a will that wants to overturn the power relations of the symbolic order. 'Commonplaces' and semantic inertia, for their part, are the potential *result* of that daring no less than its opposite. This is the sense of a memorable passage by Erwin Panofsky: 'art is not, as a point of view which excessively accentuates its opposition to the theory of imitation would like one to believe, a subjective expression of feeling or an existential occupation of certain individuals, *but rather an objectifying and realizing conflict, aiming at meaningful results, between a forming power and a material to be overcome.*'[11] Even the tone of this sentence makes it clear that, for Panofsky, there would be nothing wrong in seeing the history of art as an articulation of the history of social conflicts and violence: as a *history of conflicts in the sphere of aesthetic forms.*[12] It is no longer a question, then, of contrasting rhetorical (or ideological) 'consent' with aesthetic 'dissent', but of recognizing that there are different *moments* in the development of every system of consent, and above all different *ways* of furthering it. As I try to explain in the essays on Joyce, Eliot and Balzac – and in the fourth section of this introduction – in particular social contexts even 'open', 'non-organic', or 'obscure' aesthetic forms can function as instruments of consent.

Knowledge of the socio-historical context of a literary work or genre is not therefore an 'extra' to be kept in the margins of rhetorical analysis. In general, whether one is aware of it or not, such knowledge furnishes the starting point for interpretation itself, providing it with those initial hypothesis without which rhetorical mechanisms would be hard to understand, or would tell us very little indeed. Thus, when around ten years ago every work was implacably led back to the Nature/Culture opposition, the procedure soon wore thin, not so much because of its historical indeterminacy, but because that indeterminacy (largely encouraged by

Lévi-Strauss himself) permitted as a rule analyses that were at best elementary, and otherwise simply wrong.

Yet, although rhetorical analysis refines and extends the territory of the social sciences and the latter, for their part, provide it with that historical framework outside of which the very existence of rhetorical conventions would be meaningless, it should not therefore be thought that the connection between the two conceptual apparatuses, and the set of phenomena they refer to, is linear and predictable. True isomorphisms never occur, and from this categorial discrepancy stems the set of problems that characterizes literary history.

2. Literary Historiography – and Beyond

Literary texts are *historical* products organized according to *rhetorical* criteria. The main problem of a literary criticism that aims to be in all respects a *historical discipline* is to do justice to both aspects of its objects: to work out a system of concepts which are both historiographic and rhetorical. These would enable one to perform a dual operation: to slice into segments the diachronic continuum constituted by the whole set of literary texts (the strictly historical task), but to slice it according to formal criteria pertaining to *that* continuum and not others (the strictly rhetorical task).

To a large extent, such a theoretical apparatus already exists. It is centred on the concept of 'literary genre'. I do not think it is accidental that, in the twentieth century, the best results of historical-sociological criticism are to be found in works aimed at defining the internal laws and historical range of a specific genre: from the novel in Lukács to the baroque drama in Benjamin, from French classical tragedy in Goldmann to (in a kindred field) the twelve-note system in Adorno. Yet there is no doubt that the concept of literary genre has not yet acquired the prominence it deserves, or that it could lead to a very different structuring of literary history from the one familiar to us. I would like here to outline some of the prospects that might open up if it were to be used systematically. But first I shall suggest why criticism has put up such widespread resistance to these developments.

Let us take the case of the young Lukács. In the period when he was working on his *Modern Drama*, Lukács, under the influence of Simmel's sociology of forms, had come to formulate the problem we are concerned with in terms that still remain valid today. As he wrote in the 1911 foreword to that work: 'The fundamental problem of this book is therefore: does a modern drama exist, and what style does it have? This question, however, like every stylistic question, is in the first place a sociological one . . . . The greatest errors of sociological analysis in relation to art are: in artistic creations it seeks and examines only contents, tracing a straight line between these and given economic relations. But in literature what is truly social is form . . . . Form is social reality, it participates vivaciously in the life of the spirit. It therefore does not operate only as a factor acting upon life and moulding experiences, but also as a factor which is in its turn moulded by life.'[13] Similar concepts are expressed in the first and longer draft of the foreword, the 1910 lecture 'Observations on the Theory of Literary History': 'The synthesis of literary history is the unification into a new organic unity of sociology and aesthetics . . . . Form is sociological not only as a mediating element, as a principle which connects author and receiver, making literature a social fact, but also in its relationship with the material to be formed . . . . Form in a work is that which organizes into a closed whole the life given to it as subject matter, that which determines its times, rhythms and fluctuations, its densities and fluidities, its hardnesses and softnesses; that which accentuates those sensations perceived as important and distances the less important things; that which allocates things to the foreground or the background, and arranges them in order . . . Every form is an evaluation of life, a judgement on life, and it draws this strength and power from the fact that in its deepest foundations form is always an ideology . . . . The world view is the formal postulate of every form.'[14]

This line of research is very clear, and far richer than a couple of quotations can hope to suggest. One almost wonders what form sociological criticism might have taken had Lukács pursued his project. But, of course, things turned out differently. Already in 1910, in disconcerting synchrony with the arguments just quoted, Lukács elaborated a diametrically opposed concept of aesthetic form – a 'tragic' concept, based on the collapse of all connections between form and life, forms and history: '[Here] a fundamental question arises for aesthetics: is not what we have been accustomed to call form, and which we place a priori in front of the meanings of life and of what is being formed, the petrifaction of existence? . . . Every perfect work, precisely because of its perfection, places itself outside all communities and will not tolerate being inserted into some series of causes determining it from without. The essence of artistic creation, of formation, is just such an isolating principle: to cut every bond which tied it to living, concrete, moving life in order to give itself a new life, closed in on itself, not connected to anything and comparable to nothing. In every artistic creation there exists a kind of *Inselhaftigkeit*, as Simmel calls it, as a result of which it is reluctant to be a part of any continuous development.'[15]

As is well known, between *Soul and Forms* and *Theory of the Novel*, Lukács radicalized this second version of his concept of form. In the famous dialogue on *Tristram Shandy* the speaker who exalts formal order frightens the girl he loves and drives her into his rival's arms. By the same token, in *Theory of the Novel* the *historicity* which is consubstantial with the novel means that the formal accomplishment of a novel is always and only 'problematic': a 'yearning' for form rather than its attainment. Between Life and Form, history and forms, the young Lukács digs an ever-deepening trench. Life is 'movement', form 'closure'. Life is 'concreteness' and 'multiplicity', form 'abstraction' and 'simplification'. Form is, in a summarizing metaphor, petrified and petrifying: life is fluid, ductile, 'alive'.

However, the twentieth-century social sciences have erased this image of life for good. If one looks through the eyes of linguistics, history of the *longue durée*, anthropology and psychoanalysis, *even* life appears 'petrified'. What is unacceptable in Lukács's dichotomy is not so much the description of form as the characteristics attributed to historical existence. If, in Lukác's work between 1910 and 1920, the concept of form takes on increasingly metaphysical connotations, this happens, paradoxically, less for reasons internal to the concept of form itself than because of the image Lukács's philosophical background had imprinted on the opposing concept. Form coagulates into a cruel a priori – extreme, tragic, opposed to life – *because* Lukács wants to conserve 'life' in a state of fluid and 'open' indeterminacy. What Lukác's is aiming to avoid is a concept which is, however, essential to the analysis of culture: the concept of *convention*.[16] It is a crucial concept because it indicates when a form has taken definitive social root, entering into daily life, innervating and organizing it in ways increasingly undetected and regular – and hence more effective. But it is at the same time a concept which enforces a harsh disillusionment, because it strips historical existence of its openness to change, and aesthetic form of its pristine purity.

I believe that literary criticism has kept for too long to the terms of Lukács's dilemma: to save the warmth of life and the purity of form. This is why history and rhetoric have become totally unrelated subjects. This is why the concept of literary genre has remained confined to a sort of theoretical limbo: recognized and accepted, but little and reluctantly used. To talk about literary genres means without any doubt to emphasize the contribution made by literature to the 'petrifaction of existence' and also to the 'wearing out of form'. It means re-routing the tasks of literary historiography and the image of literature itself, enclosing them both in the idea of consent, stability, repetition, bad taste even. It means, in other words, turning the ultimate paradise – the paradise of 'beauty' – into a social institution like the others.

We can now return to the role of the concept of genre in slicing up and reordering the continuum of literary history. Something immediately strikes us. A history of literature built round this concept will be both 'slower' and more 'discontinuous' than the one we are familiar with. Slower, because the idea of literary *genre* itself requires emphasis on what a set of works have in *common*. It presupposes that literary production takes place in obedience to a prevailing system of laws and that the task of criticism is precisely to show the extent of their coercive, regulating power. The idea of genre introduces into literary history the dimension which the *Annales* school has called *longue durée*, and supports the hypothesis that 'art is without doubt more suited to the expression of *states* of civilization than moments of violent rupture.'[17]

This is a change of perspective whose consequences it is difficult, and in part also idle, to predict. But one thing is certain: it will force one to re-examine from the foundations upwards the historiographical status of literary criticism. Tottering and obsolete in this respect, literary history has never ceased to be *histoire évenementielle*, where the 'events' are great works or great individuals. Even the great historical controversies, when all is said, turn almost exclusively on the reinterpretation of an extremely small number of works and authors. This procedure condemns the concept of genre to a subaltern, marginal function, as is indicated most starkly in the formalist couple convention-defamiliarization, where genre appears as mere *background*, an opaque plane whose only use is to make the *difference* of the masterpiece more prominent. Just as the 'event' breaks and ridicules the laws of continuity, so the masterpiece is there to demonstrate the 'triumph' over the norm, the irreducibility of what is really great.

The problems here are many and intertwined. But keeping to the essential, let us at least ask two questions. First, how far has empirical research borne out the antithesis between norm and masterpiece on which literary historiography continues to rest? In what sense does Shakespeare 'violate' the conventions of Elizabethan tragedy? Why not say the opposite: that he was the only writer able to realize them fully, establishing as it were the 'ideal type' of an entire genre? Does *Wilhelm Meister's Apprenticeship* 'defamiliarize' the conventions of the *Bildungsroman*? Is not the opposite the case: that with his novel Goethe founds them and makes them reproducible? Examples could be multiplied. Here again, in essence, is the problem we dealt with in discussing the relation between the 'commonplace' and the 'daring' in rhetoric. What is at issue once more is the orientation of the historian's gaze: whether one should look only at what is *behind* the masterpiece, unilaterally emphasizing a break, a rupture of the historical tissue – or whether, by showing the consequences of every great work, one should accentuate its function as a genuine producer of historical 'stability'.

It seems evident to me that the first orientation is still the more common; and the reason is not hard to find. The fact is that criticism has not entirely freed itself of its old task: that of being a sort of cultivated accompaniment to reading – to the reading we are doing here and now. Since certain works continue to be read, the desire spontaneously arises of showing that they are 'contemporary', and thus of emphasizing what allows them to be wrenched out of the hard earth of the past and laid in our lap. This betokens a relationship with texts whose distant roots lie in Greek, and above all in Christian allegorical exegesis.[18] It is based on the belief, however banalized nowadays, that there are messages in the past that not only concern us but which in a sense were written *for us and us alone*, and whose meaning will be fully revealed only in the light of *our* exegesis. An agreeable superstition indeed and a highly useful one 'for life': but for precisely this reason it concerns the student of the contemporary mentality, not the historian. The latter – unless desirous of turning into that legendary figure whose only pleasure lay in contemplating his own reflection – must concentrate on the dissimilarities and ruptures: on what has been lost and become irretrievably unfamiliar, and which we can 're-familiarize' only by doing such violence to it that we distort the objective, material consistency of every work which it is the task of scientific knowledge to reconstruct and 'salvage'.

The improper and distorting centrality that contemporary 'taste' has won at the expense of historical criticism brings us to the second question. At the end of the nineteenth century hundreds of ghost stories were written, but *The Turn of the Screw* is something else. Agreed; or rather, it is something else 'for us', the tiny minority that acts in each case as the depository of prevailing taste. But is the task of the historian of culture always and only to ask what, in the past or the present, makes possible the 'separation' of an elite from the mass of the public? Is it not rather to deal with the mass conventions, the great ideological agreements by which each age is distinguished from others? But – it might be objected – the average production of a given genre is unreadable and boring now. I do not doubt it. But it is precisely this unbearable 'uncontemporaneity' that the historian must seek out. (We might reflect in passing that if everyone behaved like literary critics who only study what they 'like', doctors might restrict themselves to studying only healthy bodies and economists the standard of living of the well-off.) And then, are we so sure that we know those 'other' ghost stories, the 'conventional' ones? Have these conventions really been studied, or do we not rather confine ourselves to evoking them hurriedly for the sole purpose of adding lustre to their 'destroyer'? If one wants to keep the couple convention-innovation and give the latter term the full historical and formal weight it deserves, it is all the more important to realize that the first term of the pair has not yet become an 'object of knowledge' in a true sense for literary criticism. The idea of 'normal literature' – to paraphrase another *Annales* expression – has no place in criticism. The result is that, at present, our knowledge of literary history closely resembles the maps of Africa of a century and a half ago: the coastal strips are familiar but an entire continent is unknown. Dazzled by the great estuaries of mythical rivers, when it comes to pinpointing the source we still trust too often to bizarre hypotheses or even to legends.

Faced with an unknown continent, one does not of course know beforehand whether it is going to be worth exploring. I can only say that each time I have studied 'low' genres, 'mass literature' (and despite having done it in a way I no longer find satisfactory: looking for their laws of operation in a single work I thought was exemplary – *Dracula*, *The Paul Street Boys*, the Sherlock Holmes cycle – and not in a broader and more systematic corpus of 'middle-range' products) I have always ended up finding meanings that were in no sense 'predictable' or 'banal'. Very often, in fact, they were different or even antithetical to what one generally supposes at first sight.

Mass literature is not the undifferentiated and meaningless expanse most critics – still – say it is. It holds many surprises, and not just because of the meanings *within* it, but also because of the light it sheds on works of a different kind. The rhetoric of the detective story enables us to understand better the formal and cultural problematic on which the narrative solutions of Joseph Conrad (which are opposed to those of the detective story) depend. Reading Baudelaire in the light of Bram Stoker, one finds that the function of the oxymoron takes on unexpected connotations. In the essays on mass literature collected here, unfortunately, this aspect of the question is insufficiently developed. Only a few years ago, to write about *Dracula* meant being taken for an eccentric loafer, and one's main worry was to prove that one's work was legitimate: 'You see: *Dracula* is part of literary history *too*'. To wonder whether the study of Stoker might contribute towards changing the contours of 'great' literature was really going a bit too far. But I am convinced now that this is a path to pursue, and that it will perhaps allow us to reconstruct the literary system of the past with great theoretical precision and historical fidelity.

A 'slower' literary history; and a more 'discontinuous' one. At present, criticism relies on too many and too varied criteria in order to slice up the continuum of history: the individual author's life, 'style-period' concepts like mannerism or naturalism, the ruptures occurring in other areas of history, the explicit or implicit recourse to an all-pervasive 'Spirit of the age' – as well as, naturally, the concept of genre itself. The end result is in most cases a large and sticky web where historical breaks lose all clarity. If the concept of literary genre can be elaborated pertinently and systematically, it might contribute towards hardening the edges of historical research, since a history redrawn according to strictly formal principles will also be a more rigid, more interrupted history. Not only (as is already partly the case) on the diachronic plane, but also and perhaps above all on the synchronic: in every age, different and even mutually conflicting symbolic forms co-exist, each one endowed with a different diffusion and historical duration. The history of literature must aim to represent its own object as a kind of magnetic field whose overall equilibrium or disequilibrium is only the resultant of the individual forces acting within it.

It is even possible that the distinctive features of the artistic or literary 'periods' themselves will emerge profoundly modified from this re-examination, but this is to raise questions that I cannot tackle here.[19] Instead it should be noted that, if one wants to arrive at a historical reordering of any interest and validity, the concept of 'genre' will have to be elaborated in a much more pertinent way than it is now. At present, in fact, it mixes more or less at random references to content (detective story, picaresque novel), to effects (terror, humour), and to a number of formal features (stories 'with happy endings', 'documentary' novels). Such a loose classification cannot make much of a contribution towards simplifying and specifying a field of research. Perhaps the solution will be to con-

centrate on certain major rhetorical 'dominants' and reorganize
the system of the different genres on the basis of these. I have a
specific example in mind, which to me seems the most successful
attempt to found a 'rhetorical' historiography: Erwin Panofsky's
'Perspective as a "Symbolic Form"'.

Reading this essay one understands first of all how 'strong' historical hypotheses contribute to rhetorical research ('iconological'
research in Panofsky's case), not only by fortifying it but also by
offering it preliminary *structural* hypotheses. In other words one
understands the *unity* of historical and rhetorical study. But
one also grasps the *distinction* between them: those preliminary
hypotheses are in fact only corroborated after a long and arduous
march through highly specialized territories, where the analysis is
carried out (and offers itself for refutation) on the basis of principles which can no longer be *deduced* from the extra-artistic historical knowledges. This is the necessarily 'tortuous' way in which
criticism contributes to overall historical knowledge, and I shall
return to this shortly. Let us dwell for the moment on another
aspect of 'Perspective' that may turn out to be essential for a
renewal of historical methodology. As is well known, Panofsky
believes that pictorial perspective emerges in relation to a new
concept of space and of the 'ordering' function the human subject
comes to assume within it. This concept originated in experimental physics and was given its definitive codification in Kantian
philosophy. Thus an artistic procedure takes on its fullest significance in the light *not* of other artistic phenomena but of the products of scientific and philosophical thought. In fact it is in correlation with the latter that its 'form' becomes comprehensible and
reveals its own cultural function. But in that case, a history of
rhetorical forms carried through to its logical conclusion will very
probably lead to the *dismemberment of the aesthetic field*. And this
dismemberment will no longer take the historicist form of bracket-
ing off the technical peculiarities of works so as to fuse them into a
generic 'Spirit of the Age'. Rather, it is precisely from the material-
ity of their form that criticism will derive the theoretical need to
'unfix' the histories of art and of literature, and rewrite them as
merely a component of a history of values, of the structures of
thought in which these values are organized and of the institutions
designed to promote them.[20]

An example will help to clarify what I mean. The Elizabethan sonnet and the *roman-feuilleton* both belong to the area of literature, and are 'therefore' both dealt with by the same discipline, literary criticism. But things belong to the same field and are studied by the same discipline if their characteristics are held largely in *common*. Now the sonnet and the *feuilleton* certainly share that double negation by which Kant marked off the aesthetic sphere: they do not have a cognitive character, and they do not have immediate practical ends. But that is all. They have *nothing else* in common. And anyone who studies sonnets or *feuilletons* knows very well that their common 'aesthetic function' provides little or no help in interpreting them. A study of the sonnet will set no store by the critical categories valid for the *feuilleton*. It will draw instead on 'kindred' conventions to the sonnet, without these necessarily having to belong to the literary sphere: certain forms of prayer for example, or certain aspects of heraldic custom, or the theory of 'world harmony'. Conversely, in the case of the *feuilleton*, one will have to study early to mid-nineteenth-century journalism, post-Revolutionary melodrama, the conventions of a certain kind of 'popular' historiography. In both cases the work will proceed that much better the more the person conducting it – without knowing it, even maybe without wanting it – manages to 'forget' the traditional purposes of the history of 'literature' (whose theoretical horizon *demands* that, one way or another, the unnatural marriage of the sonnet and the *feuilleton* be consummated) and considers it 'enough' to make a contribution, by studying a form or a group of related forms, to the history of society.

Moreover, not enough consideration is given to a most curious fact: the adamantine lack of interest that historians 'proper' have always displayed towards literary (and, more generally, artistic) historiography. Even the 'total history' of the *Annales* school has as it were stopped short on the edge of this field of studies, without ever managing to become significantly interested or involved in it. Now, if we rule out the possibility that historians hate literary critics for private and unmentionable reasons, as well as the possibility that the latter are so much more inept than other historians as to merit their utter contempt, this state of affairs can only be explained by suggesting that literary historians do not manage to be 'real' historians because they deal with an *imaginary* object.

They call this object 'literary history', but it is traversed by such a jumble of internal contradictions, Ptolemaic epicycles, ad hoc explanations and downright eccentricities (Gibbon belongs to English literature but not Conan Doyle) that their discipline is rendered totally unusable by any historical research equipped with a modicum of scientific self-control.

So a history of literature able to rewrite itself as a sociology of symbolic forms, a history of cultural conventions, should perhaps finally find a role and a dignity in the context of a total history of society. As is always the case, this would solve some problems and create others, starting with that raised by expressions like 'total history' or 'social history': concepts too broad to regulate any given piece of research. It is impossible to deny that human society is a multifarious, complex, overdetermined whole; but the theoretical difficulty obviously lies in trying to establish the *hierarchy* of different historical factors. The solution to this problem is, in turn, broadly an historical, empirical one. In an essentially agrarian society, climatic changes will have a far greater importance than in a basically industrial one. If the majority of the population is illiterate, the written culture will oscillate between playing a wholly negligible part and having an overwhelming and traumatic function (as the printing of the Bible demonstrated). If, on the other hand, everyone is able to read, the written culture is unlikely to turn up such extreme effects, but in compensation it will become the regular and intimate accompaniment to every daily activity.

As historical periods change, then, the weight of the various institutions, their function, their position in the social structure change too. When, therefore, the historian of literary forms begins to look for those extra-literary phenomena which will help him (whether he knows it or not) orient and control his research, the only rule he can set himself is to assess *each instance* carefully. A few examples will help here too to clarify what I mean, and I hope they will show that the criterion of 'each instance' is not meant to encourage arbitrariness, but to subject it to the only kind of control possible in this context.

Let us take the knowledge of state structures and politico-juridical thought. This will be very helpful – and theoretically 'pertinent' – for analysing tragic form in the age of absolutism, but it will be a lot less so for studying comic form in the same period. In the eighteenth century it will remain important for analysing the 'satiric' form of the novel, and yet be almost totally irrelevant for analysing the 'realist' novel. Or again, a study of sexual prohibitions and certain dream symbols deriving from them can provide many suggestions about the literature of terror and practically nothing about detective fiction of the same decade. Conversely, the emotional reactions to the second industrial revolution will be pertinent to the analysis of science fiction, rather less so to that of detective fiction, and quite insignificant for the literature of terror.

Rather than multiply the examples, it will be useful to point out that the 'pertinence' of a historical factor or event to literary analysis does not of itself imply any judgement about its importance in the *overall* mechanism of history. The Second World War – to take a strident example – does not seem to have much usefulness for literary periodization or interpretation: this does not, obviously, make it a secondary episode or one without enormous explanatory power in other areas. The different institutions of history have uneven rhythms of development, and in this respect the primary task of criticism is to outline the evolution of its own area of analysis, even if this leads it to move away from or contradict periodizations operating elsewhere. The reconstruction of a unified historiographical map is a subsequent, and typically interdisciplinary, problem. But it can be successfully tackled only if one possesses knowledge corroborated against the specific criteria of each particular area.

A final point of specification, even if the scope of the argument makes it superfluous: an extra-literary phenomenon is never more or less important as a possible 'object' or 'content' of a text, but because of its impact on systems of evaluation and, therewith, on rhetorical strategies. The phenomenon of popularized science is not 'part' of detective fiction because the detective works 'scientifically' (which is true enough but banal). Rather, we can say (taking a greater risk) that 'science' enters crime fiction by way of a particular semiotic mechanism (the decipherment of clues) and a narrative function reserved for it alone (the final dénouement). If we analyse these two rhetorical choices further (and increase the risk of being wrong even further) we can say that the decipherment of clues presupposes that 'science' is identified with an organicist ideology based on the 'common-sense' notion that differences in status cannot be altered; that the ending of the detective novel sketches an image of temporality where 'science', instead of being an activity which solicits some sort of 'progress', plays a drastically stabilizing role, guaranteeing the immutability of the given social order, or at least reducing its changes to a minimum.

With these observations, as was inevitable, the strictly historiographical issue has become mingled with the question of validity, or better perhaps 'testability', of critical interpretations. Albeit summarily, we must now ask in what ways hermeneutics and historiography interact, and what their respective spheres of validity are.

3. For a 'Falsifiable' Criticism

In principle, the criteria for testing literary interpretations should be the same as those already in use in every other scientific discipline. One should in other words demand of an interpretation that it is coherent, univocal and complete. And the test will consist in comparing it with data which – in the text or texts that constitute its object – appear contradictory or inexplicable in the light of the hypothesis itself. Nothing new here, one might say; and indeed this is nothing other than the elementary formulation of that principle of falsification used by all the empirical sciences, including, with a few additional problems, the historico-social sciences. All, that is, except twentieth-century literary criticism, whose methodological framework has for a long time rested on concepts like 'polysemy', 'ambiguity', 'openness', 'difference', all of which stress the non-univocal semantic character of the literary text. If a text is by definition non-univocal, even self-contradictory, then none of its elements can ever 'falsify' an interpretation. Because of the semantic peculiarities of the literary text, it is taken for granted from the outset that interpretive hypotheses will be negated and this state of affairs is accepted as unavoidable. But if the text has no falsificatory power, then any interpretation becomes legitimate, or, more exactly, none will ever be *il*legitimate. The rivalry between different hypotheses, the pathos of refutation, the passion for discussion – the ideals that animate every scientific undertaking – lose all foundation, appear superfluous and almost inconceivable. Interpretations tend to become mutually 'incommensurable', they do not appear to have any 'problems' in common. The claim that one of them is superior to another sinks almost to the level of a judgement of taste, whose empirical foundation is felt as an unseemly and prolix pedantry.

I have exaggerated, but not all that much. So long as it continues to revolve around concepts such as 'ambiguity' and the like, criticism will always, inexorably, be pushed into multiplying, rather than reducing, the obstacles every social science encounters when it tries to give itself a testable foundation. And all for nothing! For Hecuba!, one feels inclined to add. For the point is not whether the literary use of language is particularly polysemic or not. It is. But this in no way makes it impossible to conduct univocal and potentially complete – and thus refutable – analyses. It only means that these analyses must approach the text not as if it were a vector pointing neatly in one direction, but as if it were a light-source radiating in several directions or a field of forces in relatively stable equilibrium. These are more complex objects than a simple arrow, but an empirical and testable analysis of them is entirely possible, on condition that one aims to analyse and describe them as structures. By this token, adding, subtracting or transforming the meaning of each of their elements will not longer be treated (as is normally the case these days) as an operation which is 'always legitimate' because of the weak logical connections instituted by the literary structure (which is therefore the promised land of all deconstructionist thinking). Rather, it will be treated as a legitimate act *only if* it contributes towards improving the total knowledge of the text, and thus towards *strengthening* these connections, those 'prohibitions' which, as an organized whole, it imposes on the interpreter.

The day criticism gives up the battle cry 'it is *possible* to interpret this element in the following way', to replace it with the much more prosaic 'the following interpretation is *impossible* for such and such a reason', it will have taken a huge step forward on the road of methodological solidity. This does not in the least mean giving up unpredictable or daring interpretations: as Popper observed, the value of a theory is in direct proportion to its improbability. It merely means subjecting this improbability to rigorous checks, since what is bizarre or outlandish is not always also true. *Pecca fortiter, sed crede fortius* is a good way of summing up the spirit of scientific research.

If it is both possible and necessary for critical interpretations to be falsifiable, it needs to be added that the fundamental area where they should be tested is their analysis of rhetorical mechanisms. The reason for this is simple: if one wants to initiate a history of rhetorical forms, the validity of a hypothesis can be measured only by comparing it with other interpretations of the same form. This seems obvious – but it may be asked at this point, what has happened to the unity of rhetorical analysis and socio-historical analysis which we took as our starting point? To return to the interpretation of detective fiction put forward earlier: a historian of mentalities, or science, might object that in Conan Doyle's time the most widespread image of science was not at all the one we 'deduced' from the rhetorical structure of the Sherlock Holmes cycle. Is it possible for an objection of this kind to have no falsificatory value?

It is, because the objection contains both a portion of truth (which constitutes, as we shall see, a falsification of a rather peculiar kind) and a portion of error. To start with the latter, let us suppose that a demographer discovers that the birth rate, in a given place and period, assumes a configuration that contradicts what one would reasonably expect of the relationship between population increase and, say, the relations of production, climatic conditions, habits of sanitation and religious beliefs in that same time and place. Would a specialist in these other areas of history believe the demographer's statistics to be wrong *because* they do not tally with the results of his own research (which – let us suppose – have been fully confirmed and are now considered correct beyond question)? Certainly not: he might have his doubts, be surprised, suspect a mistaken calculation, pretend the figures do not exist. But he can only really reject them when they have been replaced by a different arrangement of the data which improves on them in terms of the principles established by demographic history, and not by the history of landed property or religion. Now there is no reason why the same principle should not apply to the field of rhetoric. A given rhetorical configuration – however absurd it might seem in the light of other historical findings – can only be negated in the fullest sense by a better rhetorical configuration.

Two considerations arise here, which I will mention very briefly. It is of course entirely true to say that the language of demography is much more nearly univocal than that of literary criticism. But this is largely because criticism, for the reasons mentioned earlier, has always taken its own empirical foundations lightly, and, instead of struggling to set up a scientific community with common aims and clear rules, has tacitly preferred to legitimate a state of affairs where everyone is free to do as they like. The lexico-grammatical euphoria of the last few years is only the latest episode in a long and illustrious tradition of intellectual irresponsibility. Yet in principle this sort of thing can always be remedied. The second consideration opens up a slightly different area. If criticism can give itself a reasonably testable foundation, then rhetorical analysis will necessarily acquire a different status within the 'stronger' social sciences. If a literary critic were to attend an interdisciplinary conference on totalitarianism and speak for an hour about, say, the mechanisms of allegory, the performance would seem strange and entertaining. And yet it is the only valid contribution our imaginary participant could offer. I believe it is time to put an end to the embarrassing pantomime where the literary historian is in fact the person who expounds the commonplaces everybody knows in a string of well-turned and persuasive sentences. Historians know how to use computers; they will have no difficulty learning the difference between metaphor and metonymy – assuming , naturally, that one is able to demonstrate that the choice between these two figures entails cultural differences of some significance.

We now come to the portion of truth contained in the objection set out above. I feel slightly uneasy here, because I know that more than once I myself have been guilty of the error I am about to describe, which is this. A satisfactory level of rhetorical analysis is reached. The configuration obtained seems to refer unambiguously to a particular hierarchy of values. So one performs the conclusive welding-together of rhetoric and social history. Let us suppose that up till now the argument has been flawless. It is precisely at this point that one makes a mistake. One succumbs to the allure of the sweeping generalization and falls into what we could call the '*Zeitgeist* fallacy'. Does the rhetoric of detective fiction imply a certain attitude towards science? Right then: 'the society of Conan Doyle's time', 'England in the eighteen nineties', 'the imperialist phase of capitalism' – whatever else one cares to invoke – all '*share that attitude*'. In relation to this turn in the argument, the objections of the historian of mentalities obviously have falsificatory value. But only in relation to this. What becomes arbitrary when it is generalized may perfectly well not be so if it aims for a more restricted sphere of validity.

This universalizing immodesty, which follows literary historiography about like a shadow, has a secret cause which it is helpful to know because it points by contrast to a possible way out. The cause is named Georg Wilhelm Friedrich Hegel. Few things have been so exhilarating for aesthetic studies – and so fatal to their empirical solidity – as Hegel's marriage of philosophy of history with idealist aesthetics. In the *Aesthetics*, every historical epoch has in essence *one* ideal content to 'express', and it gives 'sensible manifestation' to it through one artistic form. It was practically inevitable that – following the argument in reverse – once one had defined a rhetorical form one felt authorized to link it directly to *the* idea – single, solitary, resplendent – in which a whole epoch is supposedly summed up. Inevitable, and wrong – or at least, nearly always. Although from time to time moments of extraordinary intellectual and formal compactness occur, as a rule the opposite happens in history, and no system of values has ever been able to represent a *Zeitgeist* without being challenged by rival systems. Besides, if it were otherwise the whole of the present argument, from the opening lines onwards, would be totally absurd, because *rhetoric should not even exist*. Remember Kenneth Burke: the aim of rhetoric – promoting adherence to specific values – presupposes its opposite – division. All rhetorical forms aspire to *become* the 'Spirit of the Age', but their very plurality shows us that this term indicates an aspiration rather than a reality, and should therefore be employed as a highly useful conceptual tool – but not as a fact.

Conversely, it is precisely a respect for the specificity of each individual form that seems to offer the best guarantee of restraint in the historico-social links that criticism seeks to establish. The more one manages to differentiate a given form from 'rival' forms, the more social and ideological connections one will find are *prohibited*. The advantages of this both for historical concreteness and empirical testability are obvious. This brings us back to the situation outlined in the previous section. If the history of literature ever transforms itself into a history of rhetorical forms, the latter will in turn have to start from the realization that a form becomes more comprehensible and more interesting the more one grasps the conflict, or at least the difference, connecting it to the forms around it. And this should not be understood – as has in fact already started to happen – as a diachronic criterion: or at least not only, and not primarily. As well as grasping the succession of different and mutually hostile forms, literary history must aim at a synchronic periodization which is no longer 'summed up' in individual exemplary forms, but is set up for each period, through a kind of parallelogram of rhetorical forces, with its dominant, its imbalances, its conflicts and its division of tasks.

At this point the relations between the history of forms and the history of society will perhaps lose their uncertain and episodic character, and that same heterogeneity of extra-literary references that has characterized (until now in a casual and untestable way) the activity of interpretation will appear as a necessary path to follow. The disparate and discontinuous nature of those references does not (necessarily) depend on the instability of the categories used by criticism, but on its search for concreteness. It has to draw on those aspects of social life which enable one to explain that specific material object that is the text under analysis. Heterogeneity of connections is in the nature of this work because it is *in the nature of literature itself*. Literature is perhaps the most omnivorous of social institutions, the most ductile in satisfying disparate social demands, the most ambitious in not recognizing limits to its own sphere of representation. One cannot ask that heterogeneity to disappear, but only (and it is no small request) to reflect faithfully the real diversity, in terms of their destination and function, of the texts under examination.

4. Literature, 'Consent'

This historical project lies almost entirely in the future. Who knows whether it will ever be carried out? Who knows whether it is a reasonable project and not just a little personal utopia (which, moreover, I am still a long way from having begun to put into practice)? Whatever the case, it is idle to speculate too much on the best of all possible criticisms. Let us try instead to complete the argument by going back to a number of characteristics of what we call 'literature' which justify that project. We need in other words to isolate those elements of that 'real object', literature, which suggest that it becomes an 'object of knowledge' according to the criteria outlined so far.

Picking up the points raised in the first section, let us say that the substantial function of literature is to *secure consent*. To make individuals feel 'at ease' in the world they happen to live in, to reconcile them in a pleasant and imperceptible way to its prevailing cultural norms. This is the basic hypothesis. To corroborate it, however, it will be necessary to try it out on the one hand with a literary phenomenon – tragedy – that seems to indicate the exact opposite, and on the other with the number of particularly significant articulations of modern aesthetic and critical thought.

In one of the essays that follow I have tried to show that Elizabethan and Jacobean tragedy contributed, more radically than any other cultural phenomenon of the same period, to discrediting the values of absolute monarchy, thereby paving the way, with wholly destructive means, for the English revolution of the seventeenth century. What I have just claimed about literature as consent and conciliation seems to be completely negated. And in fact it is, because that hypothesis was proposed in a historically indeterminate form, whereas its validity should be restricted to western capitalist society. This society is separated from the age of tragedy – the age of absolutism – by a historical rupture that radi-

cally altered two decisive aspects of literary, and more generally
artistic, activity. First, tragedy belongs to a world that does not yet
recognize the inevitability of permanent conflict between opposing
and immitigable interests or values, and therefore does not feel
any need to confront the problem of reconciling them. And second
– there is, as we shall see, a link between the two – the age in which
tragedy flourished did not recognize aesthetic activity as having
any autonomy, but believed it should always cooperate directly,
immediately, in moral or cognitive purposes.

Sixteenth- and seventeenth-century tragedy thus belongs to a
world which the dominant ideology still wants to present as an
organism, where between the various social classes there is a functional difference but not a conflict of interests. It is a world that
still thinks of itself as an organic whole, but is ceasing – clamorously – to be so. Tragedy springs from this unrepeatable historical
conjuncture. Its elementary structure always consists in showing
how two values that should be in a relationship of dominance and
subordination suddenly, mysteriously (the mystery of Iago, of the
witches in *Macbeth*, of passion in *Phèdre*) become autonomous
and take on equal violence. As all Shakespeare's and Racine's
tragic heroes discover to their consternation, the traditional
'sovereignty' of reason, or morality, over the other human faculties
suddenly and irreversibly becomes impossible.

It is a situation we can understand only if we are able to tear
ourselves away from the presuppositions of our own culture. Its
'tragic' quality does not lie (as would now be the case for us) in the
fact that the story eventually leads to the sacrifice of one of the two
values in conflict, so that the surviving value too is darkened by the
shadow of mourning. This does happen, of course, yet it is not
here, in the 'ending', that the tragedy shows itself for what it is, but
in its presuppositions: in the fact that it has been possible to
imagine, and put into words, an irreconcilable conflict. This preliminary rhetorical choice – this basic situation, which the tragic
dramatist never bothers to 'motivate', but only expound with the
utmost clarity – breaks organicist unity for ever, and is felt as
something painful, incomprehensible, 'tragic', precisely because
organicism is still felt to be the only possible form of thought.

We can invert the formula used above, and say that tragedy

presents a world which is ceasing to be organic, but which is still only able to think of itself as organic. It is the paradoxical spirit of this literary form, which always leaves us, as Goethe observed, 'with troubled minds', ill at ease, uncertain. It was for this reason an unrivalled instrument of criticism and dissent. But an unrepeatable one: once the organicist ideology disappeared, so did the formal possibility of its tragic negation.

Tragedy as an unrepeatable 'exception' in the history of literary forms: for the purposes of our argument this would be enough in itself, but there is more. Modern literature and aesthetics are born not only 'after' tragedy but also 'against' it. A metamorphosis takes place which goes beyond the realm of aesthetics and extends right across the bourgeois cultural system. Precisely because this system sees conflict as a given fact of existence in society, it no longer sets itself the task of depicting it with 'pity and terror' but of showing that mutually opposing values and interests can always reach, if not a genuine conciliation, at least some kind of coexistence and compromise. In the realm of aesthetics this anti-tragic impulse of our culture appears with particular clarity. Indeed, it appears as the real foundation, the secret raison d'être of the aesthetic sphere itself. This is attested by two works which have contributed like few others to the formation of modern aesthetic thought: the *Critique of Judgement* and *On the Aesthetic Education of Man*.

It is obviously impossible for me to discuss these two works here with the detail and care they deserve. But a few rapid references will at least serve to indicate how they are central to the path we are following. To begin with the *Critique of Judgement*, the first point to stress is that Kant wrote it, as the title of paragraph III of the introduction tells us, 'as a means of connecting the two parts of philosophy in a whole'. These two parts, analysed in the previous *Critiques*, had in other words been unable to produce a systematic, harmonious whole: 'Concepts of nature contain the ground of all theoretical cognition *a priori* and rest, as we saw, upon the legislative authority of understanding. The concept of freedom contains the ground of all sensuously unconditioned practical precepts *a priori*, and rests upon that of reason. Both faculties . . . have

. . .their own peculiar jurisdiction in the matter of their content, and so, there being no further (*a priori*) jurisdiction above them, the division of Philosophy into theoretical and practical is justified.'[21] The task attempted in the third *Critique* is thus dictated by a desire for *theoretical* completeness. But the lack of systematicity that it intends to remedy is also the sign of a *real disharmony* between the two different worlds, or ways of being, of the subject itself. In the words of a recent commentary: 'The *Critique of Judgement* proposes to resolve *the laceration that occurs in the figure of man* between the *legislation of pure reason* (which implies the idea of *necessity*) and the *legislation of practical reason* (which implies the idea of *freedom*), and to create a *middle term* (*Mittelglied*) between the two legislations. This middle term will be judgement (in its implication of the idea of *finality*).'[22]

Kant's purpose is to heal the laceration resulting from the 'disillusionment' created by the natural sciences, from which the separation between judgements of fact and value judgements stemmed. While this separation safeguards the autonomy of scientific inquiry and is thus welcomed – in that sphere – as a liberating innovation, it reverberates as a painful mutilation in the sphere where moral values and world views are generated. As Kant himself observes in paragraph IX of the introduction, the 'concept of a *finality* of nature', which is the presupposition of judgement, *must* be postulated because *only in this way* can 'freedom' become an operative and effective faculty, its 'final end . . . actualized in nature and in harmony with its laws.' Kant continues: 'The effect in accordance with the concept of freedom is the final end which (or the manifestation of which in the sensible world) is to exist, and this presupposes the condition of the possibility of that end in nature (i.e. in the nature of the subject as a being of the sensible world, namely as man). It is so presupposed *a priori*, and without regard to the practical, by judgement. This faculty, with its concept of a *finality* of nature, provides us with the mediating concept between concepts of nature and the concept of freedom. . . .'[23]

Kant's research reveals all its historical 'necessity' if one reflects that while capitalist society is unthinkable without the scientific and technical progress reflected in the separation of intellect and morality, it is equally unthinkable without the incessant attempt to annul that separation and remedy it, an attempt to which the extraordinary and apparently inexplicable proliferation of aesthetic activities that distinguishes capitalism bears witness. In our society the socialization of the individual no longer possesses the legitimacy once conferred upon it by the bonds of tradition. It appears equitable only if it satisfies – as Hegel observed in the *Philosophy of Right* – 'the right of individuals to their *particular* satisfaction'. And no 'satisfaction' is possible, for that symbolic animal, man, if existence is split between a sphere where cultural values are everything and a sphere where they have no legitimacy at all. The more the 'legislation of the intellect' increased, and the more numerous were the aspects of social life which appeared to be sustained by a rigorous symbolic 'neutrality' – the objective, alien 'second nature' typically summed up by nineteenth-century economic mechanisms – the more developed had to become the aesthetic effort to present the world as something 'finalistic', as a world-for-the-individual.

Hence the cultural centrality of Kant's attempt to establish the 'middle term' capable of reconnecting nature and reason. Hence his insistence on the 'easing and intensification of life' produced by the contemplation of the beautiful, and on the 'harmony' that aesthetic pleasure arouses both within the individual and in the relation between the individual and nature. Hence, finally, all the reflections on the 'beautiful in nature' – a problem that later aesthetic theory would consider improper but whose massive, central presence in the *Critique of Judgement* does not, I think, stem only from the peculiarities of eighteenth-century aesthetics but at least as much from Kant's awareness that the divergence between the natural sciences and practical-rhetorical culture had to find a necessary and at the same time uncertain mediation, an 'as if' of which the concept of the 'beautiful in nature', in many respects a precarious one, was to be the first version

It is well known that the letters *On the Aesthetic Education of Man* are largely limited to restating the substance of the *Critique of Judgement* while simplifying it. The novelty of Schiller's work lies in extracting from Kant's arguments what we might call 'cultural politics' (not always, it should be added, entirely in line with the intentions of the *Critique*). Thus, in the ninth letter, art is expressly presented (something which never happened in Kant's text) as an unparallelled instrument of consent: unparallelled because – the observation takes us back to the problems posed at the start of this essay – it is able to act unobserved, eluding the conscious control of its user: 'The seriousness of your principles will frighten them [your contemporaries] away, but in the play of your semblance they will be prepared to tolerate them; for their taste is purer than their heart, and it is here that you must lay hold of the timorous fugitive. In vain will you assail their precepts, in vain condemn their practice; but on their leisure hours you can try your shaping hand. Banish from their pleasures caprice, frivolity and coarseness, and imperceptibly you will banish these from their actions and, eventually, from their inclinations too. Surround them, wherever you meet them, with the great and noble forms of genius, and encompass them about with the symbols of perfection, until Semblance conquer Reality, and Art triumph over Nature.'[24]

In other places – and above all in the most famous section of the work, the sixth letter – Schiller develops Kant's theme of art as the only activity allowing man's life to regain its lost harmony: 'That polypoid character of the Greek States, in which every individual enjoyed an independent existence but could, when need arose, grow into the whole organism, now made way for an ingenious clockwork, in which, out of the piecing together of innumerable but lifeless parts, a mechanical kind of collective life ensued. State and Church, laws and customs, were now torn asunder; enjoyment was divorced from labour, the means from the end, the effort from the reward. . . . Thus little by little the concrete life of the Individual is destroyed in order that the abstract idea of the Whole may drag out its sorry existence, and the State remains for ever a stranger to its citizens since at no point does it ever make contact with their feeling. . . .One-sidedness in the exercise of his powers must, it is true, inevitably lead the individual into error; but the species as a whole to truth. . . .Athletic bodies can, it is true, be developed by gymnastic exercises; beauty only through the free and harmonious play of the limbs. In the same way the keying up of individual functions of the mind can indeed produce extraordinary human beings; but only the equal tempering of them all, happy and complete human beings.'[25]

These passages help clarify the aims and the limitations of Schiller's 'harmony'. The split suffered by each individual – the *Aesthetic Education* leaves no doubt on this – is a consequence of a *social* split (between church and state, nature and reason, 'savages' and 'barbarians'). But the reconciliation effected by art, the harmony it represents and promotes, is never seriously presented as a model to be offered to society as a whole – as an ideal that would enable the split to be healed – but only as the best way of facing up to the split and *coexisting* with it. The criterion of harmony is entirely confined to the sphere of *symbolic legitimation*, which, in fact, it institutes as an autonomous sphere. Although the material causes of the split are considered inhuman and dangerous, Schiller's harmony can exist and have a value only to the extent that they too continue to exist. The point is not to *eliminate* the conflicting tensions but to create a sphere that can *temper them*, reorganizing the perception of the split itself in such a way as to make those who must endure it 'happy'. This 'happiness' is the essence of modern 'consent': and since it is increasingly hard to attain in everyday life, a 'form' becomes necessary which can in some way guarantee its existence.

One last point, which will enable us to move on from Schiller. The laceration Kant aimed to heal with his third *Critique* had been between intellect and reason, nature and freedom. In other words it separated a realm where the concept of value was everything from an opposite realm where it was nothing. With Schiller this framework is modified. In the *Aesthetic Education* the term 'nature' no longer indicates a symbolically neutral world but a particular set of values. 'Nature' is no longer opposed to 'reason' because it lacks attributes of value, but because it is fed by *different* values. If this is true, then the aesthetic sphere fulfils two distinct cultural functions in bourgeois civilization, and Schiller's *Aesthetic Education* is situated at their meeting point. The first function is that indicated by Kant's aesthetics: to restore the connection between the world of judgements of fact and that of judgements of value by resisting scientific 'disillusionment' and instead satisfying that deep-seated need for 'magic', which is part and parcel of the desire to see values 'rooted in facts', thus avoiding responsibility for their partiality in the secure belief that they 'stem' from the very 'reality of things'.[26]

The second function has been superimposed on this and in the course of time has probably acquired even greater importance. It consists in leading *to a reconciliation between conflicting values*. Schiller's work is only half a step in this direction. The values to be harmonized in the *Aesthetic Education* are not conflictual in and of themselves. They become so only because of their *one-sided* development. But they can still be 'tempered', and in this way led back to the neo-classical concept of 'harmony'. In the picture I have in mind this is not possible any more, because the conflict no longer stems from the fact that elements once joined have become reciprocally extraneous while remaining amenable to a new synthesis, but from a real opposition, an intrinsic hostility that no longer holds out any opportunities of 'dialectical' resolution.

For this to happen, however, bourgeois society had to open up definitively, and painfully, to social conflict: the incessant and bloody conflict that runs through European history from 1789 to the present, dividing every 'people', every national culture, not so much from a 'foreign' enemy any more as from an 'internal' enemy, one that speaks the same language, lives in the same towns and often calls upon the same god. The origin of conflicts could no longer be attributed to longstanding historical or geographical differences, 'national' characters that had come to be felt as almost immutable facts of nature. No: the conflict was nearer now, and therefore more acute – and, so it seemed, unresolvable.

Nineteenth-century literature is pervaded by this new perception of the conflictual nature of society. Indeed it seems that its great historical legacy consists in indicating how – in a civilization irreparably divided between hostile interests and values – the concept of 'consent' itself has to undergo a profound transformation. It can no longer consist in the drastic and acknowledged triumph of one system of values over all the others. It must assume a more ductile and precarious form: no longer that of full dialectical synthesis but the more 'dubious' one of *compromise*.[27]

Compromise is the great theme of 'realist' narrative fiction and perhaps, even more significantly, the main rhetorical criterion of that still more enigmatic phenomenon, the 'modern lyric'. If one had to characterize the latter in one word, the term that would spring to mind is 'obscurity'. And this obscurity – which to become such is willing to risk unintelligibility – is due largely to the constraining and ineluctable attempt to make semantic 'compromises' between what have become totally heterogeneous and contradictory elements. Baudelaire's oxymoron is still the figure that best exemplifies and sums up this operation. Paul Ricoeur has written: '. . . as a man of desires I go forth in disguise – *larvatus prodeo*. By the same token language itself is from the outset and for the most part distorted: it means something other than what it says, it has a double meaning, it is equivocal. The dream and its analogues are thus set within a region of language that presents itself as the locus of complex significations where another meaning is both given and hidden in an immediate meaning. Let us call this region of double meaning "symbol". . .'.[28]

Ricoeur's words introduce the last turn to be taken here. They do not refer to the modern lyric and literary hermeneutics but to the dream and psychoanalysis. And indeed, if one wants to see in literature the cultural activity delegated to secure consent by effecting 'adjustments' between conflicting values, one cannot dispense with at least a summary discussion of certain aspects of Freudian thinking.

Freud, as is well known, saw in art the most successful form of 'compensation' for those impulses which civilization compels the individual to sacrifice.[29] At the root of aesthetic activity one therefore finds the 'return of the repressed'. But in order for the repressed psychical contents to reoccupy the stage, they must put on a 'mask', or more exactly take on a 'form' different from their original, in consequence of the conflict with a psychical force which acts in the opposite direction: '. . . the model of Freudian negation is a formal one . . . a semiotic compromise-formation which allows one to say yes and no to anything simultaneously . . . perverse desire could not [be] acceptable as content in the literary work without the latter's also accepting the formal model capable of filtering it.'[30] This Freudian view contains a number of elements which are absolutely essential to interpretative activity: the image of the text as a field of conflict between psychical and cultural forces; the idea that these forces are differently placed in relation to our self-awareness (that is, they are more or less 'unconscious'); the insistence that the conflict between them can be understood only if its specific rhetorical formalizations are analysed; the explanation of the surprising and often, indeed, 'obscure' quality of these formalizations, which is traced back to the heterogeneous and mutually hostile nature of the forces reaching a compromise within them.

These are all, in my opinion, permanent contributions to the theory of literary interpretation. The problem lies elsewhere. It consists in asking whether the theoretical horizon of psychoanalysis, having produced those contributions, does not in the end prevent them from being used in the more testable and productive way. Let me explain, starting with an essential concept for the theory of the 'formal return of the repressed': the concept of 'negation' (*Verneigung*). In his Freudian reading of *Phèdre*, Francesco Orlando has elaborated and condensed this concept into the formula 'I do not like it'. The formula expresses a conflict: (I) do not/like it'. But this conflict is expressed and interpreted in a scientifically unacceptable way, because only one of its elements is defined: the other is determined, precisely, 'by negation' only. That side of the opposition where the repressed is located possesses a content of its own – the 'like it', which refers to a specific object or image. The other side, by contrast, is nothing more than a 'do not'. This shows that it is considered of entirely secondary importance to determine it *for what it is*. It can be described and possesses theoretical relevance only by virtue of what it is *not*: 'If a desire of a certain kind or intensity can be expressed through negation by the declaration I DO NOT LIKE IT, an even more unavowable or greater desire will give rise, for example, to I DO NOT LIKE IT AT ALL. A still more unavowable or greater desire might be rendered as I HATE IT, I DETEST IT, or other, similar expressions that remain clear negations though incorporated into a verb without a negative participle. We could compare this to a container whose contents exert a more or less explosive pressure on its walls; the greater the pressure, the more resistant or numerous the walls must be.'[32] The opening sentence of *Eros and Civilization* comes to mind here: 'The methodical sacrifice of libido, its rigidly enforced deflection to socially useful activities, *is* culture.' Culture is *'nothing else'* than the repression of instincts. It can take whatever form it likes. The *only* thing that counts is that it fulfil *that* function. Hence, evidently, the historically indeterminate anthropology that has always vitiated the psychoanalytic enterprise. But hence also an unforeseen consequence at the strictly hermeneutic level. What had been presented as a conflict between opposing forces is actually transformed – following the 'negation' hypothesis – into a single-sided process, much closer to the typical 'overturnings' of Hegelian dialectic (the term 'negation' should in any case have put us on our guard) than to the materialist view of a clash between specific entities.

In the presence of the 'negation', only one thing deserves attention: what becomes of the emergent desire, how it is modified and transformed. As for the metamorphoses of the other pole of the pair, there is nothing to say, despite the fact that they should be of some interest to cultural historians. Yet it is inevitable it should be like this, because that other pole never really existed, being just the 'alienated' figure of the repressed. And so the a priori lack of interest in the 'repressive' side of the pair (in 'civilization', in 'history') ends up by devaluing the intuition of the text as a 'compromise', diluting it into that far more jaded idea of the text as a place where an 'essence' is more or less fully 'expressed'. The simile of the 'container' whose 'form' (the 'walls') is altered by the 'pressure of content' leaves no room for doubt on the matter.

This is a relapse into a monistic conception of artistic phenomena, one that is in any case detectable in the concept of 'return of the repressed' itself. If literary texts – and on this score I personally have no doubts at all – owe a large part of their enigmatic attraction to the fact that they repropose unconscious psychical contents, there is no reason, either theoretical or empirical, why one would restrict the realm of the 'unconscious' just to the 'repressed'. Freud himself suggested, with particular clarity in *The Ego and the Id*, that the unconscious includes, as well as repressed contents properly speaking, the level of the super-ego.[33] If, therefore, literature has the task of 'familiarizing' us with our unconscious selves, reviving those connections of which we normally remain unaware, there is no reason at all why this operation should not involve the super-ego too. So much the more if one remembers that the super-ego – the moral conscience in its 'cruel', inexorable form – does not at all coincide, either in Freud or in fact, with the so-called 'reality principle'. When one says, correctly, that bourgeois civilization lives on a tacit but rigid separation between what is right 'in theory' and what applies 'in practice' – between maximum principles and their minimum realization – one is saying (in Freudian terms) precisely that the relationship between super-ego and reality principle (between moral conscience and actual social behaviour) is by its nature *problematic*. 'Civilization' produces the super-ego, and makes it its 'emissary' in the individual psyche. But then it lets it down, turns it away, discourages it (and if necesssary fights it: in war, whoever abides too rigorously by the Ten Commandments is shot). Consequently, the super-ego *also* needs continually to 're-emerge' in works which variously redefine its sphere of application, and show with what other psychical and social forces it comes into conflict. Much of the realist fiction of the past century indeed revolves around this problem; and 'moving' literature for children, which is one of the final and exemplary products of this tradition, fully bears out this hypothesis.

The theory of the 'return of the repressed' therefore needs extension, first of all. But it also needs correction. For it suggests that aesthetic pleasure consists essentially in the perception of this 'return'. The formal 'compromise', according to this argument, is merely the necessary *means* for making the repressed contents re-emerge. In Orlando's words, 'I would say that the figure is the perpetual tribute paid – and how willingly it is paid – by the language of the conscious ego to the unconscious.'[34] A statement like this necessarily rests on the assumption that the greatest happiness we could find would be to express and live the unconscious contents of the psyche fully and without restraint. Since this is not possible, one 'compensates' with the compromise offered by art. But one makes it known that it would be nice to do without it.

This hypothesis seems to me untenable. Every so often, in fact, the contents of our unconscious do in fact emerge in a radical and consequential way. And, in these cases, the result is the exact opposite of pleasure. The individual finds himself radically alone, dragged into an indomitable and unequal conflict with the surrounding world. More exactly, one could say that both the id and the super-ego, although in different ways, *ceaselessly push* the individual towards this conflict. They drag him, in their intransigent one-sidedness, towards an irreparable unhappiness.

But in that case, aesthetic 'pleasure' cannot consist in the perception of a 'return' of the unconscious, but rather in its exact opposite: in the contemplation of a successful compromise. The 'formal' conciliation is not the *means*, the simple *medium* of pleasure: it is its *end*, its true and only substance. The pleasure does not lie in having 'slackened' the grip of censorship a little but in having redrawn with precision the spheres of influence of the various psychic forces. This enables one to 'tie down' their restlessness, at least for the time being, and grants the individual that 'reduction of tension' which, according to Freud, characterizes all forms of pleasure.

If we turn our attention to the 'formal compromise' effected by the text, we will also be able – in conclusion – to bring back into the limelight an element of Freudian theory which literary criticism has always left in the wings: the so-called 'reality principle'. The meaning of this concept is already uncertain and unstable in Freud himself. It is sometimes presented as the opponent of the 'pleasure principle', at other times as its 'extension'. In some cases it seems to coincide with the 'exact knowledge of reality', whereas in others its cognitive character seems entirely secondary. At times it is placed in strict connection with the moral conscience, at times in conflict with it. Yet there is no doubt that Freud wanted to indicate by this term an aspect of the psychic apparatus and of social behaviour whose importance is beyond question. The 'reality principle' is what allows one to live in a divided and conflictual world, rounding off its sharp edges and managing simultaneously to satisfy imperatives of different natures and strengths.

Such is the meaning of a famous passage where Freud describes the behaviour of the ego, the part of the psyche most closely connected to the reality principle: '. . . we see this same ego as a poor creature owing service to three masters and consequently menaced by three dangers: from the external world, from the libido of the id, and from the severity of the super-ego. . . .In its position midway between the id and reality, it only too often yields to the temptation to become sycophantic, opportunist and lying, like a politician who sees the truth, but wants to keep his place in popular favour.'[35] Like the ego, the reality principle does not, therefore, indicate an autonomous 'principle', and a self-sufficient world of objects, but that sort of 'middle-term' which always emerges from the conclusion of a conflict. It is the line of least resistance round which an equilibrium is built, a sense of the individual's wholeness and involvement in the world. This is a precarious equilibrium, sure enough, recognized as such (when it is recognized) only after it has been attained, without (we should say) one's being clearly conscious of it.

Yet the equilibrium *is* attained. To break it down into its strictly unconscious components is a necessary stage of analysis. But it must be followed by the recognition that once the 'compromise' between them has been effected, we find ourselves looking at a *new* content, which is not reducible to the sum of its parts. This content is 'implicit', not 'unconscious'. There is in fact no longer any need for consciousness to repress and distance it, since it does not violate the reigning social norms, but rather conforms to them, coincides with them. Indeed, in a sense it helps to form them, because this new content is none other than *doxa*, opinion, the commonplace, the 'world view' as it generally appears in its concrete form: not as a 'pure' and thorny system but as something persuasive, seductive, all-embracing, as something that guarantees a modus vivendi, an adjustment between conflicting thrusts.

From the reality principle to the *doxa*, and thence to literature, which is – however paradoxical it may seem – one of the clearest manifestations of the reality principle. Literature is the 'middle term' par excellence, and its 'educational', 'realistic' function consists precisely in training us without our being aware of it for an unending task of mediation and conciliation. Literature (which, like the reality principle and the *doxa*, prospers in periods of social stability and suddenly appears 'useless' or 'impossible' during wars and revolutions) indicates how deeply rooted is our desire to make the 'adjustment' to the existing order *coincide* with some idea of 'happiness'. It makes us realize that 'consent' – feeling that we 'want' to do what we 'have' to do – can be one of the highest aspirations of the individual psyche. It tells us, in other words, that in the absence of great battles (and therefore – the point cannot be suppressed – in the absence of what could be great tragedies) it is inevitable that from time to time one will try to convince oneself that this is really the best of all possible worlds.

If so undeconstructive and unliberating a notion of literature still seems disagreeable, or unconvincing, I can only draw on an image that has often come back to me in the course of this study. It is a bas-relief of an ancient Greek tomb in the British Museum. It shows a harpy – the upper half of its body a woman, the lower a bird of prey – carrying off a small human body: according to the experts, the soul of the deceased. Below, the harpy is clutching the soul tight in its claws, but higher up her Greek arms are holding her in an attentive and tender embrace. The soul is doing nothing to get out of the harpy's clutch. It seems calm, relaxed even. It probably does not like being dead: if it did there would be no need for harpies. But at the same time the soul must know that there is no escape from the grip of the claws. For this reason it does not lower its gaze, but rests its head trustingly on the harpy's arms. Precisely because there is no escape it prefers to delude itself about the affectionate, almost maternal nature of the creature dragging it away with her in flight.

Can we blame it?

The Great Eclipse

Tragic Form as the Deconsecration of Sovereignty

'That thence the *Royal Actor* born / *The Tragick Scaffold* might adorn: / While round the armed Bands / Did clap their bloody hands. / *He* nothing common did or mean / Upon that memorable Scene.'[1] Marvell's celebration of Cromwell represents the execution of Charles I as a theatrical spectacle – specifically, as a tragedy. The argument of this essay is that there are excellent reasons why this should be appropriate: Elizabethan and Jacobean tragedy was in fact one of the decisive influences in the creation of a 'public' that for the first time in history assumed the right to bring a king to justice. To acknowledge this profound historical significance, however, is not to say that English Renaissance tragedy is a 'Puritan' or 'bourgeois' or 'revolutionary' cultural form. On the contrary, there is little in English tragedy that anticipates the new age opened up by the stroke of an axe at Whitehall on 30 January 1649. Yet new ages are not brought into being merely through the development of new ideas: the dissolution or overthrowing of old ideas plays an equal part in their emergence. And in the case at hand, historians are agreed that this is indeed the decisive phenomenon.[2] In the pages that follow, therefore, I shall attempt to indicate the elements essential to a definition of tragic form, and to demonstrate that the historical 'task' effectively accomplished by this form was precisely the destruction of the fundamental paradigm of the dominant culture. Tragedy disentitled the absolute monarch to all ethical and rational legitimation. Having deconsecrated the king, tragedy made it possible to decapitate him.

1. *'Meantime, we shall express our darker purpose'*

Let us begin with the work that initiates English tragedy: *Gorboduc*, written by Thomas Norton and Thomas Sackville in 1562. The play tells the story of a king who abdicates and divides his kingdom between his two sons, Ferrex and Porrex. The latter murders his brother to seize entire control of the realm, but he in turn is murdered by his mother. At this point, the people rise up and kill both king and queen. The nobles, assembled in parliament, put down the rebellion, and although the Duke of Albany betrays their common enterprise to secure the throne for himself, the play concludes with the clear suggestion that the aristocracy-in-arms will put down the rebellion.

The bare logic of events in the play is rich in implications. One is that tragedy presents a universe in which *everything has its origin in the decision of the king*. Tragedy thus pays the monarch an ambiguous homage. If the general culture of absolutism qualified the sovereign power it conferred upon the king with countless hesitations and uncertainties (representatively summed up in Bodin[3]), tragedy surrenders such power to him wholly and without the slightest reserve. In the world of tragedy the monarch is truly *absolute*. I do not mean, either here or in what follows, that tragedy presents the absolute monarch as he really was. It would be a frustrating task indeed to seek a realistic representation of the absolutist political system in the works of English tragedy. The strength (or weakness) of absolutism did not lie in the person of the king, but rather in a system of collective institutions such as a functioning bureaucracy, a sound fiscal system, a permanent army, and an efficient juridical unification: to the point that, as Immanuel Wallerstein has written, it would be more exact to call this system 'statism'.[4] It is also true, however, that the king acted as the summa and symbol of this new system of power in the context of its own political theory, which argued for an increase of power not for the state but for the king. Tragedy, then, stages not the institutions of absolutism, but its culture, its values, its ideology. This fact by no means impairs the capacity of tragedy to perform its task of radical dissolution. On the contrary, profound historical reasons operate in the case of absolutism to make the conflict of ideas (understood as the cultural process by which power is legitimated) a decisive matter. The first of these is specifically English: the numerous structural weaknesses of the crown made it difficult to establish an absolute monarchy *de facto*. All the more reason, then, that the attempt to construct one had to rely on elements of an ideal character. The arguments of James I on the divine right of kings, Carl Schmitt observes, merely masked the dearth of hopes and prospects for his actual position.[5] When, therefore, as we shall see, tragedy performs the degradation of the cultural image of the sovereign, it deprives the monarchy of its central bastion, its ultimate weapon. There is a second, more wide-ranging reason for the crucial pertinence of the ideological field here. In the political system of absolutism, the relation between culture and power differs considerably from that obtaining in other kinds of society, capitalism in particular. In the latter, social power finds its legitimacy from the very beginning in the simple fact that it exists. The property spoken of by the philosophy of natural right – typically posited prior to the social contract – is a real datum. It exists and that suffices. It has no more meaning than the world of nature after the 'disenchantment' effected by seventeenth-century physics. For the philosophy of natural right – which is the real site of origin for the distinction between 'structure' and 'superstructure' – culture is ultimately a latecomer whose function consists in preserving the fundamental given of property. ('The Regulating and Preserving of Property' is not accidentally the classic formula that, at the beginning of Locke's Second Treatise, defines the tasks and limits of political power.) With absolutism the reverse is true. Here the legitimacy of social power derives from a form of divine investiture. Power is founded in a transcendent design, in an intentional and significant order. Accordingly, political relations have the right to exist only in so far as they *reproduce that order symbolically*. In a word, if bourgeois property can have a meaning because it exists, absolute monarchy can exist because it has a meaning. What occurs in the sphere of absolutist culture is not confined to the heights of the superstructure; it informs the base itself, the condition of existence of political rule. Hence, the cultural conflicts and modifications of the age of absolutism bear directly on the politics of this world, in whose collapse tragedy – generally neglected whenever this problem is being considered – is one of the decisive phenomena.

Sovereignty is a power that, having its origin *in itself*, is thereby released from any control; it is 'self-determined', as Hegel will say. Sovereignty is a *universal* power, reaching and defining every part of the body politic, whose destiny is therefore enveloped within it. Both attributes profoundly inform the structure of *Gorboduc*. Universal, the decision of the king will gradually affect his person, his family, the nobility, the people, and all society: in event after event, the royal act resonates over the entire political body. Self-determining, the king is the only character really free to choose and therefore to *act* in the proper sense of the word. He is the primary and, in a certain sense, the only real actor in modern tragedy. As Kierkegaard put it in his reflections on the difference between ancient and modern tragedy: in the ancient world, 'even if the individual moved freely, he still rested in the substantial categories of state, family, and destiny. This substantial category is exactly the fatalistic element in Greek tragedy, and its exact peculiarity. The hero's destruction is, therefore, not only a result of his own deeds, but is also a suffering, whereas in modern tragedy, the hero's destruction is really not suffering, but is action . . . . Our age has lost all the substantial categories of family, state, and race. It must leave the individual entirely to himself, so that in a stricter sense he becomes his own creator.'[6] There remains only to add that the chief example of this 'individual' freed from 'substantial categories' *within* society (and not outside it, banished like a vagabond or leper) is furnished by the absolute sovereign, who is literally *absolutus*, that is, released, free. Tragedy could re-emerge only in the late sixteenth century, when the figure of the new prince had entered the stage of history. Without the absolute sovereign, modern tragedy would not have been possible.

With these premisses established, let us return to *Gorboduc*. Here the attributes that the king would arrogate to himself are readily given over to him. But the gift is poisoned. Precisely what makes Gorboduc a sovereign – universality and self-determination – also proclaims him, in accordance with a paradigm that remains unchanged through the development of English tragedy, a *tyrant*.[7] The key to the metamorphosis comes early in the play when Gorboduc declares to his counsellors his intention of abdicating. Though the latter attempt to dissuade him with various 'rational' arguments ('Only I mean to show by certain rules,/Which kind hath graft within the mind of man'[8]), Gorboduc never bothers in the least to confute them. He is king not because he can reason and persuade, but simply by virtue of the fact that he *decides*. And he decides in a 'self-determined' way, that is, without having to worry about adducing 'motivations' or 'causes', on which he remains rigorously silent. We inevitably encounter the problem of *decision*, an obligatory one for the history of political theory and of absolute power in particular. As we have already hinted, it is here that the fundamental attribute of the monarch resides: according to Carl Schmitt's definition, sovereign authority is that which decides on 'the state of exception'.[9] This power of decision incarnates itself in dictatorship, which aims to put an end to the state of exception and which, when it succeeds in this, imposes itself on the basis of a permanent and no longer merely occasional sovereignty.[10] It is particularly striking that, from *Gorboduc* forward, English tragedy offers us a dynamic of events diametrically opposed to that described by Schmitt for the case of dictatorship. In tragedy, dictatorship (which, we recall from Benjamin, 'demands the completion of the image of the sovereign, as tyrant') is not the means to end a state of exception, but rather, on the contrary, what provokes it, what initiates civil war. In other words, the force that the king manifests in his decision proclaims him not only a tyrant, but incapable of governing as well. As a consequence, the exercise of sovereignty leads to complete anarchy, as though the two were one and the same. With effects that we will later need to register, tragedy represents absolutism as an irresolvable paradox.

In *Gorboduc*, I have claimed, the king appears as a tyrant, but, at first glance, the contrary seems true, for how can one be a tyrant if, like Gorboduc, one abdicates one's throne? The contradiction is only apparent. The principal characteristic of Gorboduc's abdication lies rather in its form than in its content, and in the fact that it manifests itself as a sovereign decision, an act of free will. In Elizabethan terms, the conflict in the abdication scene (I, ii) occurs between the *will* of Gorboduc and the *reason* of his counsellors. Both terms are crucial in sixteenth-century ethical-political treatises, which locate the difference between king and tyrant precisely in the relationship that is instituted between will and reason. Lydgate's Aristotle had already harped on the point: 'To Alysaunder he wrote in trouthe/That he shold alwaye be governed by reason.'[11] "Obstinacie', writes Thomas Elyot, 'is an affection immoueable, fixed to wille, abandonynge reason . . . . By it many a valyaunt capitayne and noble prince haue nat onely fallen them selfes, but also brought all their contrayes in daungeour and often tymes to subuercion and ruyne.'[12] 'Wo to him whose will hath wisedomes place', laments Richard II in *The Mirror for Magistrates*[13]; and Hooker, the great codifier of Elizabethan ideology, says: 'Two principal fountains there are of human action, knowledge and will . . .; the will. . . differeth greatly from that inferior natural desire which we call appetite. The object of appetite is whatsoever sensible good may be wished for; the object of will is that good which reason doth lead us to seek.'[14] Finally, we read in *The Mirrour of Policie* at the turn of the century: '[To live under a monarchy] is verie dangerous, and to be feared (considering the frailetie of man, and the great libertie that kings haue to doe what they list, whether it bee good or euil, and the great power that they haue to execute what so their will leadeth them unto).'[15] In short, as the last quotation makes clear, in the case of the king, will is power, the power to act. And, significantly, nothing ensures that such a power to act will be subordinated to the dictates of reason, since, on the contrary, absolutism aspires to emancipate such power entirely. In the 'autonomy of politics', Elizabethan organicism articulates *the principle of tyranny*. Hooker's consoling distinction between appetite and will is founded on the precedence and control accorded to reason, but once this ceases to be granted, the two forms of will become indistinguishable: 'Tyrannicall power is put into the hands of one alone who . . . tyrannizeth according to his disordinate will, . . . according to his sensuall appetite and will.'[16] Appetite and will are now placed on the same level. The 'too sullied flesh' triumphs over 'godlike reason': the tyrant subjugates the sovereign.

With *Gorboduc*, the old ethical conflict between will and reason is transformed into a political clash between executive power and consultative privilege, between Gorboduc and his counsellors, the sovereign and the aristocracy. The terms of the conflict are fully consonant with the system of correspondences that flourished in England around the middle of the sixteenth century. The king was the 'heart' of the body politic, the source of action, while the nobility were the 'eyes', or the organs of sense and intellection.[17] But what was a functional distinction in this 'world picture', a collaboration between different organs for the benefit of the whole, has in *Gorboduc* become a contest. The first movement of the first English tragedy is thus to *sever* the connections that sustained the dominant culture. At bottom, English tragedy is nothing less than the negation and dismantling of the Elizabethan world picture.

'The Elizabethan world picture', of course, is first and foremost an historiographical hypothesis. It was advanced independently at roughly the same time by Theodore Spencer in 1942,[18] and in 1943 by E. M. W. Tillyard, who 'invented' the term. Also in 1943, Leo Spitzer was writing *Classical and Christian Ideas of World Harmony*, in which he extended a similar argument to all of Western Europe.[19] The argument is basically as follows: European culture is based on the encounter between Platonism and Christianity, the fusion of which dominated it up to the scientific 'disenchantment' of the seventeenth and eighteenth centuries. There are basically, therefore, only two periods in European culture: the period that extends from antiquity through the Middle Ages to the Renaissance, and the modern period. In all its variations, this argument denies the historical and cultural specificity of the age of absolutism – a denial all the more easily accomplished in the case of England where the existence of such an age was briefer and more precarious than elsewhere. Thus, Tillyard: 'Coming to the [Elizabethan] world picture itself, one can say dogmatically that it was still solidly theocentric, and that it was a simplified version of a much more complicated medieval picture.' In this perspective, the only truly distinctive feature of Elizabethan culture becomes its capacity to integrate some modern elements into the already established medieval totality – its capacity, in short, for 'compromise'. 'Though the general medieval picture of the world survived in outline into the Elizabethan age, its existence was by then precarious. There had been Macchiavelli, to whom the idea of a universe divinely ordered throughout was repugnant . . . The greatness of the Elizabethan age was that it contained so much of new without bursting the noble form of the old order. It is here that the Queen herself comes in. Somehow the Tudors had inserted themselves into the constitution of the medieval universe. They were part of the pattern and they had made themselves indispensable.'[20]

However well the theory of the Elizabethan world picture explains other phenomena, it fails to grasp the most important fact of the age. For cultural production proceeds by strange leaps and condensations; and in the period of English absolutism, this production is concentrated in the drama-within-the-drama, in tragedy. Had this drama not existed, Elizabethan culture would scarcely have assumed the importance it has for us, and for the very reasons Tillyard gives: because it would not have presented its own distinctive features, such as would make it a specific object of study different from others. If one claims to speak of Elizabethan culture, therefore, one must speak of its tragedy, but this is precisely what the theory of the Elizabethan world picture prevents us from doing. To be sure, the theory takes up the subject of tragedy, but only to assign to it the curious function of confirming its own scheme *a contrario*. The tragic negation, it is argued, goes to show the solidity of medieval organicism, and the need for radical destruction confirms the power of what is to be destroyed. It is as though it were argued that in strangling Desdemona, Othello paid tribute to her importance. No doubt he does, but he strangles her all the same, and similarly, tragedy, in its destruction of the medieval world picture, recognizes its importance, but destroys it nonetheless. And it is on the dynamic of destruction that we need to focus, not on the handsome edifice that, by the end of the fifth act, has been reduced to rubble. This dynamic, as we have seen, originates in the decision of the king – or rather in the fact that the king acts as an *absolute sovereign*. Tillyard is certainly correct to notice the many glorifications of Elizabeth that 'insert' her 'within the constitution of the medieval universe'. But this is only to say that these do not recognize her new, actual function. Only tragedy looks the new prince straight in the face, taking his absolutist claims at their word and systematically elaborating them. Alone in the Elizabethan period, tragedy is truly modern, truly rigorous.

Let us once more return to *Gorboduc* and the conflict there between kingly power and aristocratic reason. By virtue of his action, the king causes the dissolution of the entire body politic. Absolutism thus reveals its full force, which is revealed in turn, however, as a social catastrophe. *Gorboduc* will prove typical of English tragedy, but only in the kind of story it tells and the kind of logic it gives to events. What is still missing is the other essential characteristic of tragedy, its particular form of *reflection* on events. In *Gorboduc*, will emancipates itself from reason, action from speech; and the autonomy of sovereign action, primed by the inscrutable will of the monarch, gives rise to the succession of actions that makes up the story. Yet if reason has been defeated by the will of the king, it has hardly been destroyed. In the last scene of the play, Eubulus, the spokesman for the ideology of the body politic and the most ample exponent of the Elizabethan world picture, reproduces the same arguments rejected by Gorboduc at the beginning. The Elizabethan cultural establishment has stood the brunt of the dramatic action, which, moreover, fully confirms its validity: Eubulus had foreseen it all from the start. Appropriately, the values of this establishment return to the field, enriched and, this time, armed, themselves endowed with the force that in the beginning had been the monopoly of the king. The parliament-in-arms at the end of *Gorboduc* can once again intervene in the course of events and, closing the tragic scission, bring the tragedy to a conclusion. It has reunited force and reason, submitting the former to the latter. Offering us only a limited absolutism, *Gorbudoc* is never more than a half-tragedy. The restoration of reason and the restoration of the aristocracy imply one another. If the values of the Elizabethan world picture survive, this is because their political exponents survive as well. Just as the progress of absolutism will eliminate the latter, so too the progress of tragic form – in its development, a shining mirror of the 'crisis of the aristocracy' – will render impossible a closure in which reason, not only uninjured but armed, reconquers the stage. We encounter the evidence half a century later, when Shakespeare rewrites *Gorboduc* and calls it *King Lear*.

Although much more complex, the plot of *King Lear* is based on the same assumptions we saw operating in *Gorboduc*. To divide the kingdom is to act against all reason, and in the void that is thereby engendered the destructive force of the selfish 'nature' of Edmund, Goneril, and Regan can be freed. Certain conventions, however, are clearer here than in *Gorboduc*, particularly the apparently paradoxical fact that abdication is a tyrannical act. The decision to abdicate, which in Gorboduc was 'purpose' *tout court*, becomes Lear's 'darker purpose': obscure, inscrutable, arbitrary, and exhibited as such. Moreover, the simple and slight reason Lear adduces for abdicating – the weight of his old age – clearly suggests that he has betrayed his political and public function to the advantage of his physical and private person. Like Claudius or Macbeth, albeit in different form, Lear thus yields to 'fallen nature', and this yielding points to the transformation of the king into a tyrant. The entire abdication scene is dominated by Lear's arrogant absolutism. Unlike Gorboduc, Lear does not stop at simply rejecting the advice of his counsellor Kent; he banishes him from the kingdom under pain of death. What gratifies him in the speeches of Goneril and Regan is the abyss they excavate between himself and them, the unlimited dependence they declare.[21] Conversely, what infuriates him in Cordelia is her untainted feudal spirit: 'I love your Majesty/According to my bond; no more nor less' (I, i, 92–3).[22] Cordelia still inhabits a world of reciprocal obligation, of feudal rights and duties, whereas Lear aspires to absolute omnipotence. His 'madness' is in large part the inevitable issue of this aspiration, not its overthrow. Thus, in III, ii, at the height of the storm, he shouts out his absurd orders to the forces of nature ('Blow, winds, and crack your cheeks!'). Or again, in III, iv, he sets himself up in supreme judgement over all daughters. Or again, finally, in the last scene, he can do no better than cover with insults those who have tried to help him, glorifying his own powers: 'A plague upon you murderers, traitors all!/*I* might have sav'd her; now she's gone for ever!/ ... /*I* kill'd the slave that was a-hanging thee' (V, iii, 269–70, 274, my italics). Thus, as Benjamin has claimed, madness appears as the definitive sign of the sovereign's degeneration.[23]

As *Lear* heightens the absolutist claims made in *Gorboduc*, it simultaneously diminishes the counterclaims of the aristocracy. Certainly, *King Lear* quite teems with loyal nobles – Kent,

Gloucester, Albany, Edgar, not to mention the numerous Gentlemen who pass on stage simply to attest their fidelity to the old king. What has been lost is not the number of faithful nobles, but their function. They are no longer allowed, as Eubulus was in *Gorboduc*, to inscribe events within an organic and rational framework of political meaning. In the first scene of the tragedy, Kent opposes Lear merely to defend the rights of Cordelia (with whom he shares a feudal ethic), not in the name of the higher interests of the kingdom. Nor as he takes his leave from the court, does he reveal any ability to foresee future consequences. The very service he will later offer to Lear is inspired by fidelity to a person rather than to a political institution. When Gloucester, for his part, tries to give an account of conditions at the start of the play, he has recourse to what already appeared to the Elizabethan audience an empty superstition, 'the excellent foppery of the world': 'These late eclipses in the sun and moon portend no good to us. . . . Love cools, friendship falls off, brothers divide: in cities, mutinies; in countries, discord; in palaces, treason; and the bond crack'd 'twixt son and father' (I, ii, 107–108, 110–114). But the clearest instance of the nobility's inadequacy comes in the speech with which Edgar concludes the play:

> The weight of this sad time we must obey;
> Speak what we feel, not what we ought to say.
> The oldest hath borne most: we that are young
> Shall never see so much, nor live so long.
> (V, iii, 323–26)

It should not seem strange that the extraordinary dramatic efficacy of these lines consists in their chilling stupidity, in the drastic banalization they impose on the play. In the very work that has unhinged our trust in the meaning of words, there reappears the obtuse assurance of sing-song proverb and of dead metaphor: 'the weight of time', 'see so much', 'live so long'. The story that has involved the downfall of a kingdom and a pair of families (not to mention, one imagines, a good number of French and English soldiers) is summed up as a 'sad time'. Though *King Lear* has denied the transparency of feelings in language, Edmund now urges us to 'speak what we feel'. 'Old' and 'young', categories

EDGAR

which the play has deprived of all interpretive value, are now exhumed as though they might explain something. And finally, to put the seal on all, four impeccably rhymed little verses, bright with monosyllables, come to conclude a work in which a tormented prose has invaded the terrain of rhythmic decorum. The speech of Edgar is the most extraordinary – and appropriate – of anticlimaxes. Its blind mediocrity indicates the chasm that has opened up between facts and words, or more accurately, between referents and signifieds. The close of *King Lear* makes clear that no one is any longer capable of giving meaning to the tragic process; no speech is equal to it, and there precisely lies the tragedy.[24] One notes here the historical caesura that divides *Gorboduc* and *Lear*. In *Gorboduc*, reason though momentarily routed by the decisive power of the king, nonetheless succeeded in foreseeing and bestowing a meaning upon the sequence of actions. It always remained a pole in the drama, endowed with its own representatives, and it emerged from its trial enriched and surer of itself. By the end, it was equipped to begin putting the world again to rights. In *Lear*, what scant reason remains has been not only defeated, but derided and dissolved by the course of events. If at the end it is allowed the last word, this is only by virtue of that archaic, semi-miraculous duel between Gloucester's two sons; and if it returns on stage, it is only with the object of confounding us with the poverty of its reflection.

Before examining the consequences of what has just been said, let us briefly consider the semantic modifications to which the term 'tragedy' is subject in the course of only a few decades. Speaking of the Prologue to Chaucer's *Monk's Tale*, George Steiner observes that the meaning of tragedy for the high Middle Ages does not imply dramatic form. 'A tragedy is a narrative recounting the life of some ancient or eminent personage who suffered a decline of fortune toward a disastrous end.'[25] Tragedy is largely synonymous with misfortune or death, and it keeps this sense not only in the *Mirror for Magistrates*, but even in *Arden of Faversham* (1590?: 'And train thy master to his tragedy')[26] and Kyd's *Spanish Tragedy* (1590?: 'This very sword . . ./Shall be the worker of thy tragedy').[27] In this perspective, the prince is more important for what he is than for what he does. If his fall is the most clamorous, this is for 'quantitative' reasons, as it were, rather than reasons inherent in his specific political function. *Gorboduc* represents a second moment, in which tragedy, ceasing to be the story of a king opposed by fate, becomes the story of a tyrant. This new sense of tragedy is found in Elyot: 'in redyng tragoedies, [a man shall] execrate and abhorre the intollerable life of tyrantes'; in Sidney: 'the high and excellent Tragedy . . . maketh Kinges feare to be Tyrants, and Tyrants manifest their tirannicall humours'; in Puttenham: '[Princes'] infamous life and tyrannies were layd open to all the world, their wickedness reproched, their follies and extreme insolences derided, and their miserable ends painted out in playes and pageants, to shew the mutabilitie of fortune, and the just punishment of God in reuenge of a vicious and euill life.'[28] Tragedy now is the story of a tyrant who unmoors action from the hold of reason. Yet if *Gorboduc* and the sixteenth-century treatises privilege this sense of tragedy, it is always with a view to reinforcing the status of reason. Tragedy with them becomes a supremely educational aesthetic form. A last indication of this comes from a dramatic function we have not yet considered. Every act of *Gorboduc* opens with a dumb show and closes with a chorus. On the one hand, the dumb show allegorically stages what will happen in the act proper, and the allegory is so codified, even proverbial, that it will immediately be understood. On the other, the chorus sums up what has happened in the act and emphasizes its significance. Thus, even though the sovereign's decision unchains action from reason, such action continues to occur in the temporal and semantic context established by reason. The moral precedes the tale, and the general model anticipates the particular case. With *Gorboduc*, tragedy takes shape thanks to the insertion of the sovereign at its origin, but this development takes place only within a rigidly circumscribed dramatic structure still possessing certain characteristics that will remain immune from the catastrophe, delimit it, bestow sense on it, and resolve it. Finally, with the destructive power of *King Lear*, tragedy enters a third phase of evolution, in which those 'pales and forts of reason' of which Hamlet was already doubtful are unremittingly struck down. Neither characters nor other dramatic elements succeed in giving significance to the tragic plot: 'th'election lights/On Fortinbras, he has my dying voice./So tell him, with th'occurrents more and less/ Which have solicited – the rest is silence' (*Hamlet*, V, ii, 355–8). 'Th'occurrents more and less': this, for Hamlet, is all one can say at the end of his tragedy. With the mediocre conscientiousness that characterizes him, Horatio will tell Fortinbras 'of carnal, bloody, and unnatural acts,/ Of accidental judgements, casual slaugh-ters,/ Of deaths put on by cunning and [forc'd] cause,/ And in this upshot, purposes mistood/Fall'n on th'inventors' head' (V, ii, 381–5). In short, he will offer him a plot summary. But what of the 'rest', which is nothing if not the meaning of what has happened? On that falls Hamlet's prohibition: let no one presume to confer meaning on it.

From the last observation, it should be clear that the concept of tragedy I am attempting to delineate here can only be a *structural* concept, capable of simultaneously defining a syntagmatic axis (plot) and a paradigmatic axis (values), and of clarifying the uni-que relation that obtains between them in tragedy. This is to say that the 'tragic' – an expression that always refers to a single dimension of the problem, usually (even in Nietzsche) to the con-tent of actions – does not exist as a possible situation in human history, whether real or imaginary. Only *tragedy* exists – that is, a particular form of *representing* that history: a rigorously asymmet-rical structure marked by a constitutive lack. Fully realized tragedy is the parable of the degeneration of the sovereign inserted in a context that *can no longer understand it*. It is a text that lacks an adequate interpretive function and in which the final 'judgement' must be enormously poorer than that on which it is passed. From Hegel forward, this inadequation has been attributed to the disap-pearance of the chorus and, along with it, of what Hegel called 'a higher moral consciousness, aware of substantial issues, warning against false conflicts, and weighing the outcome'.[29] Whether the chorus of ancient tragedy really functioned as Hegel claims (a question open to considerable debate), in modern tragedy at any rate, the chorus, still existing in *Gorboduc* where it coincided at the end of the play with the aristocracy-in-arms, is missing. With it disappears a universal, 'higher' point of view. Or more exactly this consciousness is no longer a property of those characters who hold the tragic stage, and who are various facets of the dominant class of the time. In modern tragedy, this class appears suddenly *incapable of understanding* the course and sense of history. It has nothing to teach those who are watching and who thus find themselves deprived of that spiritual guidance to which they have been accustomed, precisely when the events they watch make such guidance absolutely necessary. The spectators are literally constrained *to think for themselves*: for the first time, nothing and nobody shows them the way. For millenia, 'ideas' had been validated not by their 'intrinsic truth' (a modern scientific criterion), but by the 'authority' of those who proffered them. With modern tragedy, the principle of authority is dissolved, and with it vanishes the chief obstacle to the existence of that *rational public* that others, in other ways, will take charge of forming fully.

2. 'A tale told by an idiot, signifying nothing'

For us the concept of theatre refers directly to aesthetic activity, but for the Elizabethans it was before all else connected with a system of political relationships. 'The world's a Theater, the earth a Stage,/Which God, and nature doth with Actors fill,/Kings have their entrance in due equipage,/And some their parts play well and others ill/ .... All men haue parts, and each man acts his owne.'[30] The idea that the world is a theatre where men simply play a role is truly meaningful only in the context of a feudal 'status society', whose fundamental characteristics, according to Macpherson's reconstruction, consist in the fact that 'the productive and regulative work of the society is authoritatively allocated to groups, ranks, classes, or persons' each of which 'is confined to a way of working, and is given and permitted only to have a scale of reward, appropriate to the performance of its or his function.'[31] The significance of the stratification of medieval society into its estates, as another scholar of medieval political thought has written, is that 'it was precisely the hallmark of a member of a particular estate that he could not move out of his own estate. ...each member of society should fulfil the functions which were allotted to him, because this was held to have been the effluence of the divine ordering of things. It was the principle of vocation . . . according to which every individual had been called (*vocatus*) to fulfil specific tasks. . . .What mattered was not the individual, was not the man, but . . . the office which that individual occupied.'[32] The individual 'exists', therefore, only insofar as he is an 'actor' in a social 'role'. Society is thinkable only as a theatre, and life as a performance. Yet in that case, strictly speaking, an actual theatre would be inconceivable. And, in fact, feudal society knows the theatre only in its religious form, as the perennial re-enactment of roles prescribed for all eternity. The rebirth of the stage can take place only when the system of roles that constitutes this status society begins to give way, and the solidity of political bonds comes undone in the course of the long crisis of the fourteenth century. Absolutism – again we see the necessity of this historiographical category – has its origin in the attempt to halt this process. The feudal hierarchy whose molecular organization was in a state of extreme disarray hoped to restore itself by concentrating power in the hands of the sovereign.[33] This utopian late-medieval project, so perfectly comprehensible in the framework of the Elizabethan world picture, had an ephemeral life, but it found an interesting dramatic incarnation in the 'dark' or 'problem' plays of the first years of the seventeenth century, plays which from a historical point of view it would be preferable to call de-problematizing plays.

The 'de-problematizing' play par excellence is Shakespeare's *Measure for Measure* (1604), which enriches and perfects the structure established the preceding year by John Marston in *The Malcontent*. This structure hinges on four elements, the nature of the protagonist, his relationship to the plot, the characteristics of the minor characters, and the final scene. The four elements define as many ideological junctures in the Elizabethan world picture, and they reappear in tragic structure only to be brought into question. It will be useful, therefore, to examine the 'programmatic' functioning of the Elizabethan world picture in order to perceive more clearly how tragedy constitutes itself as its negation. Beginning with the figure of the protagonist, the legitimate holder of supreme authority, Shakespeare's Duke or Marston's Altofront, we notice that his fundamental characteristic is *not to be subject to the pas-*

sions. This separates him from the other characters, who are not-ably weaker in this respect, and designates him as the sovereign of the Elizabethan utopia, dedicated to the public weal in so far as devoid of personal interests. To return to our earlier terms, he is subject to reason and not to will, while – for the lesson to be as clear as possible – selfish passion overwhelms both Angelo, the deputy of legitimate power, and Mendozo, its usurper. He who restores this power, then, is a figure of integrity, so whole that he can be divided without risk: into the Duke/Friar, or Altofront/Malevole. What in the tragic hero becomes sorrowful laceration and impotence is here subterfuge and canniness, the *arcanum imperii* of disguise that even Elyot could still recall to his 'governors' the better to know their subjects. Dressed up as a friar, the Duke of Vienna wanders about his city and oversees. 'I perceive your Grace, like a pow'r divine,/Hath look'd upon my passes', Angelo exclaims at the end of *Measure for Measure* (V, i, 369–70). This superior vision of authority is a crucial formal element. Tragic heroes are always conspicuously blind, and in Jacobean drama, the idea that any character can 'see' the dramatic development in its entirety is completely lost, with the result that the only one to possess a comprehensive vision of events is the audience. But in a hierarchical society, this radical reversal of what ideally would be a descending order of comprehension, in which the higher one's position, the more one sees,[34] carries with it some explosive consequences. For ultimately, those who possess the most general vision may plausibly claim the most general power, and the pre-revolutionary exaltation of the Country over the Court will be based precisely on the betrayal of the general interest by the latter.[35] The Shakespeare of the 'problem plays' seems concerned to pre-empt such consequences. By means of the Duke, the London public has its own 'representative' on stage, who can, moreover, do that which is denied the public and intervene in events. But the Duke is not merely a figure for the audience; he is also and above all the director of *Measure for Measure*, bringing characters on stage, sending them off, telling them what to do and say, suggesting tricks and devices, substitutions and disguises. The plot of *Measure for Measure* is nothing other than a comedy written by the Duke, whose object – as he clearly explains early on (I,

iii) – is to reimpose his authority on Vienna and restore the force of its institutions. With the sovereign as 'director', his intrigue as 'play', the goal of the problem plays is to reconstitute a theatrical world 'from above'. The close of *The Malcontent* is exemplary in this respect.

> MALEVOLE. (*To* Pietro *and* Aurelia.)
> You o'er joyed spirits, wipe your long-wet eyes.
> Hence with this man! (*Kicks out* Mendoza.) An
> eagle takes not flies. –
> (*To* Pietro *and* Aurelia.) You to your vows. –
> (*To* Macquerelle.) And
> thou unto the suburbs. –
> (*To* Bilioso.) You to my worst friend I would hardly give:
> Thou art a perfect old knave. – (*To* Celso *and the* Captain.)
> All-pleased, live
> You two unto my breast. – (*To* Maria.) Thou to my heart.
> The rest of idle actors idly part;
> And as for me, I here assume my right,
> To which I hope all's pleas'd. To all, good night.'[6]

According to a strategy that reappears in *Measure for Measure*, the sovereign here redistributes the social roles. The world has once again been made a theatre – and for this reason, the performance can end, declaring the theatre as such henceforward gratuitous. Unlike in the case of tragedy, the finale here is truly an apex, a conclusion. This is so even at a strictly temporal level, on account of the functional position that it occupies in the plot sequence. Here the finale is not just the last ring in the chain of events, but an act that sends its repercussions backwards, and, more than simply 'putting an end' to the plot, it negates its character as an irreversible temporal sequence, as *history*. Whereas tragedy is dominated by the perception that there is no going back, which is epitomized in the act of *dying* (both Desdemona and the Duchess of Malfi 'return to life' for a moment to give the illusion that everything can start all over again, but then they expire for good), in the last scene of the 'problem' plays, the criminal acts that the villain thought they were committing are revealed never to have happened, and those who were believed dead rise again, to the joy of all present. Thus is dramatically realized the ideal of every restoration culture: to abolish the irreversibility of history and render the past everlasting. Social relations, no longer fraudulent and productive of uncontrollable events, are reformulated in a transparent and spatial – that is, static – form.

It remains to speak of the others, who, seemingly menaced by a quite different dramatic fate, prove instead to have been pliant, compliant wax in the hands of a benevolent wizard. Except for the villain, these characters are marked by the two attributes of the ideal subject, loyalty and passivity. We meet women who seven years later still love the men who rejected them and even refused to see them afterwards; jailors who succumb to the magnetism emanating from a friar; sisters who never entertain the slightest thought of revenge for a murdered brother; fortress commanders who remain stubbornly faithful to their legitimate but dispossessed lord. Each and every one is present to perform in the drama conceived by the sovereign, on whom is conferred (as in a famous speech of James I in Parliament) 'power to exalt low things, and abase high things, to make of their subjects like men at the Chesse.' [37] Thus the sovereign achieves his real theatrical triumph not over such characters, but over the villain, Angelo in *Measure for Measure* or Bertram in *All's Well That Ends Well*. The form of his humiliation is identical in both cases: he is forced to accept the woman to whom he is bound by law or troth and to renounce the woman to whom he has been drawn by passion. He is constrained to marry the former because, imagining he was committing adultery, he has in fact made love to his wife or his legitimate betrothed. The substitution-trick dramatizes two important facts. First, it denies all autonomy to the sphere of private relationships, rendered transparent to the eyes of the sovereign and the audience. What the villain had tried to keep jealously hidden is on the contrary pitilessly exposed and ridiculed. Second, Angelo and Bertram are both aware that they have been mere 'actors' in the sovereign's design. The role they have physically impersonated imprisons them in its fixity, dissolves whatever individual aspirations they have entertained, and reconfirms the basic principle of *status society*: that man is what his sovereign makes him. Thus, everything once again finds its place and its sense – exemplarily, in the context of matrimony. The problem plays exalt the abilities of the king, wise, astute, powerful, only to reduce him in the end to a justice of the peace. Nor should this seem strange, for what was the good king of the Elizabethan utopia but the administrator of traditional justice? The problem plays conclude therefore with scenes of judgement, where the rite of punishment and retribution is perfectly enacted. It must also be noted that Shakespeare's intelligence goes still further in designating the sovereign as the figure who can realize the desired compromise between the *political constitution* of society and the first yearnings for independence on the part of *civil society*. In *Measure for Measure*, in contrast to Angelo's intransigent legalism, the Duke validates with his own authority the 'private contracts' between individuals, even though they are formally deprived of any legal sanction. In *All's Well*, the King exalts the value of merit and scientific ability over the rigid aristocratic hauteur of Bertram. The sovereign reconstitutes a network of social relationships that, precisely because they possess so solid a political base, can be open and tolerant towards a 'newness' that is ready and willing to be inserted within the old framework. The 'mixed' form of tragicomedy embodies in its dramatic structure that compromise between the sphere of the state and civil society that was one of the great Elizabethan aspirations.[38]

Let us resume our examination of tragic structure, in which the sovereign-protagonist of the 'problem' plays is transformed into the considerably more complex figure of the tragic hero. And to begin, let us look at two of the most widely known interpretations of the tragic hero. The first we find in Hegel's *Aesthetics*, where, speaking precisely of Shakespeare, Hegel locates the novelty of 'modern' tragedy in its capacity to construct 'firm and consistent characters who come to ruin simply because of this decisive adherence to themselves and their aims', figures 'without ethical justification, but upheld solely by the formal inevitability of their personality '[39] This fidelity to his own individuality makes the tragic hero the partial, one-sided character par excellence: one in whom all universality has been lost. 'The ethical powers, just like the agents, are differentiated in their domain and their individual appearance. Now, if . . . these thus differentiated powers are summoned into appearance as active, . . .then their harmony is cancelled and they come on the scene in *opposition* to one another in reciprocal independence . . . . Therefore what is superseded in the tragic dénouement is only the *one-sided* particular which had not been able to adapt itself to this harmony, and now (and this is the tragic thing in its action), unable to renounce itself and its intention, finds itself condemned to total destruction.' [40] Against this, let us now consider another critical text that also puts the essence of tragedy in the figure of the tragic hero, Lucien Goldmann's *The Hidden God*. Goldmann stands on its head the Hegelian conception of the tragic hero, who now comes on stage to counterpose 'against a world composed of fragmentary and mutually exclusive elements a demand for totality that inevitably becomes a demand for the reconciliation of opposites. For the tragic mind, authentic values are synonymous with totality.' [41] If in Hegel the tragic hero yields to partiality, in Goldmann he stands committed to universal values. The Shakespearean tragic hero, I believe, represents the point at which the two hypotheses meet: not that he manages to unite them, so much as they succeed in dividing him. Opposed and irreconcilable forces, they make of him an irreparably *split* character, like Claudius 'to double business bound', or Hamlet in his 'distraction', or Antony wandering between Rome and Egypt, or Othello 'perplex'd in the extreme'. This is, in its best summation, the conflict that lays unremitting hold of the regicide Macbeth.

It is pointless to interpret the scission that characterizes the tragic hero as a psychological datum, like the modern 'madness'. This is so because – quite apart from the fact that, as Michel Foucault has shown, the Renaissance conception of 'madness' is far removed from our own – a statement such as 'The tragic hero is a madman' defines a man whereas we are interested in defining a dramatic function. We might begin to define the tragic hero as that element of the work in which two contrary tensions meet and fight it out to the finish. And those two forces, which Hegel and Goldmann call 'particularity' and 'totality', we have called will and reason. As we have seen in *Gorboduc* and *King Lear*, their separation, along with their consequent conflict , is the necessary premiss of tragedy. It is likewise the case with the tragic hero, who exists to emphasize and intensify in his person the overall significance of tragic structure. (Note that only Shakespeare succeeds in perfectly fusing the scission that constitutes tragic structure with that constituting the tragic hero, pointing to their common origin.) Yet, to take a further step, if the tragic split is duplicated within the hero we may finally discard the popular but erroneous conception that tragedy essentially consists in a conflict between characters. This conception, too, finds its source in Hegel's *Aesthetics*, where one reads: 'What we see in front of us are certain ends individualized in living characters and very conflicting situations, and we see them in their self-assertion and display, in their reciprocal influence and design . . . . The individual does not remain shut into an independence of his own but finds himself brought into opposition and conflict with others . . . . Collision is the prominent point on which the whole turns.'[42] Hegel's suggestions were developed a century later in the first work of George Lukács: 'Drama is the poetry of the will . . . the purest expression of the will is struggle . . . all the manifestations of the will could be reduced to struggle.' And again: 'The [dramatic] conflict must be such as to allow man to realize the highest or maximum value of his life – that is, precisely that part of himself in which his entire life is condensed with the greatest force . . . tragic man is the only human type whose life is symbolized by a single adventure.'[43] As the last passage makes clear, the notion of the drama as conflict cannot be separated from the definition of the tragic hero as a unitary character. Mutually supportive of one another, the two affirmations concur to form a single argument. The argument is valid in certain cases – the tragedies of Corneille, the history plays of Shakespeare himself – but not for Shakespearean tragedy, which notwithstanding always furnishes its canonical example. Though a conflict between characters is certainly present in Shakespearean tragedy, it in no way constitutes the essence of the drama. The best example in this respect is *Hamlet*, where the outcome of the clash between Claudius and Hamlet is the reign of Fortinbras, whom we have seen for a few minutes, of whom we are given varying opinions, and who has passed by Elsinore on his return to Norway by pure chance. The result of the conflict is thus blatantly *accidental*. Hamlet himself gives it no weight and liquidates the problem of the succession in a sentence. Why? Precisely because the problem of the tragic hero is not one of acting to affirm his own individual ends, any more than the significance of tragic structure lies in the supremacy of one specific end over the others. The political dimension of tragedy does not consist in illuminating the displacements of power, as happens in the long procession of sovereigns in the histories and even in *Julius Caesar*; it lies rather in posing the question of whether a *cultural foundation* of power is still possible, and in answering it in the negative. In the histories, sovereign power is a given that no one puts in question, and hence the dramatic interest is concentrated in the development and issue of the clash that occurs over it. In the tragedies, sovereign power has instead become an insoluble *problem*: forced to face this fact, the hero can no longer believe in his struggle for power, and abandons it as a meaningless enterprise. But let us try to specify this further through the example of him who, on the eve of what ought to be 'the conflict in which his entire life is condensed', discourses on the battlements of a castle and declares himself 'a-weary of the sun'.

In reading the story of Macbeth, one cannot but be reminded of Cesare Borgia. What makes the resemblance particularly interesting is that it stops half-way. For though the actions of the Scottish sovereign can be thought to be inspired by the counsels of Machiavelli to the new prince, they in fact depart from them on a crucial point, the question of 'cruelty used well or badly': 'We can say that cruelty is used well (if it is permissible to talk in this way of what is evil) when it is employed once for all, and one's safety depends on it, and then it is not persisted in but as far as possible turned to the good of one's subjects. Cruelty badly used is that which, although infrequent to start with, as time goes on, rather than disappearing, becomes more evident. Those who use the first method can, with divine and human assistance, find some means of consolidating their position, as did Agathocles; the others cannot possibly stay in power.'[44] Macbeth is unable to follow in the first path: he hesitates, and allowing his enemies to reorganize, is lost. And he hesitates because he is divided – because he acted according to Machiavelli, while continuing to *think* like Hooker.[45] It is indicative how Macbeth speaks and makes use of his regicide – or rather, how he does not speak and make use of it. In his eyes, it is the action that must never be 'seen', never be entitled to cultural recognition. 'Stars, hide your fires,/Let not light see my black and deep desires;/The eye wink at the hand; yet let that be/Which the eye fears, when it is done, to see' (I, iv, 50–3); 'That my keen knife see not the wound it makes' (I, v, 52); 'I am afraid to think what I have done;/Look on't again I dare not' (II, ii, 48–9). Political murder, which in Machiavelli may be profitably reflected upon and even more profitably put to use as a warning to enemies, becomes in *Macbeth* the unthinkable and unprofitable deed par excellence. Though one must commit it on the way to power, one cannot discourse on it or accept it into the universe of culture. Macbeth's dilemma is that coexisting in him are the imperative of power *and* the imperative of culture, will and reason together. He cannot yet unburden the exercise of power – power as such – from the need for its cultural legitimation. This co-presence of irreconcilable drives deprives his life of a unified meaning: 'It is a tale/Told by an idiot, full of sound and fury,/Signifying nothing' (V, v, 26–8). That is to say: only a madman or imbecile (in effect, those like Edgar or Malcolm who step in claiming to 'conclude' the tragedy) can think that Macbeth's story can be 'told', ordered on the basis of comprehensible meanings. Such a combination of narrative and value-judgement has become impossible, and what remains is only 'sound', the word without force, and 'fury', force without sense. This is, in miniature, the lesson of tragic structure as a whole.

Macbeth epitomizes a whole group of Shakespearean characters who yield to that 'vicious mole of nature' of which Hamlet complains in his first two soliloquies. Claudius yields to it, tempted by the crown and Gertrude; and Lear, in the face of old age; and Antony, in the face of Cleopatra; and Othello, after Iago has dismantled the rigid defences of his Venetian culture. Just as tragedy is born from the dominating irruption of will over reason, so too the tragic hero is moved by a passion that compels him to act despite and against the cultural values that continue to inspire him. So consistent is this paradigm that in *Hamlet* Shakespeare is able to confirm it by diametrically reversing the problem. If for four centuries the tragedy of the prince of Denmark has baffled its spectators and readers, perhaps not the least reason is that *Hamlet* is a work *with the wrong protagonist*. If Claudius were its centre of gravity, everything would run far more smoothly and to pattern. Instead the protagonist is Hamlet, and nothing runs smoothly at all. It is impossible to understand Hamlet by assimilating him to Macbeth or Othello, for he represents the other principle on which the tragic hero may be constructed. The opposition is so fundamental that, unlike what happens in every other tragedy, Shakespeare does not pit Hamlet against a Macduff, or a Caesar, or an Edmund – all univocal, unified characters – but against *another tragic hero*: against Claudius, which is, in the end, merely Danish for Macbeth.

The great and notorious mystery surrounding Hamlet is that he fails to act. The reason for Hamlet's inaction, we should say, is that within the tragic universe there is never a reason for action. One recalls that in *Macbeth* action is speechless fury: one may or may not fall into it, but one cannot in good faith 'convince oneself' to enter it. Therefore when Hamlet says, 'My thoughts be bloody, or be nothing worth!' (IV, iv, 66), he perfectly expresses his dilemma, in so far as he preserves the illusion that 'thoughts' can be 'bloody'. For if reason is incapable of stopping action, it is also, symmetrically, incapable of inciting it. That tie has been severed, and though Hamlet would like to reconnect it, this very ambition, impelling him to reason in even greater depth, irremediably places him further from action.[46] Whereas Macbeth speaks of actions 'which must be acted ere they may be scann'd' (III, iv, 139), Hamlet, once more sheathing the sword he has drawn to kill Claudius, says the opposite: 'That would be scann'd' (III, iii, 75).[47] Macbeth is pulled along by the logic of his first act; Hamlet continually postpones such an act (committed, if at all, by chance, as when he kills Polonius). For Hamlet starts from the conviction (on which his first two soliloquies turn) that everything belonging to the category of 'passion' or 'nature' is for that very reason opposed to the image of the stable, metahistorical absolute sovereign – 'Hyperion to a satyr' – that he sees in his father and feels called upon – 'O cursèd spite' – to reincarnate. Hamlet requires cultural values to provide him with the Form that precedes and directs a passional Nature (just as, to take up a previous comparison, the rational good of Hooker's divine legislator precedes and directs the course of nature and guarantees its meaning). His famous precept to the actors – 'hold as 'twere the mirror up to nature' (III, ii, 22) – does not mean (as even Lukács believes) 'reflect nature', but rather the opposite: show nature the model to which it must conform. Yet this, we repeat, is now impossible. The form, reason, has lost the power to impose itself on nature: Hamlet's advice is given merely to *actors*, and only in performance (See the 'What's Hecuba to him?' soliloquy in II, ii, 559–ff.) can the head still rule the heart and an ethics foment a passion.

Hamlet's advice to the players – 'to hold as 'twere the mirror up to nature, to show virtue her feature, scorn her own image, and the very age and body of time his form and pressure' – is filled with nostalgia for a vanished relationship with the world. In effect, what Hamlet asks the players to do is what the Duke in *Measure for Measure* actually does. In Vienna, the theatrical project can be translated into an intervention in the world, an organic restoration of hierarchy and meaning; at Elsinore, it remains a performance, which, moreover, never completed, conveys to the court the opposite meaning of the one Hamlet seeks.[48] The tragic hero cannot be Hooker's legislator, the director of a play with a happy ending. And the world that he can no longer reduce to a theatre opens on to a mode of conduct that both completes and negates the theatre: *the lie*. For if in fact the individual exists socially because he plays a part, then what matters most is his performance. Fidelity is only fidelity to a role, and sincerity simply means a good performance. Othello suspects Desdemona because in her ignorance she isn't preoccupied with conforming to a social type and thus commits 'errors' of conduct; and instead, he believes blindly in Iago, who, conscious of artifice, performs to the rules of art.[49] Not the least of Shakespeare's merits is to have coolly illuminated the extent to which the ideal of the world-as-theatre had become vulnerable once a space of freedom and individual interest had opened up, creating a gap between 'person' and 'function'. To give a newly solid basis to human society, it would be necessary to abandon the ideal of 'fidelity' for that of 'interest' and to transform the social bond from a feudal 'oath' to the 'contract' of natural right philosophy:[50] a cultural shift that overturned the relation between facts and values (and in the realm of literary history replaced tragedy with the novel). But this is truly another story, which Shakespeare quite predates and one vainly tries to read in his works. He may announce the dawn of bourgeois civilization, but not by prefiguring it. On the contrary, he demonstrates inexorably how, obeying the old rules, which are the only ones he knows, the world can only fall apart.

If we place Macbeth and Hamlet against each other, we recognize the two solitary extremes into which the image of the sovereign has been decomposed. In Macbeth, we have force, impelling him to a tyranny well beyond true sovereignty; in Hamlet, we have reason, or a mad obsession with it, keeping him in the role of the 'sweet prince' well to this side of such sovereignty. As the one who, himself in equilibrium, provides the point of equilibrium for the social body, the sovereign is the missing person, the impossible being in Shakespearean tragedy. Only elsewhere does this monarch find his full dramatic incarnation, in another country and another text: in the figure of Segismundo in Calderon's *La vida es sueño*. Like Machiavelli's centaur, Segismundo holds together man and beast, the Christian philosopher and the commoner dressed in animal skins, mastery of himself and mastery of others. The emergence of such a character had to be preceded by the jesuitical meditation on 'reason of state' and the recognition of a 'technical' validity in Machiavelli's thought that could then be subordinated and brought back to a spiritual end.[51] When in the last scene of the play, Segismundo imprisons the soldier who led the very uprising that brought him to the throne, his gesture shows exactly how the illegality and violence necessary to the conquest of political power can be subsumed, then banished, in the name of the moral ends of that power. 'Force' in Calderon does not have its own independent logic: it can be transformed into an instrument of any project whatsoever. This possibility of mediating and tempering force with reason is what Shakespeare refuses to credit. For him, the 'Christian prince', wholly Christian and wholly a prince, does not exist. In this, Shakespeare is the only dramatist who rises to the level of Machiavelli, elaborating all the consequences of the separation of political praxis from moral evaluation. Not that Shakespeare conceives of this separation in the same fashion as Machiavelli: I said earlier that Macbeth acts like Cesare Borgia but thinks like Hooker, and such is also the position of Shakespeare – the position manifest in his tragic structure, where the axis of actions (the plot) is governed by one logic and the axis of values (the paradigm) by another, without either ever succeeding in overwhelming or expunging the other (as happens, in obviously different directions, in Machiavelli and Hooker). In Shakespeare's intimately paradoxical structure, two mutually exclusive positions appear equally real, and the same world seems governed by two different systems of law.

The clearest manifestation of the paradox occurs when the tragic hero is torn between conflicting claims. The radical character of Shakespeare's position emerges clearly if we compare him to a dramatist such as Corneille, who bases his entire dramaturgy precisely on the soliloquy.[52] Corneille's most typical tragedies – particularly, *Le Cid* and *Horace* — may be described as a succession of duels: first an internal duel, a soliloquy at the end of which the hero has chosen one of the lines of practical and moral conduct between which he was undecided; then, a verbal duel, a dialogue in which the hero displays to his adversary the superior firmness of his own ideal; and finally – off-stage – a physical duel, from which the hero returns victorious. The pattern is elementary, but rich in meaning. We may begin by remarking that the Cornelian hero is always perfectly conscious of the values between which he is rent. His purpose can never be 'dark' like Lear's, nor will he ever be amazed at what he has done or failed to do like Macbeth or Hamlet. That he always chooses (as Starobinski and Doubrovsky have shown) the heroic over the natural, the political over the personal, the 'luminous' over the 'obscure', is already prescribed in the fact that the choice must be expressed in the solar, omnipresent, heroic form of the Cornelian distych. When the dilemma itself is posed in the clear and distinct form of a contrast between values, one easily foresees that the ideally superior value will prevail. Since indeed it always proves so, one might say that, with the initial choice of the hero, the tragedy is already over and done with. What follows – the verbal, then the physical duel – merely repeats the outcome of the opening conflict. Doubrovsky's analysis of Corneille has frequent recourse to the Hegel of the master/servant dialectic in the

Phenomenology. One might add that Corneille's theatre is governed by the same logic that governs Hegel's philosophy of history: the progressive self-affirmation of the idea in the world. This is the profound reason why the literal duel can – rather, must – take place off-stage: it is only the material echo, inevitable and redundant, of the ideal conflict. In short, Cornelian action is always an *emanation of reason*. And, insofar as it initiates and determines every successive action, the soliloquy of the divided hero is not so much a verbal act as the sole real action.

With Shakespeare, the soliloquy fills a very different function – not of promoting the action or establishing its implications, but rather of retarding it and making its implications ungraspable. It is the site of doubt and irresolution: of 'the pale cast of thought' with which 'the native hue of resolution/is sicklied o'er' in Hamlet; of the 'words' that 'to the breath of deeds too cold breath gives' in Macbeth. Instead of the lucid Cornelian continuity between word and action, a radical discrepancy, or category difference, makes words impotent and actions mute. This mistrust in the practical force of language – so different from what his culture envisioned – makes Shakespeare's soliloquies the first manifestations of 'poetry' in the modern sense of being emancipated from a rhetoric conceived as the art of convincing. Whereas in the Cornelian soliloquy, the hero prescribed to himself the actions he would then perform, establishing in fact a complete rhetorical circuit, the Shakespearean hero by contrast addresses no one – neither a part of himself, nor another character, nor even the audience. Having no addressee, his words do not even participate in the dramatic context. Though it frequently happens (in *Hamlet*, I, iv, and III, ii, and in *Macbeth*, V, v) that the hero begins a soliloquy in the presence of other characters, these do not hear him, and the soliloquy can end only when the action – a principle now heterogeneous and hostile to his reflections – returns to claim its own rights. When, therefore, an idealist aesthetic excerpts these passages and transforms them into 'poems', the critical operation, however illegitimate, has intuitively understood the dramatically absurd character of the soliloquies. The other characters do not even hear them; they have no connection to the action; it is never clear what is the 'object' of their reflection – indeed the character who pronounces them retains no memory of them, so that Hamlet and Macbeth must begin their entire reasoning afresh every time they soliloquize. And finally, as Tolstoy once observed (in the only reasonable attitude for anybody seeking 'psychological realism' in Shakespeare), it is not Othello or Macbeth or Hamlet speaking in such passages, but 'all his characters speak, not their own, but always one and the same Shakespearean, pretentious, and unnatural language, in which not only they could not speak, but in which no living man ever has spoken or does speak'.[53] A single voice speaks in the soliloquies – or better, a single function: not referential, as in the speeches of Gorboduc's counsellors; nor expressive, as in King Lear; nor conative, as in the heroes of Corneille; but *self-referential*, forcibly released from all that surrounds it and henceforward painfully absorbed in itself.

It should be clear that this Shakespearean 'poetry' has nothing 'liberating', 'constructive', or 'universal' about it. It is made possible by, and is identical with, the stupefied perception that cultural paradigms, abruptly defaulting, are no longer capable of ordering and guiding the word. A chasm has opened up between signified and referent that, while it provides the imagination with an unexpected semantic freedom, empties reality and history of that meaning which had seemed consubstantial with them.[54] In the tragedies, this is exemplarily revealed in the fact that, from Richard II forward, only the defeated king is allowed (or better, condemned) to accede to speech thus conspicuously poetic: only the king who fails to act 'as the real "God-man"', as the *real embodiment* of the Idea'.[55] 'Poetry' is thus born from the disjunction of 'idea' and 'reality'; this disjunction in turn becomes the privileged object of poetic reflection which can neither recompose nor resolve it; and finally poetry can be 'spoken' only by one who has lived through an analogous disjunction in his own person – by the sovereign who is unable to unite history and transcendence, action and value, passion and reason, and whose fall therefore epitomizes the collapse of an entire civilization. Poetry is thus synonymous with the organic crisis of a political and cultural order, as we see if, enlarging the field of analysis, we move from the soliloquy to tragic structure as a whole. The latter blatantly violates the function that Elizabethan culture assigned to art and completely departs from its interpretive schemas (by means of which we were able, for instance, to explain *Gorboduc*, but not *King Lear*). Neither Sidney nor Puttenham ever for a moment ceases to abide by a pair of assumptions on which their key works are based: art acquires its right to exist only in so far as it performs an educational function,[56] which in turn is made possible because artistic 'beauty' consists in a *harmonious proportion* that contains within itself the image of the world as (in Sidney's phrase) 'what may be, and should be'.[57] Tragedy evokes proportion and harmony only to dissolve them, in characters as well as in the overall structure. How can an educational function be exercised by a structure that takes for its object the gap between culture and action and for its formal postulate the impossibility of abolishing it? Against the background of English culture, tragedy is that which 'eternally negates': like Goethe's Mephistopheles, it is the midwife of history.

3. *'We may go read i'th'stars . . . if we could find spectacles to read them'*

To read Jacobean tragedy with Shakespeare in mind is immediately to notice a vacancy – the tragic hero has disappeared. There is no one in whose person the meaning (or rather the loss of meaning) of the work is concentrated. A new collective protagonist stands in for the sovereign: the court. 'Court is a maze of turnings strange', wrote Thomas Churchyard in 1596, 'a laborinth, of working wits,/A princely seate, subiect to change.'[58] It is symptomatic that one of the first deprecations of the court should come from Churchyard, whose denunciations of cupidity, falsity and cruelty are typically applied to a quite different social category: the new (urban, competitive, acquisitive) *civil society*. That he reproduces these accusations in speaking of the court anticipates the image that the Jacobeans will typically bring forward: the court as the exemplary site of an unrestrained conflict of private interests. This is the venal and discredited court of the Stuarts, where the 'crisis of the aristocracy' is degraded to a tragicomedy of intrigue, a hectic and vain assault on the last remnants of power. On stage, those who belong to this court will speak like Iago and act like Edmund. The ambiguous density of Shakespeare's language divides to give rise to two characteristic forms of expression: the *sententia* and the *aside*, on one hand the profession of faith in the guise of a proverb, on the other the cool private undertones of egoism, on one hand public virtue, on the other private vice. If the tragic hero in his soliloquies waged unequal battle with a dubious and elusive meaning, the Jacobean character (except in Webster) never wants for lucid and univocal speech. Thus, in a work from the concluding years of the flowering of Jacobean drama, James Shirley has a character say: 'Alas poor lady,/I half repent me since she is so constant./But a friend's life weighs down all other love;/Beside, I thus secure my fate. Lorenzo/Threatens my spring. He is my enemy.'[59] Everyone here can perfectly distinguish good from evil, and divide himself accordingly into the two halves that the distinction requires. Social conduct, from being problematic, has become merely tortuous. 'A labyrinth of working wits': such will be the characteristic plot of Jacobean drama. 'So who knows policy and her true aspèct/Shall find her ways winding and indirect.'[60] Thus speaks Flamineo in Webster's *The White Devil*, and his maxim is repeatedly borne out in works like *The Revenger's Tragedy* or *Women Beware Women*, where the mortal conflict among characters will never issue in a direct encounter. The aristocratic duel still used, albeit modified, by Shakespeare at the end of *Hamlet*, *King Lear*, *Macbeth*, and *Antony and Cleopatra* has been replaced with the courtly intrigue. A character no longer glories in his valour, but rather in his astuteness. Though the tortuousness of individual 'designs' would attest to the superior efficacy of the new form of political dominion, yet there are now *too many* plots, overlapping and undoing one another incessantly. The obsessive lesson of Jacobean drama is that the proliferation of interests and points of view makes them all vulnerable. No one manages to control the plot, or even to understand much about it. The play now lacks a privileged point of observation, a centre such as the tragic hero had previously furnished. In this is manifest the profoundly baroque nature of Jacobean tragedy, perfectly of a piece with what is its most appropriate conclusion, the sudden mockery of slaughter. (Slaughter had already triumphed in *Ham-*

let, a work that, were it possible to expunge its protagonist, would effectively offer on all the points mentioned an insuperable model of Jacobean tragedy.) The unique 'solution' of dramatic complications, the only 'meeting place' of the dramatic agents, now consists in the reduction of everything to 'nothing', a word that frequently recurs in this drama. We no longer have even Shakespeare's bloodless heirs to give the illusion of historical continuity, as virtually the entire court expires under our eyes.

In Jacobean tragedy, the structural disappearance of the hero coincides with the political disappearance of the figure of the sovereign. Jacobean princes are almost always 'dukes' of small cities, and their power makes no universal claims and no longer poses the Shakespearean problem of its cultural foundation. Thus divested of all prominence or exemplarity, they become much more like the other characters, from whom they are only separated by a merely quantitative difference. As our remarks on the plot have already suggested, it is as though the barriers of status had fallen and every character were endowed with the same power, the same dignity, and finally (with Webster) the same language. Yet the equality that emerges from this metamorphosis is highly paradoxical, for the principle that governs such a process proves to be the destructive impulse par excellence: lust, the sexual desire or passion to which everyone – duke and merchant, cardinal and professional killer, brother and sister, procuress and duchess – equally succumbs. 'L'amour', says Corneille in *Le Cid*, 'est un tyran qui n'épargne personne'.[61] Like Cornelian love, Jacobean lust spares no one and thereby renders everyone equal. This very fact makes it an agent of destruction[62] in a social hierarchy based on the diametrically opposed principle of *inequality*. The opposition between a principle of passion and a principle of status, between lust and wealth, subtends the entire corpus of Jacobean drama. The incest in Ford's *'Tis Pity She's a Whore* (anticipated in *Women Beware Women* and, more obscurely, *The Duchess of Malfi*) may be thought to be its extreme and conclusive incarnation, ironically predicted by the father of Giovanni and Annabella when he declares: 'I would not have her marry wealth, but love'.[63] Incest is that form of desire which makes impossible the matrimonial exchange that, in a society in which power is still connected with physical persons, reinforces and perpetuates the network of wealth. But the conflict between lust and wealth had already, in play after play, claimed illustrious victims: the Duke of Bracciano and Vittoria Corombona, the Duchess of Malfi and Isabella in *The Changeling*, the entire court in *The Revenger's Tragedy* and *Women Beware Women* – all of them follow a single itinerary to destruction that they embark upon as soon as they let desire lead them.

All of them follow a single itinerary because lust is an obsession. In *The Atheist's Tragedy*, Levidulcia speaks of her 'affection' in these terms: 'I would unbrace and entertain/The air to cool it.' Lust appears external and objective, a burden that overwhelms its bearer. A few lines later Levidulcia says: 'Lust is a spirit which whosoe'er doth raise,/The next man that encounters boldly lays.'[64] Lust has become the very name of spectral obsession, a transformation that irrevocably dispels the ribald epicureanism that could still prompt Viscount Conway to exclaim, 'what is a gentleman but his pleasure?'[65] In the heavy Jacobean atmosphere, such pleasure, lacking entirely the essential dimension of freedom, becomes a repetition compulsion. On this account, it is preferable to define lust as 'passion' rather than 'desire', for it is clearly something that one passively undergoes. In Jacobean drama, a single glance suffices to bring about one's capture. Characters don't fall in love by 'looking' (a subjective action of discerning and observing), but by 'seeing', in the passive act of *being dazzled*. Examples abound: the Duke with Bianca and Livia with Leantio in *Women Beware Women*; Alsemero and Deflores with Isabella in *The Changeling*; Lussurioso with Castiza in *The Revenger's Tragedy*; Levidulcia with Sebastiano and then with Fresco in *The Atheist's Tragedy*. Lust changes from an enjoyment into a sign of destiny – or rather, into destiny *tout court*. In the first lines of *'Tis a Pity*, the Friar says to Giovanni, 'Death waits on thy lust' (I, i, 59). To which Giovanni replies, 'my fate's my god'. A destiny, a curse, a supreme example of *allegorical deception*, lust promises pleasure, but procures its opposite. In its name, the parable prefigured in the notorious ambiguities of the verb 'to die' (to climax/to expire) is brought to completion.

GIOVANNI   One other kiss, my sister.
ANABELLA   What means this?
GIOVANNI   To save thy fame, and kill thee in a kiss. *Stabs her*
             Thus die, and die by me, and by my hand.

                              ('*Tis a Pity*, V, v, 83–85)

'What means this?' Anabella's perturbation echoes that of Tour-neur's Duke, who, as he realizes he is kissing a poisoned skull, lamely cries, 'Oh! what's this? Oh!'[66] At the moment of death, lust reveals itself for what it has always been, a destiny that derides its victims. And at this moment, also, allegory triumphs in its defini-tive gesture of overturning meanings. The lover becomes a killer; the apparently faithful servant proves a mortal enemy; what seemed vital and attractive (the beautified skull in *The Revenger's Tragedy*) is shown to be dead and lethal. One woman is murdered by her husband as she kisses the portrait he himself has poisoned; another by a cardinal as she kisses his Bible in token of fidelity. Signifieds are reversed and (in another typically allegorical metamorphosis) fixed once for all in death, the only signified that is truly stable and universal. The characteristic emphasis is carried in Bosola's words: 'Though we are eaten up of lice, and worms,/ And though continually we bear about us/A rotten and dead body, we delight/To hide it in rich tissue.'[67] An ephemeral paren-thesis, life is nothing more than a wait for the ultimate and irrevoc-able transformation, the negation of every mask: the skull. The skull of Yorick, which after thirty years shows up in the hands of Hamlet; the skull of Vindice's wife, which he transforms into an instrument of revenge; the unidentified skulls on which Charlem-ont and Castabella go to sleep; the skull menacingly displayed to Flamineo by Bracciano's ghost. The skull of which Walter Benja-min has penetratingly written: 'in allegory, the observer is con-fronted with the *facies hippocratica* of history as a petrified, primordial language. Everything about history that, from the very beginning, has been untimely, sorrowful, unsuccessful, is ex-pressed in a face – or rather in a death's head. . . . The greater the significance, the greater the subjection to death, because death digs most deeply the jagged line of demarcation between physical nature and significance. But if nature has always been subject to the power of death, it is also true that it has always been allegorical. Significance and death both come to fruition in historical development, just as they are closely linked as seeds in the creature's graceless state of sin.'[68]

'But if nature has always been subject to the power of death, it is also true that it has always been allegorical.' Benjamin's argument finds its dramatic translation in the Rocambolesque peripety of Jacobean theatre, whose victims – by arrangement of those who have ensnared them – discover in their last moments both the 'truth' of the real state of affairs and the 'mendacity' of what it had appeared to be. As he begins the process of killing the Duke, for instance, Tourneur's Vindice shocks him with the revelation that neither his murderer nor the instrument of his death (the poisoned skull) are what they seemed: and then, sword in hand, compels him to watch the adultery by which, at that very moment, he is about to be betrayed. The deceptiveness of life, clarified only by slow death, coincides exactly with the operations of 'allegorical nature' in Benjamin. It is no accident that Puttenham defines allegory as 'the figure of [false semblant or dissimulation]', having just reminded us: *'Qui nescit dissimulare nescit regnare.'*[69] The Jacobean villain's supreme euphoria comes with his success in elaborating an 'allegorical' scheme to entrap his enemy. His rhetorical voluptuousness is nicely caught in the words of D'Amville concerning the stone with which he has murdered his brother: 'Upon this ground I'll build my manor house,/And this shall be the chiefest corner-stone' (*Atheist's Tragedy*, II, iv, 99–100). Yet such success is typically short-lived, for allegory always ends by revenging itself on whosoever aspired to keep it under his control. Though in Tourneur the villain's 'manor-house' remains intact and impenetrable almost to the end (so much so that some rather clumsy expedients – an involuntary confession, an axe that slips from the executioner's hands – are required to bring it down), the later developments of Jacobean drama offer more satisfying solutions. Contrary to what happens in Tourneur, the proliferation of plots in later tragedies allows no one to take control over events. The allegorical construction of one character becomes only an element already taken into account in the conflicting construction of another, and where one character proposes to write *finis* to 'his' tragedy, another is already prepared to begin his own. As in Benjamin's argument, allegory is not a subjective deception to which someone might be imagined to hold the semantic key, but the objectively deceptive condition of the nature of history by which everyone is ultimately betrayed. This is borne out if we compare the two supremely allegorical masques that respectively conclude *The Spanish Tragedy* and, three decades later, *Women Beware Women*. In Kyd's tragedy, Hieronimo arranges for everyone's role to be replicated in the masque where it is given its moral explanation and judgement. If the masque is the 'figure of dissimulation' permitting Hieronimo and Bel-Imperia to be avenged, it is also at the same time the symbolic re-elaboration of the whole tragic course of events on which it confers a luminous and unequivocal comprehensibility. In Middleton's tragedy, Livia too elaborates a scheme of murder and, putting it into action, assigns every character the role he has already played in the four preceding acts. But this time the actors betray their parts and – before the Duke who, mildly annoyed, deplores these departures from the programme, and then, distracted by the performance, casually drinks from a cup brimming with poison – the masque concludes with the murderous pyrotechnics of Cupids launching envenomed arrows and nymphs releasing lethal vapours. The clear, distinct allegory of Kyd (and of the entire Christian Middle Ages) has given way to the obscure, elusive allegory examined by Benjamin. Like the principal theme of lust, the plot too undergoes this transformation, which it remains for us to follow in the main 'character' of the Jacobean stage as well.

The plot of Jacobean drama requires two newly prominent, complementary functions: one in charge of *mediating* between various conflicting designs in an attempt to avoid catastrophe, the other in charge of *executing* a given such design without hesitation or delay. In Shakespeare, these tasks were assigned to minor and often ridiculous characters – Polonius, Rosencrantz and Guildenstern, Macbeth's hired killers. With the Jacobeans, these go-betweens and assassins (both functions often united in a single figure) occupy centre stage – Flamineo, Bosola, Livia, Deflores, in part even Vindice. The displacement of the dramatic centre of gravity toward persons of lower rank adds another item to the discredit that proceeds to accumulate on the Jacobean ruling class, who are implicitly not only degenerate, but cowardly as well, unable to look their own actions in the face. Macbeth does not hire a killer to murder Duncan, and Othello knows he must strangle Desdemona with his own hands, but the petty Jacobean lord ingloriously discharges all responsibility for his projects onto someone else–whom he will later blame, moreover, for having followed his orders (Ferdinand with Bosola, or Isabella with Deflores). Thus these servile figures are pushed to a 'central' position in the plot, as much as such a position is possible – think of the grand but brief pacification effected by Livia in the third act of *Women Beware Women* – and they become the only characters who from time to time possess a comprehensive knowledge of events. Their supremacy, however, is ambiguous, connected to and even dependent on their lack of autonomy, on their being mere instruments in the hands of others: 'I am your creature', Bosola tells Ferdinand (*Duchess*, I, i, 296). As Flamineo observes, they are constrained to an incessant 'varying of shapes' if they are to be 'great men's apes' (*White Devil*, IV, ii, 244–45). They are constrained never to be 'themselves', but always something else, artificial and deceitful: constrained to strut and fret on stage as nothing more than personified allegories. 'What the bondsman does is really the action of the lord', writes Hegel: 'this action of the second [consciousness] is the first's own action.'[70] At the heart of Jacobean tragedy we find a consciousness devoid of autonomy, an agency devoid of freedom. It is not surprising that these figures impersonate the essence of melancholy: 'I have lived/Riotously ill, like some that live in court,/And sometimes when my face was full of smiles,/Have felt the maze of conscience in my breast./Oft gay and honoured robes these tortures try:/We think caged birds sing when indeed they cry' (*White Devil*, V, iv, 118–23). This is the lament of inauthentic existence that, as Hegel was right to say, finds its most nearly complete objectification in the servant. And this inauthenticity does not find (as Goldmann's theory would have it) its counterweight in some authentic value, however defeated it might in actuality be. The maze in Flamineo's breast never comes to light, and when his *confrère* Bosola, now dismissed from the service of power, is 'free' to act, an error causes him to kill the 'good' half of himself in the person of Antonio. Jacobean tragedy does not in the least intend to seek a different basis for human society, but only to follow the trajectory of inauthenticity all the way to its inevitable self-dissolution. It is a drama whose subject is not questing, but only straying.

The curse of allegory that in various ways hangs over the Jacobean court finds perhaps its best 'spokesman' in John Webster, where the curse radically invests the domain of language itself. 'When I look into the fish-ponds, in my garden,/Methinks I see a thing, arm'd with a rake/That seems to strike at me' (*Duchess*, V, v, 5–7). The Cardinal's words are a splendid example of Webster's rhetoric: the uncertainty of appearances, the vagueness of 'a thing' oddly matched with the precision of the 'rake' it is armed with, the whole uncanny vision located in the familiar waters of 'the fish-ponds in my garden'. Suddenly, and in the most unexpected place, there appears a sign, an equivocal sign. Its equivocation, moreover, is not that of the classical oracle, the cool ambiguity of Apollo that, if it deceives, does so to reveal in the end its true and single meaning. In Webster, meaning does not deceive, but rather dissolves: into appearance ('methinks'), indeterminancy ('a thing'), and inexplicable detail ('arm'd with a rake'). Nor is the problem even how to interpret such signs, but, more basically, to determine whether or not they are in fact signs. Where does the melancholic's *imagination* (a key word in Webster) end and the manifestation of a transcendental reality begin? Webster's characters waver between the need to find metaphysical 'confirmation' in the form of a transcendent signified and a discouraged scepticism about its actual existence and comprehensibility. For instance, though the horoscope Antonio has cast at the birth of his son predicts for the child a violent death, it is Antonio who dies violently, while his son inherits his dukedom. Or again, as he reads the horoscope, his nose bleeds onto the monogram of his handkerchief: 'One that were superstitious', he notes, 'would count'/This ominous: when it merely comes by chance' (*Duchess*, II, ii,

127–28). Yet in saying this, he is distracted and drops the horoscope, which, picked up by Bosola, betrays the Duchess. In the end, then, blood has indeed been an ominous sign, but for the Duchess and Antonio rather than their son. This semantic uncertainty and imprecision is typical of Webster as a whole. There is supposed to be some relationship between human existence and the stars, but what it is, or how one might comprehend it, remains unclear. Ghosts apparently exist, but they may be mere projections of the imagination. St. Gregory's description of hellfire should be beyond disputing for the Cardinal, who instead, 'puzzled', finds it contradictory. At one point in *The White Devil*, Flamineo recites a lengthy apologue, glosses it, confesses that the comparison may not hold 'in every particle', and then once more proceeds to trust in it and apply it to the situation at hand (IV, iii, 218f). The specific curse on Webster's characters is that they can never dispense with speech, with sense-making, with the rhetorical amplification of their experience. This one discovers he is a cuckold because an 'emblem' is thrown in at his window; that one arranges a murder by staging dreams and riddles. Characters die with a metaphor in their mouths: Marcello, Flamineo, Julia, the Duchess, the Cardinal, Bosola. Yet so much 'poetry' (of all the Jacobeans, Webster is the one who in this respect most recalls Shakespeare), though it never abandons the character, never enlightens his way. Instead it maintains him in an uncertain and equivocal state that makes him the resigned victim of the trap of others. 'Fate's a spaniel', Flamineo says (*White Devil*, V, vi, 179), always at our heels, nor will we ever succeed in getting away from it. Pursued by spirits – 'haunted', as they say to one another –, these courtiers go round in circles in the vain attempt to escape that 'thing' they are so hard put to define. Their fate is no longer Macbeth's tale told by an idiot or Hamlet's vicious mole of nature, but a spaniel – or at least seems to them such. Their world survives without vitality, exhausted by the search for an illusory *ubi consistam* in the midst of countless deceptive signs. This is a world whose deepest desire is for oblivion. Flamineo says before he dies, 'To prate were idle. I remember nothing' (*White Devil*, V, vi, 206). And the Cardinal: 'And now, I pray, let me/Be laid by, and never thought of' (*Duchess*, V, v, 90). The palace of the prince is truly haunted, and the inflexible allegorical destiny suspended above every aspect of it (love and ambition, masters and servants, actions and words) makes it a site at once dilapidated and threatening. To the imagination of the Jacobeans, this was a court that, incapable of being set to rights, had to be dispersed, exorcised. A few years later . . .

Dialectic of Fear

1. Towards a Sociology of the Modern Monster

The fear of bourgeois civilization is summed up in two names: Frankenstein and Dracula. The monster and the vampire are born together, one night in 1816, in the drawing room of the Villa Chapuis near Geneva, out of a society game among friends to while away a rainy summer. Born in the full spate of the industrial revolution, they rise again together in the critical years at the end of the nineteenth century, under the names of Hyde and Dracula.[1] In the twentieth century they conquer the cinema: after the First World War, in German Expressionism; after the 1929 crisis, with the big RKO productions in America; then in 1956–57, Peter Cushing and Christopher Lee, directed by Terence Fisher, again, triumphantly, incarnate this twin-faced nightmare.

Frankenstein and Dracula lead parallel lives. They are two indivisible, because complementary, figures; the two horrible faces of a single society, its *extremes*: the disfigured wretch and the ruthless proprietor. The worker and capital: 'the whole of society must split into the two classes of *property owners* and propertyless *workers*.'[2] That 'must', which for Marx is a scientific prediction of the future (and the guarantee of a future reordering of society) is a forewarning of the end for nineteenth-century bourgeois culture. The literature of terror is born precisely *out of the terror of a split society*, and out of the desire to heal it. It is for just this reason that Dracula and Frankenstein, with rare exceptions, do not appear together. The threat would be too great: and this literature, having produced terror, must also erase it and restore peace. It must restore the broken equilibrium, giving the illusion of being able to stop history: because the monster expresses the anxiety that the future will be monstrous. His antagonist – the enemy of the monster – will always be, by contrast, a representative of the present, a distillation of complacent nineteenth-century mediocrity: nationalistic, stupid, superstitious, philistine, impotent, self-satisfied. But this does not show through. Fascinated by the horror of the monster, the public accepts the vices of its destroyer without a murmur,[3] just as it accepts his literary depiction, the jaded and repetitive typology which regains its strength and its virginity on contact with the unknown. The monster, then, serves to displace the antagonisms and horrors evidenced *within* society *outside* society itself. In *Frankenstein* the struggle will be between a 'race of devils' and the 'species of man'. Whoever dares to fight the monster automatically becomes the representative of the species, of the whole of society. The monster, the utterly unknown, serves to reconstruct a universality, a social cohesion which – in itself – would no longer carry conviction.

Frankenstein's monster and Dracula the vampire are, unlike previous monsters, dynamic, *totalizing* monsters. This is what makes them frightening. Before, things were different. Sade's malefactors agree to operate on the margins of society, hidden away in their towers. Justine is their victim because she rejects the modern world, the world of the city, of exchange, of her reduction to a commodity. She thus gives herself over to the old horror of the feudal world, the will of the individual master. Moreover, in Sade the evil has a 'natural' limit which cannot be overstepped: the gratification of the master's desire. Once he is satiated, the torture ceases too. Dracula, on the other hand, is an ascetic of terror: in him is celebrated the victory 'of the desire for *possession* over that of *enjoyment*'[4]; and possession as such, indifferent to consumption, is by its very nature insatiable and unlimited. Polidori's vampire is still a petty feudal lord forced to travel round Europe strangling young ladies for the miserable purpose of *surviving*. Time is against him, against his conservative desires. Stoker's Dracula, by contrast, is a rational entrepreneur who invests his gold to expand his dominion: to conquer the City of London. And already Frankensteins's monster sows devastation over the whole world, from the Alps to Scotland, from Eastern Europe to the Pole. By comparison, the gigantic ghost of *The Castle of Otranto* looks like a dwarf. He is confined to a single place; he can appear once only; he is merely a relic of the past. Once order is re-established he is silent for ever. The modern monsters, however, threaten to live for ever, and to conquer the world. For this reason they must be killed.[5]

Frankenstein

Like the proletariat, the monster is denied a name and an individuality. He is the Frankenstein monster; he belongs wholly to his creator (just as one can speak of a 'Ford worker'). Like the proletariat, he is a *collective* and *artificial* creature. He is not found in nature, but built. Frankenstein is a productive *inventor*-scientist, in open conflict with Walton, the contemplative *discoverer*-scientist (the pattern is repeated with Jekyll and Lanyon). Reunited and brought back to life in the monster are the limbs of those – the 'poor' – whom the breakdown of feudal relations has forced into brigandage, poverty and death.[6] Only modern science – this metaphor for the 'dark satanic mills' – can offer them a future. It sews them together again, moulds them according to its will and finally gives them life. *But at the moment the monster opens its eyes,* its creator draws back in horror: 'by the glimmer of the half-extinguished light, I saw the dull yellow eye of the creature open . . . How can I describe my emotions at this catastrophe . . . ?' Between Frankenstein and the monster there is an ambivalent, dialectical relationship, the same as that which, according to Marx, connects capital with wage-labour.[7] On the one hand, the scientist cannot but create the monster: 'often did my human nature turn with loathing from my occupation, whilst, still urged on by an eagerness which perpetually increased, I brought my work near to a conclusion.' On the other hand, he is immediately afraid of it and wants to kill it, because he realizes he has given life to a creature stronger than himself and of which he cannot henceforth be free. It is the same curse that afflicts Jekyll: 'to put your good heart at rest, I will tell you one thing: the moment I choose, I can be rid of Mr

Hyde.' And yet it is Hyde who will become master of his master's life. The fear aroused by the monster, in other words, is the fear of one who is afraid of having 'produced his own gravediggers'.

The monster's explicit 'demands' cannot in fact produce fear. They are not a gesture of challenge; they are 'reformist'/'Chartist' demands. The monster wishes only to have rights of citizenship among men: 'I will not be tempted to set myself in opposition to thee. I am thy creature, and I will be ever mild and docile to my natural lord and king, . . . I was benevolent and good; misery made me a fiend. Make me happy, and I shall again be virtuous.' Furthermore, when all friendly relations with humans have failed, the monster humbly accepts his marginalization, begging only to have another creature who is 'as deformed and horrible as myself'. But even this is denied him. The monster's sheer *existence* is frightening enough for Frankenstein, let alone the prospect of his producing children and multiplying. Frankenstein – who never manages to consummate his marriage – is the victim of the same impotence that Benjamin describes: 'Social reasons for impotence: the imagination of the bourgeois class stopped caring about the future of the productive forces it had unleashed . . . . Male impotence – key figure of solitude, in which the arrest of the productive forces is effected'.[8] The possibility of the monster having descendants presents itself to the scientist as a real nightmare: 'a race of devils would be propagated upon the earth who might make the very existence of the species of man a condition precarious and full of terror.'

'Race of devils': this image of the proletariat encapsulates one of the most reactionary elements in Mary Shelley's ideology. The monster is a historical product, an artificial being: but once transformed into a 'race' he re-enters the immutable realm of Nature. He can become the object of an instinctive, elemental hatred; and 'men' need this hatred to counterbalance the force unleashed by the monster. So true is this that racial discrimination is not superimposed on the development of the narrative but springs directly from it: it is not only Mary Shelley who wants to make the monster a creature of another race, *but Frankenstein himself*. Frankenstein does not in fact want to create a man (as he claims) but a monster, a race. He narrates at length the 'infinite pains and care' with which he had endeavoured to form the creature; he tells us that 'his limbs were in proportion' and that he had 'selected his features as beautiful'. So many lies: in the same paragraph, three words later, we read: 'His yellow skin scarcely covered the work of muscles and arteries beneath; his hair was of a lustrous black, and flowing; his teeth of a pearly whiteness; but these luxuriances only formed a more horrid contrast with his watery eyes, . . . his shrivelled complexion and straight black lips.' Even before he begins to live, this new being is already monstrous, already a race apart. He must be so, he is made to be so: he is created, but on these conditions. There is here a clear lament for the feudal sumptuary laws which, by imposing a particular style of dress on each social rank, allowed it to be recognized at a distance and nailed it physically to its social role. Now that clothes have become commodities that anyone can buy, this is no longer possible. Difference in rank must now be inscribed more deeply: in one's skin, one's eyes, one's build. The monster makes us realize how hard it was for the dominant classes to resign themselves to the idea that all human beings are – or ought to be – equal.

But the monster also makes us realize that in an unequal society they are *not* equal. Not because they belong to different 'races' but because inequality really does score itself into one's skin, one's eyes and one's body. And more so, evidently, in the case of the first industrial workers: the monster is disfigured not only because Frankenstein wants him to be like that, but also because this was how things actually were in the first decades of the industrial revolution. In him, the metaphors of the critics of civil society become real: the monster incarnates Adam Ferguson's helots, the dialectic of estranged labour described by the young Marx: 'the more his product is shaped, the more misshapen the worker; the more civilized his object, the more powerless the worker; the more intelligent the work, the duller the worker and the more he becomes a slave of nature. . . . It is true that labour produces . . . palaces, but hovels for the worker. . . . It produces intelligence, but it produces idiocy and cretinism for the worker.'[9] Frankenstein's invention is thus a pregnant metaphor of the process of capitalist production, which forms by deforming, civilizes by barbarizing, enriches by impoverishing – a two-sided process in which each affirmation entails a negation. And indeed the monster – the pedestal on which Frankenstein erects his anguished greatness – is always described *by negation*: man is well proportioned, the monster is not; man is beautiful, the monster ugly; man is good, the monster evil. The monster is man turned upside-down, negated. He has no autonomous existence; he can never be really free or have a future. He lives only as the other side of that coin which is Frankenstein. When the scientist dies, the monster does not know what to do with his own life, and commits suicide.

The two extremes of *Frankenstein* are the scientist and the monster. But it is more precise to say that they become extremes in the course of the narration. Mary Shelley's novel rests in fact on an elementary scheme, that of simplification and splitting ('The whole of society must split into the two classes. . .'). It is a process that demands its victims: and indeed, all the 'intermediate' characters perish one after the other by the monster's hand: Frankenstein's brother William, the maid Justine, his friend Clerval, his wife Elizabeth, his father. This is a sequence echoed in the sacrifice of Philemon and Baucis, as Faust's entrepreneurial dream dictates the destruction, in the figures of the two old people, of the family unit and small independent property. In *Frankenstein* too, the victims of the monster (or rather of the struggle between the monster and the scientist, a struggle which prefigures the social relations of the future) are those who still represent the ethical and economic ideal of the family as an 'extended' unit: not just the relatives, but also the maid and the fraternal friend Clerval. Clerval, in comparison with his contemporary, Victor, is still placidly traditionalist: he, unlike Frankenstein, has chosen to stay in his parent's town, in his family home, and keep their values alive. These values are corporative, localistic, unchanging: the ethic of the 'common road' praised by Robinson Crusoe's father.[10] Frankenstein himself ends up being converted to them, but by then it is too late: 'how much happier that man is who believes his native town to be the world, than he who aspires to become greater than his nature will allow . . . . Farewell, Walton! Seek happiness in tranquility and avoid ambition, even if it be only the apparently innocent one of distinguishing yourself in science and discoveries.'

Frankenstein's last words reconnect with Mary Shelley's preface, which gives the aim of the work as 'the exhibition of the amiableness of domestic affection'. Nor is it by accident that his words are spoken to Walton, since Walton is essential for the communication of the work's message. Like Frankenstein, Walton starts out as the protagonist of a desperate undertaking, spurred on by an imperious as well as aggressive and inhuman idea of scientific progress: 'One man's life or death were but a small price to pay for the acquirement of the knowledge which I sought'. But Frankenstein's story puts him off. At the end, Walton accedes to the protestations of the sailors, who are frightened for their lives, and agrees to come back 'ignorant and disappointed' to his homeland and his family. Thanks to his conversion, Walton survives. And this confers on him a dominant function in the narrative structure, in the book's system of 'senders' of messages. Walton both begins the story and ends it. His narrative 'contains', and thus subordinates, Frankenstein's narrative (which in turn 'contains' that of the monster). The broadest, most comprehensive, most *universal* narrative viewpoint is reserved for Walton. The narrative system inverts the meaning of *Frankenstein* as we have described it, exorcising its horror. The dominant element of reality is not the *splitting* of society into two opposing poles, but its symbolic *re-unification* in the Walton family.[11] The wound is healed: one goes back home.

The universality attributed to Walton by the system of narrative senders applies not only to the story at hand but to the whole course of history. Through Walton, Frankenstein and the monster are relegated to the status of mere historical 'accidents'; theirs is only an episode, a 'case' (Stevenson's title will be *The Strange Case of Dr Jekyll and Mr Hyde*). By this means Mary Shelley wants to convince us that *capitalism has no future*: it may have been around for a few years, but now it is all over. Anyone can see that Frankenstein and the monster die without heirs, whilst Robert Walton survives. It is a glaring anachronism, but one for which Mary Shelley has prepared us. The sociological fulcrum of *Frankenstein* – the creation of the proletariat – responds neither to economic interests nor to objective needs. It is the product of a solitary, subjective and entirely disinterested piece of work: Frankenstein expects no personal advantage from creating the monster. Or rather, he *cannot* expect it, because in the world of the novel there is no way of *utilizing* the monster.[12] And there is no way of utilizing him because there are no factories. And there are no factories for two very good reasons: because for Mary Shelley the demands of production have no value in themselves, but must be subordinated to the maintenance of the moral and material solidity of the family; and because, as she understood, the factories would undoubtedly multiply the feared 'race of devils' to an infinite number. Wishing to exorcise the proletariat, Mary Shelley, with absolute logical consistency, erases capital from her picture too. In other words, she erases history.

And indeed, the end result of the peculiar narrative structure employed is to make the story of Frankenstein and the monster resemble a *fable*. As in a fable, the story proceeds in *oral* form: Frankenstein speaks to Walton, the monster to Frankenstein, Frankenstein to Walton again (whereas Walton, who embodies history and the future, *writes*). As in a fable, there is an attempt to create a cosy, trusting, *domestic* situation: even the monster, at the beginning of his narrative, suggests that he and Frankenstein take refuge in a mountain cottage so as to be more comfortable. As in a fable, by an iron law, what has happened must be considered an *imaginary* occurrence. Capitalism is a dream – a bad dream, but a dream nonetheless.

Dracula

Count Dracula is an aristocrat only in manner of speaking. Jonathan Harker – the London estate agent who stays in his castle, and whose diary opens Stoker's novel – observes with astonishment that Dracula lacks precisely what makes a man 'noble': servants. Dracula stoops to driving the carriage, cooking the meals, making the beds, cleaning the castle. The Count has read Adam Smith: he knows that servants are unproductive workers who diminish the income of the person who keeps them. Dracula also lacks the aristocrat's conspicuous consumption: he does not eat, he does not drink, he does not make love, he does not like showy clothes, he does not go to the theatre and he does not go hunting, he does not hold receptions and does not build stately homes. Not even his violence has pleasure as its goal. Dracula (unlike Vlad the Impaler, the historical Dracula, and all other vampires before him) does not *like* spilling blood: he *needs* blood. He sucks just as much as is necessary and never wastes a drop. His ultimate aim is not to destroy the lives of others according to whim, to waste them, but to *use* them.[13] Dracula, in other words, is a saver, an ascetic, an upholder of the Protestant ethic. And in fact he has no body, or rather, he has no shadow. His body admittedly exists, but it is 'incorporeal' – 'sensibly supersensible' as Marx wrote of the commodity, 'impossible as a physical fact', as Mary Shelley defines the monster in the first lines of her preface. In fact it is impossible, 'physically', to estrange a man from himself, to de-humanize him. But alienated labour, as a *social* relation, makes it possible. So too there really exists a social product which has no body, which has exchange-value but no use-value. This product, we know, is money.[14] And when Harker explores the castle, he finds just one thing: 'a great heap of gold . . . – gold of all kinds, Roman, and British, and Austrian, and Hungarian, and Greek and Turkish money, covered with a film of dust, as though it had lain long in the ground.' The money that had been buried comes back to life, becomes capital and embarks on the conquest of the world: this and none other is the story of Dracula the vampire.

'Capital is dead labour which, vampire-like, lives only by sucking living labour, and lives the more, the more labour it sucks.'[15] Marx's analogy unravels the vampire metaphor. As everyone knows, the vampire is dead and yet not dead: he is an Un-Dead, a 'dead' person who yet manages to live thanks to the blood he sucks from the living. *Their* strength becomes *his* strength.[16] The *stronger* the vampire becomes, the *weaker* the living become: 'the capitalist gets rich, not, like the miser, in proportion to his personal labour and restricted consumption, but at the same rate as he squeezes out labour-power from others, and compels the worker to renounce all the enjoyments of life.'[17] Like capital, Dracula is impelled towards a continuous growth, an unlimited expansion of his domain: accumulation is inherent in his nature. 'This', Harker exclaims, 'was the being I was helping to transfer to London, where, perhaps for centuries to come, he might, amongst its teeming millions, satiate his lust for blood, and create a *new and ever widening* circle of semi-demons to batten on the helpless' (my italics). 'And so the circle goes on *ever widening*', Van Helsing says later on; and Seward describes Dracula as 'the father or furtherer of a *new* order of beings' (my italics). All Dracula's actions really have as their final goal the creation of this 'new order of beings' which finds its most fertile soil, logically enough, in England. And finally, just as the capitalist is 'capital personified' and must subordinate his private existence to the abstract and incessant movement of accumulation, so Dracula is not impelled by the *desire* for power but by the *curse* of power, by an obligation he cannot escape. 'When they (the Un-Dead) become such', Van Helsing explains, 'there comes with the change the curse of immortality; they cannot die, but must go on age after age adding new victims and multiplying the evils of the world'. It is remarked later of the vampire that he 'can do all these things, *yet he is not free*' (my italics). His curse compels him to make ever more victims, just as the capitalist is compelled to accumulate. His nature forces him to struggle to be unlimited, to subjugate *the whole of society*. For this reason, one cannot 'coexist' with the vampire. One must either succumb to him or kill him, thereby freeing the world of his presence and him of his curse. When the knife plunges into Dracula's heart, in the moment before his dissolution, 'there was in the face a look of peace, such as I would never have imagined might have rested there'. There flashes forth here the idea, to which we shall return, of the *purification* of capital.

If the vampire is a metaphor for capital, then Stoker's vampire, who is of 1897, must be the capital of 1897. The capital which, after lying 'buried' for twenty long years of recession, rises again to set out on the irreversible road of concentration and monopoly. And Dracula is a true monopolist: solitary and despotic, he will not brook competition. Like monopoly capital, his ambition is to subjugate the last vestiges of the liberal era and destroy all forms of economic independence. He no longer restricts himself to incorporating (in a literal sense) the physical and moral strength of his victims. He intends to make them his *for ever*. Hence the horror, for the bourgeois mind. One is bound to Dracula, as to the devil, for *life*, no longer 'for a fixed period', as the classic bourgeois contract stipulated with the intention of maintaining the freedom of the contracting parties. The vampire, like monopoly, destroys the hope that one's independence can one day be brought back. He threatens the idea of individual liberty. For this reason the nineteenth-century bourgeois is able to imagine monopoly only in the guise of Count Dracula, the aristocrat, the figure of the past, the relic of distant lands and dark ages. Because the nineteenth-century bourgeois believes in free trade, and he knows that in order to become established, free competition had to destroy the tyranny of feudal monopoly. For him, then, monopoly and free competition are irreconcilable concepts. Monopoly is the *past* of competition, the middle ages. He cannot believe it can be its *future*, that competition itself can *generate* monopoly in new forms. And yet 'modern monopoly is . . . the true synthesis . . . the negation of feudal monopoly insofar as it implies the system of competition, and the negation of competition insofar as it is monopoly.'[18]

Dracula is thus at once the final product of the bourgeois century and its negation. In Stoker's novel only this second aspect – the negative and destructive one – appears. There are very good reasons for this. In Britain at the end of the nineteenth century, monopolistic concentration was far less developed (for various economic and political reasons) than in the other advanced capitalist societies. Monopoly could thus be perceived as something extraneous to British history: as a *foreign threat*. This is why Dracula is not British, while his antagonists (with one exception, as we shall see, and with the addition of Van Helsing, born in that other classic homeland of free trade, Holland) are British through and through. Nationalism – the defence to the death of British civilization – has a central role in *Dracula*. The idea of the nation is central because it is collective: it coordinates individual energies and enables them to resist the threat. For while Dracula threatens the freedom of the individual, the latter alone lacks the power to resist or defeat him. Indeed the followers of pure economic individualism, those who pursue their own profit, are, without knowing it, the vampire's best allies.[19] Individualism is not the weapon with which Dracula can be beaten. Other things are needed – in effect two: money and religion. These are considered as a single whole, which must not be separated: in other words, money at the service of religion and vice versa. The money of Dracula's enemies is money that *refuses to become capital*, that wants not to obey the profane economic laws of capitalism but to be used *to do good*. Towards the end of the novel, Mina Harker thinks of her friends' financial commitment: 'it made me think of the wonderful power of money! What can it not do when it is properly applied; and what might it do when basely used!' This is the point: money should be used according to justice. Money must not have its end *in itself*, in its continuous accumulation. It must have, rather, a *moral*, anti-economic end to the point where colossal expenditures and losses can be calmly accepted. This idea of money is, for the capitalist, something inadmissible. But it is also the great ideological lie of Victorian capitalism, a capitalism which is ashamed of itself and which hides factories and stations beneath cumbrous Gothic superstructures; which prolongs and extols aristocratic models of life; which exalts the holiness of the family as the latter begins secretly to break up. Dracula's enemies are precisely the exponents of *this* capitalism. They are the militant version of Dickens's benefactors. They find their fulfilment in religious superstition, whereas the vampire is paralysed by it. And yet the crucifixes, holy wafers, garlic, magic flowers, and so on, are not important for their *intrinsic* religious meaning but for a subtler reason. Their true function consists in setting impassable limits to the vampire's activity. They prevent him from entering this or that house, conquering this or that person, carrying out this or that metamorphosis. But setting limits to the vampire-capital means attacking his very raison d'être: he must by his nature be able to expand without limit, to destroy every restraint upon his action. Religious superstition imposes the same limits on Dracula that Victorian capitalism declares itself to accept spontaneously. But Dracula – who is capital that is not ashamed of itself, true to its own nature, an end in itself – cannot survive in these conditions. And so this symbol of a cruel historical development falls victim to a handful of whited sepulchres, a bunch of fanatics who want to arrest the course of history. It is they who are the relics of the dark ages.

At the end of *Dracula* the vampire's defeat is complete. Dracula and his lovers are destroyed, Mina Harker is saved at the last moment. Only one cloud darkens the happy ending. In killing Dracula, Quincy P. Morris, the American who has been helping his British friends to save their nation, dies too, almost by accident. The occurrence seems inexplicable, extraneous to the logic of the narrative, yet it fits perfectly into Stoker's sociological design. The American, Morris, *must* die, because Morris is a vampire. From his first appearance he is shrouded in mystery (a friendly sort of mystery, it is true – but isn't Count Dracula himself likeable, at the beginning?). 'He is such a nice fellow, an American from Texas, and he looks so young and so fresh [he *looks*: like Dracula, who looks it but isn't] that it seems almost impossible that he has been to so many places and has had such adventures.' What places? What adventures? Where does all his money come from? What does Mr Morris do? Where does he live? Nobody knows any of this. But nobody suspects. Nobody suspects even when Lucy dies – and then turns into a vampire – immediately after receiving a blood transfusion from Morris. Nobody suspects when Morris, shortly afterwards, tells the story of his mare, sucked dry of blood in the Pampas (like Dracula, Morris has been round the world) by 'one of those big bats that they call vampires'. It is the first time that the name 'vampire' is mentioned in the novel: but there is no reaction. And there is no reaction a few lines further on when Morris, 'coming close to me, . . . spoke in a fierce half-whisper: "What took it [the blood] out?"' But Dr Seward shakes his head; he hasn't the slightest idea. And Morris, reassured, promises to help. Nobody, finally, suspects when, in the course of the meeting to plan the vampire hunt, Morris leaves the room to take a shot – missing, naturally – at the big bat on the window-ledge listening to the preparations; or when, after Dracula bursts into the household, Morris hides among the trees, the only effect of which is that he loses sight of Dracula and invites the others to call off the hunt for the night. This is pretty well all Morris does in *Dracula*. He would be a totally superfluous character if, unlike the others, he were not characterized by this mysterious connivance with the world of the vampires. So long as things go well for Dracula, Morris acts like an accomplice. As soon as there is a reversal of fortunes, he turns into his staunchest enemy. Morris enters into competition with Dracula; he would like to replace him in the conquest of the Old World. He does not succeed in the novel but he will succeed, in 'real' history, a few years afterwards.

While it is interesting to understand that Morris is connected with the vampires – because America will end up by subjugating Britain in reality and Britain is, albeit unconsciously, afraid of it – the decisive thing is to understand why Stoker does *not* portray him as a vampire. The answer lies in the bourgeois conception of monopoly described earlier. For Stoker, monopoly *must* be feudal, oriental, tyrannical. It cannot be the product of that very society he wants to defend. And Morris, naturally, is by contrast a product of Western civilization, just as America is a rib of Britain and American capitalism a consequence of British capitalism. To make Morris a vampire would mean accusing capitalism directly: or rather accusing Britain, admitting that it is Britain herself that has given birth to the monster. This cannot be. For the good of Britain, then, Morris must be sacrificed. But Britain must be kept out of a crime whose legitimacy she cannot recognize. He will be killed by the chance knife-thrust of a gypsy (whom the British will allow to escape unpunished). And at the moment when Morris dies, and the threat disappears, old England grants its blessing to this excessively pushy and unscrupulous financier, and raises him to the dignity of a Bengal Lancer: 'And, to our bitter grief, with a smile and in silence, he died, a gallant gentleman.' (the sentence significantly abounds in the clichés of heroic-imperial English literature). These, it should be noted, are the *last* words of the novel, whose true ending does not lie – as is clear by now – in the death of the Romanian count, but in the killing of the American financier.[20]

One of the most striking aspects of *Dracula* – as of *Frankenstein* before it – is its system of narrative senders. To begin with, there is the fact that in this network of letters, diaries, notes, telegrams, notices, phonograph recordings and articles, the narrative function proper, namely the description and ordering of events, is reserved for the British alone. We never have access to Van Helsing's point of view, or to Morris's, and still less to Dracula's. The string of events exists only in the form and with the meaning stamped upon it by British Victorian culture. It is those cultural categories, those moral values, those forms of expression that are endangered by the vampire: it is those same categories, forms and values that reassert themselves and emerge triumphant. It is a victory of convention over exception, of the present over the possible future, of standard

British English over any kind of linguistic transgression. In *Dracula* we have, transparently, the perfect and immutable English of the narrators on the one hand, and Morris's American 'dialect', Dracula's schoolbook English and Van Helsing's bloomers on the other. As Dracula is a danger because he constitutes an unforseen variation from the British cultural code, so the maximum threat on the plane of content coincides with the maximum inefficiency and dislocation of the English language. Half way through the novel, when Dracula seems to be in control of the situation, the frequency of Van Helsing's speeches increases enormously, and his perverse English dominates the stage. It becomes dominant because although the English language possesses the word 'vampire', it is unable to ascribe a meaning to it, in the same way that British society considers 'capitalist monopoly' a meaningless expression. Van Helsing has to explain, in his approximate and mangled English, what a vampire is. Only then, when these notions have been translated into the linguistic and cultural code of the English, and the code has been reorganized and reinforced, can the narrative return to its previous fluidity, the hunt begin and victory appear secure.[21] It is entirely logical that the last sentence should be, as we saw, a veritable procession of literary English.

In *Dracula* there is no ominiscient narrator, only individual and mutually separate points of view. The first-person account is a clear expression of the desire to keep hold of one's individuality, which the vampire threatens to subjugate. Yet so long as the conflict is one between human 'individualism' and vampirical 'totalization', things do not go at all well for the humans. Just as a system of perfect competition cannot do other than give way to monopoly, so a handful of isolated individuals cannot oppose the concentrated force of the vampire. It is a problem we have already witnessed on the plane of content: here it re-emerges on the plane of narrative forms. The individuality of the narration must be preserved and at the same time its negative aspect – the doubt, impotence, ignorance and even mutual distrust and hostility of the protagonists – must be eliminated.[22] Stoker's solution is brilliant. It is to collate, to make a systematic integration of the different points of view. In the second half of *Dracula*, that of the hunt (which begins, it should be noted, only *after* the collation), it is more accurate to speak of a 'collective' narrator than of different narrators. There are no longer, as there were at the beginning, *different* versions of a single episode, a procedure which expressed the uncertainty and error of the individual account. The narrative now expresses the *general* point of view, the official version of events. Even the style loses its initial idiosyncrasies, be they professional or individual, and is amalgamated into Standard British English. This collation is, in other words, the Victorian compromise in the field of narrative technique. It unifies the different interests and cultural paradigms of the dominant class (law, commerce, the land, science) under the banner of the common good. It restores the narrative equilibrium, giving this dark episode a form and a meaning which are finally clear, communicable and universal.

2. The Return of the Repressed

A sociological analysis of *Frankenstein* and *Dracula* reveals that one of the institutions most threatened by the monsters is the family. Yet this fear cannot be explained wholly in historical and economic terms. On the contrary, it is very likely that its deepest root is to be found elsewhere: in the eros, above all in sex. 'Dracula', David Pirie has written, '. . . can be seen as the great submerged force of Victorian libido breaking out to punish the repressive society which had imprisoned it; one of the most appalling things that Dracula does to the matronly women of his Victorian enemies (in the novel as in the film) is to make them sensual.'[23] It is true. For confirmation one only has to reread the episode of Lucy. Lucy is the only protagonist who falls victim to Dracula. She is punished, because she is the only one who shows some kind of *desire*. Stoker is inflexible on this point: all the other characters are immune to the temptations of the flesh, or capable of rigorous sublimations. Van Helsing, Morris, Seward and Holmwood are all single. Mina and Jonathan get married in hospital, when Jonathan is in a state of prostration and impotence; and they marry in order to mend, to forget the terrible experience (which was also sexual) undergone by Jonathan in Transylvania: 'Share 'my ignorance' is what he asks of his wife. Not so Lucy, who awaits her wedding day with impatience. It is on this restlessness – on her 'somnambulism' – that Dracula exerts leverage to win her. And the more he takes possession of Lucy, the more he brings out her sexual side. A few moments before her death, 'She opened her eyes, which were now dull and hard at once, and said in a soft voluptuous voice, such as I had never heard from her lips: . . .'. And Lucy as a 'vampire' is even more seductive: 'The sweetness was turned to adamantine, heartless cruelty, and the purity to voluptuous wantonness. . . . the face became wreathed with a voluptuous smile . . . she advanced to him with outstretched arms and a wanton smile . . . and with a langorous, voluptuous grace, said: –"Come to me, Arthur. Leave these others and come to me. My arms are hungry for you. Come, and we can rest together. Come, my husband, come!"' The seduction is about to work, but Van Helsing breaks its spell. They proceed to Lucy's execution. Lucy dies in a very unusual way: in the throes of what, to the 'public' mind of the Victorians, must have seemed like an orgasm: 'The Thing in the coffin writhed; and a hideous, blood-curdling screech came from the opened red lips. The body shook and quivered and twisted in wild contortions; the sharp white teeth champed together till the lips were cut and the mouth was smeared with a crimson foam.' Surrounded by his friends who goad him on with their cries, Arthur Holmwood Lord Godalming purges the world of this fearful Thing; not without deriving, in distorted but transparent forms, enormous sexual satisfaction: 'He looked like a figure of Thor as his untrembling arm rose and fell, driving deeper and deeper the mercy-bearing stake, whilst the blood from the pierced heart welled and spurted up from around it.'

Dracula, then, liberates and exalts sexual desire. And this desire *attracts* but – at the same time – frightens. Lucy is beautiful, but dangerous. Fear and attraction are one and the same: and not just in Stoker. Much of nineteenth-century bourgeois high culture had already treated eros and sex as *ambivalent* phenomena. Their rhetorical figure is the oxymoron, the contradiction in terms, through which Baudelaire sings the ambiguity of amorous relations. Among the condemned poems of *Les Fleurs du Mal* – a title which is itself an oxymoron – is 'Les métamorphoses du vampire', where the irresistible female seducer is described 'writhing like a snake over charcoal'. And Stendhal noted in the margin of the first page of *De l'Amour*: 'I undertake to trace with a mathematical precision and (if I can) truth, the history of the illness called *love*.' Love is an illness: it entails the renunciation of man's *individuality* and *reason*.²⁴ For Stendhal, the devotee of enlightenment, this means denying one's very reason for existing: love becomes a *mortal* danger, and only a *greater* danger (Dracula!) can cure the person who falls victim to it: 'The leap from Leucates was a fine image in antiquity. In fact, the remedy for love is almost impossible. It requires not only that danger which sharply recalls a man's attention to his own preservation; it also requires – something far more difficult – the continuity of an enticing danger.'²⁵ *An enticing danger*, just as that of love is *a dangerous enticement*: fear and desire incessantly overturn into one another. They are indivisible. We find this confirmed in Sade, in Keat's Lamia, in Poe's Ligeia, in Baudelaire's women, in Hoffmann's woman vampire. Why is this?

Vampirism is an excellent example of the identity of desire and fear: let us therefore put it at the centre of the analysis. And let us take the psychoanalytic interpretation of this phenomenon, advanced for example by Marie Bonaparte in her study of Poe. Commenting on Baudelaire's remark that all Poe's women are 'strikingly delineated as though by an adorer', Marie Bonaparte adds: 'An adorer . . . who dare not approach the object of his adoration, since he feels it surrounded by some fearful, dangerous mystery.'²⁶ This mystery is none other than vampirism:

'the danger of sexuality, the punishment that threatens all who yield, is shown, as in *Berenice*, by the manner in which Egaeus is obsessed by her teeth. And indeed, in psychoanalysis, many cases of male impotence reveal, though more or less buried in the unconscious – strange as it may seem to many a reader – the notion of the female vagina being furnished with teeth, and thus a source of danger in being able to bite and castrate. . . . Mouth and vagina are equated in the unconscious and, when Egaeus yields to the morbid impulse to draw Berenice's teeth, he yields both to the yearning for the mother's organ and to be revenged upon it, since the dangers that hedge it about make him sexually avoid all women as too menacing. His act is therefore a sort of retributive castration inflicted on the mother whom he loves, and yet hates, because obdurate to his sex-love for her in infancy. . . . This concept of the *vagina dentata* and its consequent menace is, however, also a displacement (in this case downwards) of a factor with roots deep in infantile experience. We know that babes which, while toothless, are content to suck the breast, no sooner cut their first teeth than they use them to bite the same breast. This, in each of us, is the first manifestation of the aggressive instinct, . . . later, when the sense of what 'one should not do' has been instilled by ever severer and more numerous moral injunctions . . . the memory, or rather the phantasy of biting the mother's breast must have become charged, in the unconscious, with past feelings of wickedness. And the child, having learnt by experience what is meant by the law of retaliation when he infringes the code . . . begins, in his turn, to fear that the bites he wished to give his mother will be visited on him: namely, retaliation for his "cannibalism".'[27]

This passage identifies with precision the *ambivalent* root, interweaving hate and love, that underlies vampirism. An analogous ambivalence had already been described by Freud in relation to the taboo on the dead (and the vampire is, as we know, also a dead person who comes back to life to destroy those who remain): 'this hostility, distressingly felt in the unconscious as satisfaction over the death . . . [is displaced] on to the object of the hostility, on to the dead themselves. Once again . . . we find that the taboo has grown up on the basis of an ambivalent emotional attitude. The taboo upon the dead arises, like the others, from the contrast between conscious pain and unconscious satisfaction over the death that has occurred. Since such is the origin of the ghost's resentment, it follows naturally that the survivors who have the most to fear will be those who were formerly its nearest and dearest.'[28]

Freud's text leaves no doubt: the ambivalence exists *within the psyche of the person suffering from the fear*. In order to heal this state of tension one is forced to *repress*, unconsciously, one of the two affective states in conflict, the one that is socially more illicit. From the repression arises fear: 'every affect belonging to an emotional impulse, whatever its kind, is transformed, if it is repressed, into anxiety'.[29] And fear breaks out when – for whatever reason – this repressed impulse returns and thrusts itself upon the mind: 'an uncanny experience occurs either when infantile complexes which have been repressed are once more revived by some impression, or when primitive beliefs which have been surmounted seem once again to be confirmed.'[30] Fear, in other words, coincides with the 'return of the repressed'. And this brings us perhaps to the heart of the matter.

The literature of terror is studded with passages where the protagonists brush against the awareness – described by Freud – that the perturbing element is *within them*: that it is they themselves that produce the monsters they fear. Their first fear is – inevitably – that of *going mad*. 'Remember, I am not recording the vision of a madman.' (*Frankenstein*). 'God preserve my sanity . . . there is but one thing to hope for: that I may not go mad, if, indeed, I be not mad already.' (*Dracula*, Harker's words). '[Dr Seward] says that I afford him a curious psychological study' (*Dracula*, Lucy). 'I have come to the conclusion that it must be something mental.' (*Dracula*, Seward, who is also the director of a mental hospital). Jekyll has to defend himself from the suspicion of being mad, just like Polidori's Aubrey a century earlier. In these novels, reality tends to work according to the laws that govern dreams – 'I wasn't dreaming', 'as in a dream', 'as if I had gone through a long nightmare'.[31] This is the return of the repressed. But *how* does it return? Not as madness, or only marginally so. The lesson these books wish to impart is that one need not be afraid of going mad; that is one need not fear one's own repressions, the splitting of one's own psyche. No, one should be afraid of the *monster*, of something *material*, something *external*: '"Dr Van Helsing, are you mad?" . . . "Would I were!" he said. "Madness were easy to bear compared with truth like this."' *Would I were*: this is the key. Madness is nothing in comparison with the vampire. Madness does not present a problem. Or rather: madness, in itself, *does not exist*: it is the vampire, the monster, the potion that creates it.[32] *Dracula*, written in the same year that saw Freud begin his self-analysis, is a refined attempt by the nineteenth-century mind not to recognize itself. This is symbolized by the character who – already in the grip of fear – finds himself by chance in front of a mirror. He looks at it and jumps: in the mirror is a reflection of his face. But the reader's attention is immediately distracted: the fear does not come from his having seen his *own* image, but from the fact that the *vampire* is not reflected in the mirror. Finding himself face to face with the simple, terrible truth, the author – and with him the character and the reader – draws back in horror.

The repressed returns, then, but disguised as a monster. For a psychoanalytic study, the main fact is precisely this metamorphosis. As Francesco Orlando has remarked of his analysis of Racine's *Phèdre*, 'the relationship between the unconscious and literature was not postulated according to the presence of contents, whatever their nature, in the literary work ... perverse desire could not have been acceptable as content in the literary work without the latter's also accepting *the formal model capable of filtering it*.'[33] This formal model is the monster metaphor, the vampire metaphor. It 'filters', makes bearable to the conscious mind those desires and fears[34] which the latter has judged to be unacceptable and has thus been forced to repress, and whose existence it consequently cannot recognize. The literary formalization, the rhetorical figure, therefore has a double function: it *expresses* the unconscious content and at the same time *hides* it. Literature always contains *both* these functions. Taking away one or the other would mean eliminating either the problem of the unconscious (by asserting that everything in literature is transparent and manifest) or the problem of literary communication (by asserting that literature serves *only* to hide certain contents). Yet while these two functions are always present in the literary metaphor, the relationship between them can nevertheless change. One can stand out more than the other and win a dominant position within the overall signification of the work. These observations have a direct bearing on our argument, because the metaphor of the vampire is a splendid example of how the equilibrium of literary functions can vary. The problem can be posed thus: what is the sex – in literature, naturally, not in reality – of vampires? Vampires, unlike angels, do have sex. But it changes. In one set of works (Poe, Hoffmann, Baudelaire: 'elite' culture) they are women. In another (Polidori, Stoker, the cinema: 'mass' culture) they are men.

The metamorphosis is by no means accidental. At the root of vampirism, as we have seen, lies an ambivalent impulse of the child towards its mother. To present the vampire as a *woman* therefore means to make relatively little distortion of the unconscious content. The literary figure still retains the essential element – the sex – of that which is at the source of the perturbation. The defences that literature puts up to protect the conscious mind are relatively elastic: D. H. Lawrence (as Baudelaire, implicitly, before him) passes with ease from the vampire theme back to Poe's perverse erotic desires.[35] But if the vampire becomes a man, the unconscious source of the perturbation is hidden by a further layer of signifieds. The link becomes more tenuous. The conscious mind can rest easy: all that remains of the original fear is a word, 'Dracula': that splendid and inexplicable feminine name. The metamorphosis, in other words, serves to protect the conscious mind, or more precisely to keep it in a state of greater unawareness. The vampire is transformed into a man by mass culture, which has to promote spontaneous certainties and cannot let itself plumb the unconscious too deeply. Yet at the same time and for precisely this reason, the repressed content, which has remained unconscious, produces an irresistible fear. Spurious certainties and terror support each other.

3. The Strategy of Terror

Marxist analysis and psychoanalytic analysis have permitted us to isolate two prominent groups of signifieds which come together in the literature of terror and which render it, so to speak, necessary. They are, clearly, different signifieds, and it is hard to unite them harmoniously. I do not propose here to reconstruct the many missing links that might connect socio-economic structures and sexual-psychological structures in a single conceptual chain. Nor can I say whether this undertaking – attempted many times and in many different ways – is really possible: whether, that is, it is permissible to 'integrate' Marxism and psychoanalysis into a much broader and much more solid science of modern society. It is a highly complicated scientific problem, and I do not intend to broach its general aspects. I would merely like to explain the two reasons that – in this specific case – persuaded me to use two such different methodologies. The first is rather obvious. The central characters of this literature – the monster, the vampire – are *metaphors*, rhetorical figures built on the analogy between *different semantic fields*. Wishing to incarnate Fear as such, they must of necessity combine fears *that have different causes*: economic, ideological, psychical, sexual (and others should be added, beginning with religious fear). This fact seems to me to make it possible, if not obligatory, to use different tools in order to reconstruct the multiform roots of the terrorizing metaphor. But the monster and the vampire are metaphors for another reason too. Not only in order to synthesize phenomena of different natures, but also to *transform them*: to change their form, and with it their meaning. In Dracula there is monopoly capital and the fear of the mother: but these meanings are *subordinated* to the literal presence of the murderous count. They can be expressed only if they are hidden (or at least transformed) by his black cloak. Only in this way can the social consciousness admit its own fears without laying itself open to stigma. Marxism and psychoanalysis thus converge in defining the function of this literature: to take up within itself determinate fears in order to present them *in a form different from their real one*: to transform them into *other* fears, so that readers do not have to face up to what might really frighten them. It is a 'negative' function: it distorts reality. It is a work of 'mystification'. But it is also a work of 'production'. The more these great symbols of mass culture depart from reality the more, of necessity, they must expand and enrich the structures of false consciousness: which is nothing other than the dominant culture. They are not confined to distortion and falsification: they form, affirm, convince. And this process is automatic and self-propelling. Mary Shelley and Bram Stoker do not have the slightest intention of 'mystifying' reality: they interpret and express it in a spontaneously mendacious manner. This becomes clearer if we go back once again to the fact that monsters are metaphors. Now generally, in literature, metaphors are constructed (by the author) and perceived (by the reader) precisely as metaphors. But in the literature of terror this rule no longer applies. The metaphor is no longer a metaphor: it is a character as real as the others. 'The supernatural', Todorov has written, 'often appears because we take a figurative sense literally.'[36] Taking the figurative sense literally means considering the metaphor as an *element of reality*. It means, in other words, that a particular intellectual construction – the metaphor and the ideology expressed within it – really has become a 'material force', an independent entity, that escapes the rational control of its user. The intellectual no longer builds the cultural universe; rather, this universe speaks through the intellectual's mouth. After all, this is a familiar story: it is the story of Dr Frankenstein. In Mary Shelley's novel, the monster, the metaphor, still appears, at least in part, as something constructed, as a product. The monster, she warns us, is something 'impossible as a physical fact': it is something metaphorical. Yet the monster *lives*. Frankenstein's first moment of terror arises precisely in the face of this fact: a metaphor gets up and walks. Once this has happened, he knows that he will never be able to regain control of it. From now on, the metaphor of the monster will lead an autonomous existence: it will no longer be a product, a consequence, but the very origin of the literature of terror. By the time of *Dracula* – which carries the logic of this literature to its farthest consequences – the vampire has existed since time immemorial, uncreated and inexplicable.

There is another point on which the works of Shelley and Stoker diverge radically from one another: the *effect* they mean to produce on the reader. The difference, to paraphrase Benjamin, can be put like this: a description of fear and a frightening description are by no means the same thing. *Frankenstein* (like *Jekyll and Hyde*) does not want to *scare* readers, but to *convince* them. It appeals to their reason. It wants to make them reflect on a number of important problems (the development of science, the ethic of the family, respect for tradition) and agree – rationally – that these are threatened by powerful and hidden forces. In other words it wants to get the readers' assent to the 'philosophical' arguments expounded in black and white by the author in the course of the narration. Fear is made subordinate to this design: it is one of the means used to convince, but not the only one, nor the main one. The person who is frightened is not the *reader*, but the *protagonist*.

The fear is resolved within the text, without penetrating the text's relationship with its addressee.[37] Mary Shelley uses two stylistic expedients to achieve this effect. She fixes the narrative time in *the past*: and the past attenuates every fear, because the intervening time enables one not to remain a prisoner of events. Chance is replaced by order, shock by reflection, doubt by certainty – all the more completely in that (the second expedient) the monster has nothing *unknown* about him: we watch Frankenstein assemble him piece by piece, and we know from the start what characteristics he will have. He is threatening because he is alive and because he is big, not because he is beyond rational comprehension. For fear to arise, reason must be made insecure. As Barthes puts it: '"suspense" grips you in the "mind", not in the "guts".'[38]

The narrative structure of *Dracula*, the real masterpiece of the literature of terror, is different. Here the narrative time is always the present, and the narrative order – always paratactic – never establishes causal connections. Like the narrators, the readers have only clues: they see the effects, but do not know the causes. It is precisely this situation that generates suspense.[39] And this, in its turn, reinforces the readers' identification with the story being narrated. They are dragged forcibly *into* the text; the characters' fear is also theirs. Between text and reader there no longer exists that distance which in *Frankenstein* stimulated reflection. Stoker does not want a thinking reader, but a frightened one. Of course, fear is not an end in itself: it is a means to obtain consent to the ideological values we have examined. But this time, fear is the *only* means. In other words the conviction is no longer in the least rational: it is just as unconscious as the terror that produces it.[40] And thus, while professing to save a reason threatened by hidden forces, the literature of terror merely enslaves it more securely. The restoration of a logical order coincides with unconscious and irrational adherence to a system of values beyond dispute. Professing to save the individual, it in fact annuls him. It presents society – whether the feudal idyll of *Frankenstein* or the Victorian England of *Dracula* – as a great corporation: whoever breaks its bonds is done for. To think for oneself, to follow one's own interests: these are the real dangers that this literature wants to exorcise. Illiberal in a deep sense, it mirrors and promotes the desire for an integrated society, a capitalism that manages to be 'organic'. This is the literature of *dialectical* relations, in which the opposites, instead of separating and entering into conflict, exist in function of one another, reinforce one other. Such, for Marx, is the relation between capital and wage labour. Such, for Freud, is the relation between super-ego and unconscious. Such, for Stendhal, is the bond between the lover and the 'illness' he calls 'love'. Such is the relationship that binds Frankenstein to the monster and Lucy to Dracula. Such, finally, is the bond between the reader and the literature of terror. The more a work frightens, the more it edifies. The more it humiliates, the more it uplifts. The more it hides, the more it gives the illusion of revealing. It is a fear one *needs: the* price one pays for coming contentedly to terms with a social body based on irrationality and menace. Who says it is escapist?

Homo palpitans

Balzac's novels
and Urban Personality

This essay will endeavour to demonstrate three hypotheses.* First, that the metropolis (in our case, Paris in the middle of the nineteenth century) calls for a change in the perception not so much of space as of the *flow of time*. To come to terms with the urban experience, literature must excogitate a new rhetoric of temporality which is to reach its most complete manifestation not in poetry, but in the suspense plot of the novel, and specifically in Balzac's work. Second, I will maintain that this peculiar rhetorical arrangement moves from literature into the daily life of urban dwellers, becoming one of the most relevant intellectual filters they can use to ascribe a meaning to their world and accept it with a good deal of satisfaction. The third hypothesis – which is closely interwoven with the first two and depends entirely upon their validity – is that the connection Benjamin established between the urban experience and literary production in his essays on Baudelaire (the *sancta sanctorum* of literary criticism, in the last decade) is probably far less convincing and exemplary than one would tend to believe, and therefore must be re-examined.

1. Images of the City

It is not in the least obvious that the relationship between city and novel manifests itself especially at the level of plot. At least, it has not been so on various occasions, all of them significant in their own ways.

* This paper was presented at the convention *Città e metropoli*, Ferrara 2–4 October1981.

August Endell, 'Die Schönkeit der grossen Stadt', 1908: 'The age that produced the grand development of cities also created painters and poets who began to feel their beauty and to be inspired by them. But they were overcome by a wave of suspicion, lies, and moralism. They are accused of having lowered themselves into the mud of the streets and nobody even suspects that their glory lies precisely here: they find beauty and greatness exactly in those places the majority of people passed by with indifference.'[1]

Robert E. Park, 'The City: Suggestions for the Investigation of Human Behaviour in the Urban Environment', 1925: 'The same patient methods of observation which anthropologists like Boas and Lowie have expended on the study of the life and manners of the North American Indian might be even more fruitfully employed in the investigation of the customs, beliefs, social practices, and general conceptions of life prevalent in Little Italy on the lower North Side in Chicago, or in recording the more sophisticated folkways of the inhabitants of Greenwich Village and the neighbourhood of Washington Square, New York.

'We are mainly indebted to writers of fiction for our more intimate knowledge of contemporary urban life. But none of our cities demands a more searching and disinterested study than even Émile Zola has given us in his experimental novels. . .'.[2]

Erich Auerbach, *Mimesis*, 1946: 'The description of Madame Vauquer is controlled by a leading motif, which is several times repeated – the motif of harmony between Madame Vauquer's person . . . and the room . . . the harmony between her person and what we (and Balzac too, occasionally) call her milieu . . . . The motif of the unity of a milieu has taken hold of him so powerfully that the things and persons composing a milieu often acquire for him a sort of second significance . . . – a significance which can be best defined by the adjective demonic.

    . . . In his entire work . . . Balzac feels his milieux, different though they are, as organic and indeed demonic unities, and seeks to convey this feeling to the reader . . . to him every milieu becomes a moral and physical atmosphere . . . .'[3]

The culture and intentions of Endell, Park, and Auerbach are as different as they could be. Their overlapping treatment of the connection between literature and the city is, therefore, all the more striking: it is essentially through *description* that the city penetrates literature, and literature our perception and understanding of the city. To convey information about the city, the text must stop the story, temporarily suspend the action, and describe places and spaces: Park prefaces his remarks with a whole list of neighbourhoods; Endell's paragraph is entitled 'The city as landscape', and Auerbach's chapter 'In the Hôtel de la Mole'.

Neighbourhoods, streets, houses: places to describe. Literary description, however, is never a replica of something else, but rather a way of building and conveying a meaning, and establishing a *classification* of high and low, beautiful and ugly, old and new and so on. Classification (a concept that will be picked up at various points) is useful as long as time does not alter it: by ordering given elements, it postulates their immobility. Not surprisingly, literary criticism has always allotted a particular status to the analysis of description, whether by dubbing it 'symbolic interpretation' or 'institution of paradigms'. According to both versions, description stops the flow of the plot and reveals the fundamental meanings of the text. Better still, description reveals these meanings precisely by halting that succession of events which potentially confuses or hides them.

One is tempted to concede that such an attitude has common sense on its side. It would seem inevitable, or even obvious, that in coming to grips with the city, literature exalts description: the city is ultimately and above all a spatial entity where the value and meaning of every component – human or other – crystallize in the form of objects, houses, entities that can be variously described and classified. All this is true. But it is also true of the village, the country, or of any other form of human residence. What *distinguishes* the city – however, and this will find its way into the technique of the novel – is that its spatial structure (basically its *concentration*) is functional to the intensification of *mobility*: spatial mobility, naturally enough, but mainly *social* mobility. The dazzling rapidity of success and ruin is the great theme of the nineteenth-century novel from Balzac to Maupassant: with it the city enters modern literature and becomes, as it were, its obligatory context. Yet it is such precisely because the city as a physical place – and therefore as a support to descriptions and classifications – becomes the mere backdrop to the city as a network of developing social relationships – and hence as a prop to narrative temporality. The novel reveals that the meaning of the city is not to be found in any particular place, but manifests itself only through a temporal trajectory. Whereas the great aspiration of mythic narration exacts the metamorphosis of time into space, the urban novel turns the axiom on its head and seeks to resolve the spatial in terms of the sequential.

Analysis yields evidence that description plays an entirely secondary role in Balzac's Paris. Confirmation is not difficult to come by. Indeed, Auerbach had already observed – without furnishing explanations – that when Balzac tried to transform space into 'a total atmosphere which envelops all its several milieux . . . he did his best and most truthfully for the circle of the middle and lower Parisian bourgeoisie and for the provinces; while his representation of high society is often melodramatic, false, and even unintentionally comic . . . he is unable to create the true atmosphere of the higher spheres – including those of the intellect.'[4] This is a legitimate observation and would be even more so for, say, Zola – with due modification of the sociological references. The 'best and most truthful' realizations in this sense stem from the fact that certain characters, or certain situations, can be entirely made out through the description of the environment because – and only because – the time of their metamorphoses is irrevocably over. It is no accident that descriptive force reaches its maximum with the 'poor' of naturalism and with Balzac's memorable 'elderly' (Vauquer, Séchard, Goriot, Gobseck, Grandet, Hulot). Their future can only duplicate their present: their essence is what they *are*, not what they might become. They will never be objects of a narration, in so far as the latter always and necessarily implies change.

All this can be confirmed *e contrario*. An early scene in *Lost Illusions* establishes which of the two young friends will be the novel's protagonist. Davide Séchard, who has been invited, through Lucien, to an evening at the de Bargeton's, moves to the sidelines: '. . . you are neither ticketed nor docketed. Take advantage of being socially uncommitted. . . . You are well-built, have a graceful figure, you carry your clothes well. . . . In such a circle I should look like a working man. I should be awkward, ill at ease. I should talk nonsense. . . .' Thus, Lucien can – or must – become the protagonist precisely because he is not 'describable': his beauty will be the means to social ascent not, in the banal sense, as seductive beauty, but because it singles him out as the physically unmarked ('virgin') being, the man without signs. Lucien is 'neither ticketed nor docketed'. His beauty is his polyvalence, his transformability, his intrinsic predisposition to shift from one role to another, from one attachment to another (and even from one surname to another).

Beauty is beauty, and can aim at success, because it is not chained to any definite and hence binding content: as a rule, beauty is never described, but simply affirmed and reiterated. The reason for this leaps to the eye during Lucien's first encounter with that phenomenon which links together beauty, success, and the city: fashion. Strolling through the Tuileries – it is his first day in Paris – Lucien, and Balzac, muse over the passers-by and their clothes. They divide them into two categories: those whose dress indicates some form of *status* (social, geographical, generational), and those whose dress reveals only fashion. In the first case dress is – in the terms of *Système de la mode* and *S/Z* – a clue: it inexorably assigns a place, an age, a job, a condition from which the individual cannot extricate himself even physically. It pins down, it betrays, it boxes in. It engenders a classification; or rather it indicates that, in this case, the principle of classification is valid. Again, this principle is fixed in time: it predicts and prescribes the immutability of everything that falls under its jurisdiction.

In fashion, just the opposite is true. In this case sensory perception cannot lead us to classification. Fashionable dress is not a clue: it is, rather, a tautological sign. For example, twenty-odd years ago faded blue jeans were a clue to at least three things: a poorly paid job (the material is coarse and cheap), a job requiring a lot of rough movement (the material is strong), and one done out of doors (hence, the discoloration). Yet these very same blue jeans, once they have become fashionable, no longer furnish clues. They indicate the man of fashion not *because they are made of rough, bleached-out denim* (as was the case with the cowboy), but because fashion randomly and fecklessly exacts rough, bleached-out denim. In other words, they denote fashion because they are in fashion. Of course, tautologies are never particularly satisfying, especially when already implicit in an essay of 1895. . . . Yet, in his brilliant examination of fashion Simmel missed a necessary step. The expression 'this object is fashionable because it is in fashion' is incomplete. We should add its truly essential qualification: 'this object is fashionable because it is in fashion now'. To 'describe' a fashionable object is useless. But to ascertain whether it is fashionable now, in the past, or in some predictable future – this, on the contrary, is essential. Fashion, as Leopardi hinted in his *Dialogue between Fashion and Death*, is the daughter of time. It is *nothing but* time. The man of fashion is not 'boxed in' by his clothing in the same way as the cowboy was. To remain in the same slot – 'man of fashion' – he must refurbish his wardrobe incessantly, always 'keeping up with the times'. Let us then turn once and for all to the question of the representation of time in literature.

2. Plot, Shock, Surprise, Suspense

In that splendid book *Tempus*, Harald Weinrich observes that narration must avail itself of what Goethe called the 'unheard-of'. 'Unheard-of' is exactly the right term, especially because it superimposes two distinct references: the *novelty* of a particular occurrence and the *violation* of a particular rule (which often constitutes the premiss of novelty itself). While all narration demands the unheard-of, not all cultural systems produce it in the same way. It would seem that for an entire phase of the novel's development, the narrative unheard-of (novelty) was based on the moral unheard-of (violation). That is, the novel told stories that could exist only because of the presence of some kind of Super-villain or monster *tout court*. Take away Blifil, Lovelace, Heathcliff, Moby Dick, and some of the most gripping plots of eighteenth- and nineteenth-century novels would never have been written. And without that merry brigade of fake and real friars, obscene marquises, mellifluous cardinals, hunchbacks of great cathedrals, hideous bats, thieves, poisoners, hardened schoolboys, three-

footed cannibals, *not one* of all the main genres of popular literature would exist.

Now, the relationship of all this to the city is that the urban
narrative environment makes it possible, for the first time, to
create an enthralling plot without having to resort to the freak.[5]
The monster, in fact, is perceived as such only on the basis of a
taxonomy, of an extremely rigid classification that distinctly separates what is normal[6] from what is not. But the underlying rule of
the big laissez-faire city has the peculiarity of furthering *an incessant shift in classification*: especially in that tumultuous development of heterogeneous forms of power – financial, political, and
cultural: each in turn divided between conflicting groups – which
characterized Paris in the mid nineteenth century.

A constantly shifting classification implies at least two consequences. First of all, it becomes almost impossible to define the monstrous (in the double sense of exceptional and repugnant). Who
comes closest: Vautrin or Nucingen, Rastignac or Goriot?
(Besides, the concept of 'monstrous' had already been questioned
by Romantic culture). But the second, and much more far-
reaching consequence is that what engages the reader is no longer
the 'state of exception' of the symbolic system (the monster indicates a taxonomy that is no longer obeyed: the falling apart of all
symbolic 'laws') and, thereby, of represented life – but the unpredictability harboured *in ordinary administration and 'everyday
life'*.

Balzac's extraordinary invention was to show that a young man's
life could be exciting without his having to get shipwrecked on a
desert island, sign a pact with the devil, or create homicidal life-
size dolls. It is sufficient to write a theatrical review, lose one's
heart to a light-headed actress, and lack an iron will. A touch of
quite banal speculation transacted by not terribly trustworthy
friends, the bank regulations on promissory notes, and the court
will take care of the rest. Indeed, with Balzac the 'prose of the
world' ceases to be boring. It is precisely the very prosaic social
relationships of incipient capitalism that constitute his plots and
confer on them their gripping syntagmatic – temporal – features.
To arouse the protagonist and the reader it is no longer necessary
to embark on a journey: much better to stay in town. Here,

indeed, everyday life can – and, in a sense, must – transform itself into adventure.

This conclusion calls for a re-examination of the relationship that Benjamin established between urban life, shock, and individual experience. 'Some Motifs in Baudelaire' is, unfortunately, ambiguous precisely on the point that has made it famous: that is, whether the objective intention of Baudelaire's poetry is 'to produce' or rather to 'parry' shock is not clear.[7] 'Parry' or not, however, Baudelaire's poetry indubitably confronts us with a series of shocks. Or rather – to reformulate the concept of shock in terms more consonant with the literary object – it proffers particularly audacious rhetorical figures. Even aside from the question – which incidentally is in no way secondary – whether such figures can be traced back to metaphor, to allegory, or to yet something else, they are in any case indubitably audacious. For once, let us forget the notorious *passante*, and recall the swan, the seven old men, the demons that wake up as businessmen and the other kindred images of the *Tableaux parisiens*. But what precisely is an audacious figure? It is a peculiarly contradictory classifying act. It is the 'state of exception' of the semantic system. It is, indeed, the monster: all the more perceivable when made to leap out of the faultless background of alexandrines or sonnets.

The monster is the *sans pareil* of shock, no doubt about it. This seems to tally perfectly with *Beyond the Pleasure Principle*. Trauma and monstrosity are one and the same. Yet there is a problem. It is not accidental that Freud's text takes its cue from traumas undergone in wartime: the concept of shock can originate only from the analysis of *exceptional* experiences. Baudelaire's figures are also exceptional, true enough. But the question we have to ask is whether the category of the traumatic and exceptional event is really the most appropriate for the analysis of the experiences of urban life.

Benjamin, implicitly, answers that it is. In a famous passage, he describes city life as 'a series of shocks and collisions'. I shall return to this specific aspect of urban life later: here, let it suffice to say that Benjamin has unduly extended the Freudian concept of shock and by so doing has misunderstood what is essential to the urban experience. Shock, to be such, presupposes on the one hand an extremely rigid and poor system of expectations and, on the other, an event that clamorously violates it in an essentially unrepeatable way. City life, however, has modified both aspects of the relationship: the apparatus of reception and prediction has become much more elastic and much richer – while the external stimuli either present themselves as 'chances' to be seized (the exact opposite of a potential offence) or, when threatening, are always rather easy to foresee, whereas total unpredictability is essential to shock.

To be suspended between unswerving habit and sudden catastrophe is much more typical of traditional rural societies, villages, and the provinces. By comparison, city life mitigates extremes and extends the range of intermediate possibilities: it arms itself against catastrophe by adopting ever more pliant and provisional attitudes. It is no accident that the city dweller has always appeared as a typically 'adaptable' animal. The rigid separation between internal and external, which is at the root of the theory of shock, in urban life tends to transform itself into that continuum rendered in Leopold Bloom's amble. And another continuum – the temporal – overcomes the rigid partition dividing experience and tradition: in the organized and yet ephemeral life of the city no event possesses all the characteristics of full-fledged experience, but no event ever lacks them completely.

If, in fact, every individual's dependence on every other's activities does not actually originate in the metropolis (Smith and Hegel had already mentioned it with reference to other contexts), Simmel is not mistaken in placing this general interdependence at the centre of the urban experience where it is not only absolutely inevitable, but noisy, visible, and unforgettable. This ties in with what has already been said, for generalized mutual dependence implies a constant increase of the variables in play, and this clearly means that no outcome of any action can be given as certain, or be discarded a priori as incapable of promoting experience. The isolated and unrepeatable event – Baudelaire's apparitions that break the flow of time – lose their pre-eminence which is, instead, taken over by those events which, while in themselves repeatable and predictable, by *combining* together always end up by breeding something unusual.

In effect, Balzac's plots are such combinations – with an addition: that urban life generally strives to reduce and contain unpredictability, while in the novel, the opposite occurs. Thus, the mechanism of urban social relationships, though a *necessary* condition, is not in itself sufficient to account for the emergence of the novelistic plot. The novel adds the convention of suspense. And, as it is really very hard to imagine the city dweller's culture *without* that convention, it is worth specifying what constitutes it.

Rhetoric has tended to oppose *suspense* and *surprise*, equating the first with tragic irony, and, therefore, to a certain extent, with destiny, and the second with the unexpected, that is, with historical and sublunar development. After a certain point, however, this distinction no longer reaches the core of the problem. Balzac, as a rule, operates simultaneously on both planes. Towards the end of *Lost Illusions*, for example, we foresee Lucien's ruin. But there is a substantial difference between his fall and, say, Oedipus's or Macbeth's. In tragedy everything conspires concertedly *in only one direction*. In Balzac, although the basic tendency is clear, the high number of variables inherent to the systems of the city and the novel brings about the conclusion through a continuous and highly unpredictable series of ups and downs. In this way, suspense and surprise encourage city dwellers to believe that only rarely is 'everything lost'. Even in the middle of catastrophe they are induced to perceive, and hence rejoice in, all surviving potentiality. There is no need to illustrate how pleasant this sensation is.

Another hiatus separates tragic irony and modern suspense. In the first, time has no prominence. It makes no difference whether the shepherd of Cithaeron reaches Thebes a month sooner or later – nor when Birnam wood be come. But in Balzac it makes an enormous difference that a certain promissory note expires today and not next week. This suggests that the main effect of suspense consists in sharpening our perception of passing time. Because of the rhetoric of suspense, time always appears as either too fast or too slow: in both cases, however, time *moves*, and forces us to come to terms with this fact. It is no longer the non-perceivable time of 'classified' life, incapable of experience, nor that concentrated and exploded in the unique instant of the sudden shock.

We must, finally, clarify what throwing oneself headlong into the flow of time means for the city dweller's 'spiritual life' or 'psychic economy'. First of all, this has *nothing* to do with that 'anxiety' which, according to *Beyond the Pleasure Principle*, prepares us to 'parry' shock. Anxiety always presupposes that we are in the dark as regards the threat hanging over us, and this is certainly not the case in Balzac's novels. (It is the case in several specific sub-genres of nineteenth-century literature, but that is another matter). It is not anxiety but rather a bittersweet – and highly irrational[8] – blend of *curiosity* and *haste*. The city dweller's life is dominated by a nightmare – a trifling one, to be sure – unknown to other human beings: the terror of 'missing something', and specifically of missing it because of 'getting there too late'. Suspense, with its incitement to go full steam ahead because there are novelties in store, confirms this conviction; and at the same time, by allowing it to be experienced vicariously and with the certainty of always arriving on time, furnishes psychic protection in the losing race with the time of the city.

It might not be much: and certainly 'anxiety' offers a much fiercer model of the struggle between humans and their environment. Yet nineteenth-century readers – the good citizens of their time – soon learned to moderate their expectations: and besides, if one wants to perceive ordinary life as something potentially exciting, one implicitly accepts that excitement becomes a trifle ordinary. Only rarely does that reader – 'Hypocrite lecteur' – stay put in his armchair, *fumant son houka* and dreaming about the gallows. More often, and more simply, he wishes to retrieve the feeling that tomorrow, if not exactly another day, will at least be different from today.

3. The Red, the Black, and the Others

Lost Illusions: 'In Paris, it is first of all the general pattern that commands attention. . . . The ever-present contrast between extreme luxury and extreme indigence, all these things are particularly striking.' The laissez-faire city is not only *founded* on social inequality: its main goal is to *intensify* it. Concentration plus mobility means precisely that disequilibrium is bound to sharpen,

and in a relatively restricted space, thus becoming more percep-
tible and more conspicuous. In Paris, differences immediately
strike the eye. . .

The proximity of luxury and penury – the brazen manifestation
of social violence – is tolerated by the city dweller for reasons
completely different from those which made it acceptable in, say,
the feudal era. Then it was legimated by the *immutability* of social
relationships: the lord and the beggar could fit into the same picture because that had always been – and would always be – the way
of the world. On the contrary, in the bourgeois city, spatial contiguity is accepted because it is automatically 'translated' into, and
legitimated by, a chronological contiguity, the idea of an unexpected and sudden reversal of fate: '"So the wheel turns," said
Vautrin; "yesterday night at a duchess's ball, this morning in a
money-lender's office, on the lowest rung of the ladder – just like a
Parisienne!"' (*Père Goriot*). As if to say: here in the city, the
change of status can easily take on extreme and virulent forms.

This is one of the major urban myths of the nineteenth century:
yesterday at the duchess's, today at the usurer's. These are the
Parisians – this is Paris. Once again, to 'show', it is useless to
'describe': one has to *narrate* what happens there – yesterday
today tomorrow – because only through this succession does the
'meaning' of Paris emerge. It is often an extreme meaning – Balzac's 'excess' and 'melodrama'. Yet, this has nothing to do with the
production of the effect of shock. Shock always presupposes an
irremediable fracture in the course of experience: a full 'recovery'
from it is impossible. Balzac, on the contrary, emphasizes his
characters' perennial *resurgence*, and always focuses the narration
on those still capable of recovery, those for whom shock, if there was
one, was only an *Augenblick*. Balzac is not interested in Goriot,
but in Rastignac; not in Coralie, or Eva, or Davide Séchard,
but in Lucien: when the latter is about to kill himself Balzac
puts Vautrin-Herrera in his path, to bring him back to Paris richer
and more powerful than before. The 'definitive' has no place in
Balzac's great ideological construction: only alternation enthralls
him. Not triumph *per se*, nor defeat: only the perpetual appearance of one in the other.

In *Homo Ludens* Huizinga maintains that people played less in the nineteenth century than in any other. Perhaps. Yet this could occur only because the taste for risk had never penetrated so deeply into the very fabric of everyday life. The expression 'to play the stock market' – not to mention the thing in itself – originates in the nineteenth century: and the readiness with which, in Balzac's novels, the characters try to compensate for the disasters of their professional lives by gambling is indicative of the confusion between the two realms.

Among all games of chance – in Balzac no less than in Baudelaire – the place of honour doubtlessly goes to roulette. This could be because roulette best reflects the potential rapidity of urban social change – or perhaps because it is set apart from all other games by a decidedly puzzling detail. Games normally have a binary scheme. There are two sides: one wins, the other loses; one wins *because* the other loses. Obviously, this is also true of roulette: red wins because it has 'beaten' black: the two movements are inseparable. Yet anyone who has played roulette will recall the general atmosphere of irresponsibility, innocence almost, that hovers over the green table. No one ever has the sensation of betting against another player. One always has the impression of winning against or losing to the bank. The bank really has no money of its own: it limits itself to circulating the chips, taking them on consignment from x, and passing them over to y. Still, this exiguous extra passage, this slight deviation from the model of direct face-to-face conflict masks the true nature of the relationship that links the players. *Roulette* is crude mutual looting, in which no one looks the other in the eye; rather, everyone automatically turns to an impeccably dressed intermediary who, in the blind-folded goddess's stead, never looks anyone in the face.

This situation seems perfectly natural to us now. But it is probable that for the gambler's psychology (and not only his), roulette constituted an enormous novelty; perhaps this explains its dazzling and demonic diffusion. To appreciate the nature of the change one need only go back a few years to Pushkin's *Queen of Spades*, where faro is played. Faro – along with games like baccarat or chemin de fer, and to some extent poker – is the exact opposite of roulette. The players are so explicitly direct adversaries that Pushkin himself observes, shortly before narrating the last hand, how

'It was like a duel'. The observation is exact, and the naturalness with which it is made reveals how, in Pushkin (who was, in this and other ways, a transitional figure), the link between social power, the game, and the duel was deemed obvious. With roulette, the situation changes and in moving away from the model of the duel one already perceives a certain analogy with the urban mechanism, as well as with Balzac's novels. In both cases, the system of power relationships becomes more and more pervaded by the act of *mediation*: you can ruin or be ruined by someone without ever having looked them in the face, even remaining unaware of their existence. Still, the mediation of the croupier is not the only, nor even the most interesting, of the ways in which roulette replaces the model of the duel with a completely different kind of conflict. Let us return to the basic situation – the 'struggle' between red and black. An infinite number of options are superimposed on this initial conflict. For instance, whoever plays red is implicitly the enemy of all those who have played single black numbers and, conversely, the ally of all those who have played single red numbers. Then there are those who have played a predominantly black or predominantly red combination; and those who have bet on combinations based on an absolute balance between red and black. Thus an extremely complicated parallelogram of forces emerges, a combination of 'friends' and 'enemies' and 'accomplices', graded into a thousand nuances. There is even a sort of universal brotherhood (also, however, never completely lacking in exceptions) against zero.

Thus, in roulette, the model based on binary opposition – the 'duel' model – is not exactly discarded: rather, it undergoes a process of multiplication and overdetermination. It is never wholly clear who the enemy is, to what extent, or why. And here the analogy with the mechanism of Balzac's novels enters into play. His narrative also stems from several simple irreducible oppositions (whether of sentiment or of interest is secondary here) which are mixed in so dense and asymmetrical a combination that the moment of direct conflict – conclusive precisely because open and direct – inevitably becomes more and more marginal: whether it be a conflict between social, or political, or cultural fields, or a conflict between individuals. It is well known that the last page of

Père Goriot contains Rastignac's famous cry from the heights of the Père Lachaise: '"We'll fight this out, you and I".' A gauntlet has been flung down with ostensible certainty. Less well known, but far more relevant, are the two lines that follow: 'And, as the first move in the challenge he was flinging at society, he went back to dine with Madame de Nucingen.' *Finis*. The duel will never occur. As for the challenge, it is to be a highly tolerable sentimental triangle.

Absolute sovereigns had already attempted to prohibit duels (to little effect); but only the novel was really capable of dismantling the ethic of the duel.[9] The novel, and the city. City legislation had already outlawed the duel; but people merely rented a carriage and went off to the Bois. No, the city managed to banish the idea that the duel constituted the summit of human existence, the action that epitomized the entire meaning of life, in a way that was certainly not deliberate and was at first sight paradoxical. By exposing the individual to such an unending succession of little and big 'duels' it convinced him once and for all that they must be avoided for survival's sake. The 'duels' I refer to arise directly from the coupling of concentration and mobility: living in a crowded city one must learn to escape thousands of small and large physical and social clashes. In particular, urban life becomes safer and, paradoxically, even quicker if the individual learns to give up the *short cut* (the straight line, which is also the typical direction of the duel) and to follow a tortuous path, a continuous slalom between objects, people, and institutions. This is extremely evident with traffic, but it is just as true for social movement.[10]

Thus, in the city – unless (in Vautrin's words) one has the force of a cannon ball or is committed to martyrdom – one must learn how to get round thousands of unmoveable objects. Against Benjamin, however, the novel, and the city dweller's entire 'education', do not hinge on the shock image of potential impact – but rather on the know-how necessary to avoid it, on competence in 'alternative paths' of every kind, and on the ability to latch on immediately to the possibilities that these very often disclose. This suggests a further consideration regarding the relationship between the novel's plot and the duel. In the duel the target is right there, straight ahead, and the ground is clear: one mustn't, one 'can't' miss it. In the novel, and in urban life, because of the myriad of detours, mediations, and adjustments, the target blurs. The long detour undertaken to reach it has transformed us, and when we get there we no longer recognize it. We have already chosen another aim which in turn will be supplanted by yet another. The duel gravitates towards the solution: it aspires to conclude as soon as possible and the outcome, whatever it is, will always appear adequate. Painful perhaps, but exact: a verdict, like destiny, permitting no appeal. The novel tends in the opposite direction: it is all in the process; it can only 'digress', and the conclusion, whatever it is, will always be perceived as unsatisfying. Balzac's most characteristic endings – those which leave the reader flabbergasted – are *preludes* to successive narrations. The novel, just like the city, can never stop.

4. On the Road

For the last time let us pick up the connection between the variety and complexity of urban life and the suspense of plot. So far we have seen how a given form of social relationships and of spatial aggregation transforms itself – in order to acquire a meaning and be accepted with pleasure – in the strictly temporal structure of the plot. It is necessary to work our way backwards and understand how one who is so thoroughly immersed in the time flow 'sees' the city and its social relationships: understand, that is, what kind of vision of the whole is implicit in the novel with a suspense plot.

I shall try to clarify this with two examples, one concerning the social dimension of the modern city, the other its spatial features. Lukàcs has written that *Lost Illusions* narrates a story set in a period of extremely rapid expansion of capitalist social relationships, which invest and subjugate even the field of 'spiritual production'. Second: when Lucien tries to sell the manuscript of his historical novel he is forced to turn to several publishers, and thus compelled to roam Paris's entire intellectual milieu and observe its urban and architectonic peculiarities, local slang, representative individuals, and so on. These two statements – one 'on' and one 'from' *Lost Illusions* – are, doubtless, true. But then it would seem that what has been said thus far needs revision. It would seem that the suspense plot – as depositary of the meaning of the text – is yielding to social history on the one hand, and to some form of description and classification on the other. One is led to believe that the plot is simply an *instrument*, the necessary means to the emergence of much more substantial realities.

Yet this is not the case. In the Balzacian novel, social relationships and the urban landscape, far from disputing the primacy of the plot, have a right to citizenship only within the limits *dictated by the plot itself*. They are evoked only to reinforce the plot *as plot*: to intensify its complexity and unpredictability. Thus, the plot is not at their service, but they at the plot's. The syntagmatic axis is not functional to the institution or the explication of paradigms (as in the case of myth): rather, the paradigms are the springboard for the story. It is not a 'story' at the service of a 'moral' capable of summarizing it, but thousands of 'morals' aimed at developing the taste for suspense, that is, for the temporal flow abstracted from the content of individual episodes in and for themselves.

If we now translate these observations into terms of urban psychology we perceive that the novel accustoms us to 'seeing' the city in a glance – not so much 'absent-minded' as intermittent. We see the city to the extent that it hinders a specific action, interposes between us and something else, and makes us 'waste *time*'. This situation culminates in some of Hitchcock's films, but it is experienced daily by anyone who lives in the city. It is precisely this interlocking of time and space that explains one of the city dweller's most bizarre perversions: his unswerving, arrogant and deliberate *ignorance* of the place he lives in. The urban dweller seems to make a point of honour of knowing as little as possible about his city, and is capable of walking a hundred times past a church by Borromini without ever going inside. How so? Because, the city dweller complains, I have no time. He lies; no one has ever had more free time. It is not that he has no time, but that city life does not allot time to contemplation. It allows time only for *activity*, of whatever kind. It allows for a time always dedicated to weaving relationships, obtaining things, and carrying out duties. It conceives of the flow of time and of the organization of life as the most gripping story possible, compared to which the city cannot stand out as an object worthy of attention in and for itself. It is only background: perceived perhaps clearly and violently, but always framed and defined by exigencies of a temporal order.

The city does not allot time to contemplation. It is clear that the point also runs up against Benjamin's reflections and, even more so, Simmel's[11]. Seeking the specific and distinctive features of the urban personality, both cite the acts of crossing the street and (with an unjustified extension, as we shall see) of going for a walk as emblematic events. On these occasions the deep structure of the urban situation, supposedly surfaces with greater evidence in the form of a chaotic and incessant succession of stimuli; and it is in this selfsame sphere that the individual psyche presumably reacts by engendering the *flâneur* – who 'was addicted . . . to the phantasmagoria of space'[12] – and his successor, the 'blasé type' for whom '. . . the meaning and the value of the distinctions between things, and therewith of the things themselves, are experienced as meaningless. They appear . . . in an homogenous, flat and gray colour with no one of them worthy of being preferred to another.'[13]

It is clear that both these figures, though in different ways, are characterized by a hypertrophy of the sense of sight. Whether to enjoy themselves with the urban phantasmagoria, or to belittle it, they define themselves in the act of looking. To observe becomes an end in itself, the emblematic compendium of modern existence. And this, obviously, is performed where sight can best be put to the test, that is, on the road. Thus, walking along the street becomes the metropolitan act par excellence, in which the sense of an entire environmental and social structure emerges in exemplary form.

This typology is erroneous. I have partially explained why above, maintaining that the spatial dimension – in the novel and in ordinary urban experience – is always instrumental: it can be perceived as an obstacle to something else, but never in and for itself. This objection can, however, be reformulated more substantially and emphatically: the street is, clearly enough, the public dimension par excellence. In the street, we become visible to others and they to us; the street itself (and many of the means of transportation on it) are public property; and in using it we must all respect a public set of rules, or laws even – the street 'code'. The street is therefore a part of the 'public sphere'. Our problem, then, consists in establishing the relevance of this sphere in the city dweller's life, and in particular the degree to which the 'public sphere' can be translated for him in the action of 'being in the street'. I would say that – if we compare city life to other types of communities – the significance of this public situation appears to have enormously *diminished*. The village road was certainly a thousand times poorer in stimuli than the city street. On the other hand, however – and this is the point – the near-totality of life occurred in the road, or in places of work, or even in homes which were normally exposed to the eye of the passer-by (and therefore to the entire social structure: Balzac has written very cogent pages about the 'visibility' of life in the provinces). But then, compared to the village, the city has certainly given full value to the street as a channel of communication (and also of communication of information, that is, of stimuli) – but it has drastically and irreparably devalued it *as a place of social experience*. Not because in the city 'experience' in the strong sense becomes impossible (as Simmel and Benjamin contend): more simply, because in the city experience is had *elsewhere*.

The great novelty of urban life, in fact, does not consist in having thrown the people into the street, but in having raked them up and shut them into offices and houses. It does not consist in having intensified the public dimension, but in having invented the private one – and especially in having transferred the meaning of individual life, and thus also the standard for evaluating what constitutes experience, into this new domain.

This, therefore, is the reason why the city – in its public dimension, of which the street is one of the most appropriate symbols – inevitably appears in the novel only as background. It is also the reason why it has been difficult for *the state* to acquire prominence in the narrative of the last centuries: bourgeois culture is fundamentally a culture of private life, which is reluctant to identify and resolve itself entirely in great collective institutions. Obviously, I have no intention of maintaining that private life is subtracted from and extraneous to social laws, nor that the meaning ascribed to it is something totally personal and unrepeatable. But to understand the social significance and function of the private sphere it is pointless to take short cuts and attempt to resolve it in explicitly public instances. Rather, one could further analyse the meaning intrinsic to the plot's sequence of actions: here, I have limited myself to formulating the necessity of such an analysis and to a few premisses. A semantics of the plot (or rather of plots, as they are hardly all of the same type) is perhaps the best way to establish how literature has contributed to forming the image modern man has of his life.

One last remark. It is clear that all my hypotheses work especially for the laissez-faire city. Literature, and the novel, have considerably changed since then. But this is not because the cities have changed. The really new element is the change in the system of expectations concerning private life. I have cited Leopold Bloom's walk. Joyce already intuited that the exemplary urban act consisted no longer in *crossing* the street – an action always indicative of an individual aim, and of the irreversible temporality in 'turning one's back' upon one side, even if it is only a sidewalk – but in strolling without any specific aim. Joyce himself traced this metamorphosis back to something that had nothing to do with the structure of the city: to the re-emergence of that 'mythic' culture which characterizes our century precisely in relation to private life, its perception and what the individual expects from it.[14]

Things have changed, no doubt. But we must inquire if this change has produced an equally sturdy way of perceiving the urban context as that delineated in this essay. and therefore one capable of substituting for it in lasting forms. I do not believe that this has occurred, in literature at least. The most explicit attempts in this direction – Döblin's and Dos Passos's – had little following; or, in the case of certain avant-garde movements, developed and concluded outside the literary domain. As for mass culture, all of its principal genres have maintained the nineteenth-century model with minor adjustments. But even with Joyce, or Proust, or Musil, or the 'detective story' trend of twentieth-century 'high' literature (Borges, Gadda, Robbe-Grillet, Pynchon), or even Kafka – we find no new convention, but rather a hollowing out of former conventions. It is as if the developments of the literary image of the city were strictly of a negative and critical character: a model exists which must be mangled and enervated, treated with irony, further and further removed – but never abandoned once and for all. It is an ambivalent attitude towards the old image of city life which perhaps has something in common with what, in a completely different realm and with completely different aims, produced the semi-exodus to the suburbs. This obviously does not mean that twentieth-century literature is only the cultivated and sceptical parasite of nineteenth century models: but that its major innovations – of which there are many – are to be found in areas which are substantially extraneous or indifferent to the changes in the urban context.

But, then, every form of social existence experiences a moment in which its potentialities and its meaning emerge in an exemplary and, as it were, definitive form. Why not accept the idea that – as far as the experience of the city goes – this moment has escaped us for the very good reason that it took place more than a hundred years ago?

Clues

1. Methods of Analysis

'A notion can be defined in two ways: either in terms of its internal organization or in terms of its function. In the first case, one deals with a system of which this notion is the external limit; in the second, it is a constitutive element in another system . . . let us call the first type of definition structural and the second functional. We shall say that the structural description of linguistic facts is dependent on linguistics, their functional description on a (scarcely existent) linguistic anthropology. Let us note that there is no necessary correlation between the two domains – structural and functional.'[1] A sociology of literature – a functional analysis of a structured system – makes sense only if it demonstrates that the correlation negated by Todorov actually exists. What is in question is *correlation*, not necessarily *homology*. It is not, therefore, a question of *equating* structure and functional analyses, which are, and remain, distinct. (Nor is it a matter of being theoretically nonchalent: we can quell our fear by whistling in the dark, but this doesn't make us see any more clearly.) A shift from one field of investigation to another implies a relationship between different methods, and, hence, constitutes a *problem*.

Against Todorov's theoretical position it can be said that a structure carries out a specific function in a larger system because it is *that* structure and not another. So, too, the function carried out by a structure is *one particular* function, specified and delimited by the structure it depends upon. Structure and function define one another: they constitute their specific identities through their relationship. The sociology of literature must reproduce these two identities and their connection conceptually. That is, it must run structural and functional hypotheses against one another, using each as the 'potential falsifier' of the other. For example, certain sociological premises lead to the postulation of a functional hypothesis ('detective fiction fosters the values of liberal democracy because it embodies the ideal of habeas corpus'): if contradicted by the structural analysis of the texts (as is the case), it proves false *both* as a literary *and* as a sociological hypothesis. The same holds true for structural hypotheses. Within this frame of reference, the sociology of literature does not emerge as *a critical method*, but rather as a way of *relating* independent methodologies: not of adding them up, but of testing and specifying their validity.

Structural hypotheses cannot be *deduced* from functional hypotheses or vice versa. They must be worked out separately by developing two independent lines of reasoning and must be continuously checked against one another in the hope that, in the end, all tallies. The appeal of the venture lies in this divarication, which is its only raison d'être, and explains its distance from current sociological criticism. Even when this critical trend uses structural analysis (which is rarely the case, but for argument's sake, let's suppose it is), it does so only to *confirm* its sociological premises, which have been built upon and verified by *different* disciplines.[2] Literary research *adds nothing* to what is already known about society. It merely allows for the usual: '*also* in Mallarmé one can discover the mechanism of alienation'. Literary criticism becomes a parasitical embellishment. Literature itself, in this light, also seems superfluous: it seems to exist only to voice in a round-about way concepts expressed elsewhere with greater precision. In effect, the deepest desire of the current sociology of literature is to 'forget' literature; a clear example is Asor Rosa's early work. If this is the case, then literary criticism can only hope to be the novelesque surrogate for more substantial disciplines. This would then reconfirm the role of cultural filler assigned to literary studies – which aimed at being ever so subversive – by the ministries of public education over the past century. At this point, it would be more logical and more honest to take up a different profession.

Today one can study literature only by aiming higher. Specifically, the hypothesis of this study is that the interweaving of functional and structural analyses, when properly carried out, *adds* to our knowledge of society; therefore, it can contribute to *changing* and *specifying* the conceptual framework of those disciplines of which literary criticism has long been a passive tributary. This is a hypothesis; what follows is not yet a satisfactory application. What is, however, important is to prefix a theoretical aim, for this is the life-blood of all real research. *On s'engage*: and then we will see.

A similar problem arises even in the most rigorous analyses of narrative structure with the opposition between syntagmatic and paradigmatic models, whose respective major exponents are Propp and Lévi-Strauss. These two critical hypotheses – the first of which aims at establishing the syntax of a work and the formal succession of its elements, the second, at defining the cultural values which make up its meaning – have essentially developed separately or even in opposition – as Lévi-Strauss's splendid attack on *The Morphology of the Fable* demonstrated. The idea of attempting to connect them has taken form only in recent years: 'It is postulated that the underlying structure of all narratives consists of two sub-structures, which will be referred to here as the syntagmatic and the paradigmatic. The former relates to plot, the latter to character (and theme). Paradigmatic structure consists of two elements in opposition. . . . The two elements constitute, in effect, sets or groupings of all the *dramatis personae* that appear in the narrative (with the possible exceptions of certain 'mediating' characters . . .)'.[3]

Yet his proposal for synthesis oversimplifies the problem. In the first place, the unification of the two 'sub-structures' is not, contrary to appearances, a sum total of independent entities – but the result of a process. The choice of paradigms alters the selection and the order of narrative 'functions' and hence, the syntax. (Narcejac, for example, by placing the opposition writing/reading at the root of detective fiction inevitably assigns a negligible role to the criminal in the plot.) On the other hand, the construction of a syntax influences the choice of paradigms: since an obligatory function of the detective story is a '*mysterious* crime', all 'obvious' crimes are excluded, and elementary oppositions such as life/death or legality/illegality become unacceptable. As with the relationship between functional and structural hypotheses, the only exact procedure seems to consist in a continual transposition and checking of the hypotheses worked out for the paradigmatic area by the syntagmatic axis and vice versa.[4] The two must be brought progressively closer and closer. This process can be considered complete only when the data collected in the two spheres integrate each other and the most complete description possible of the text has been reached.

But there is another problem. According to Hendrick's line of reasoning – which is the most common – the 'cultural meaning of narrative' resides only in the 'paradigmatic sub-structure'. The plot and the syntax are considered purely formal phenomena and totally without meaning. Semantic analysis – cultural research – seems to be able to afford to push them aside. In this essay I shall attempt to demonstrate the opposite; the syntax of the detective story – even in its most abstract aspect, that is, in the relationship between *sjužet* and *fabula* – will prove *essential* in defining its meaning.

Thus the two sides of these prefatory remarks come together. Functional analyses of literature have always emphasized the paradigmatic. In a sense, this is obvious: paradigms refer to the cultural universe *outside* the work and this is the natural field of action of functional criticism. Further: the paradigms are instituted *in absentia* through a process of 'selection and substitution' (to use Jakobson's terms) which involves 'the entities associated in the code but not in the message'.[5] The institution of paradigms can therefore easily elude the verification on the 'axis of concatenation', that is, on the actual *in praesentia* structure of the message. In other words, by emphasizing the paradigms, functional analysis avoids dealing fully with the actual structuration of the text. The connection of these two aspects of the *structural* analysis – paradigms and syntax – is therefore the decisive factor in guaranteeing the precision of the *functional* analysis. This also resolves the supposed antithesis between 'description' and 'interpretation'. Interpretation is not an arbitrary act subject to the interpreter's 'values': it means testing the possibility of inserting a structural description into a larger system (which in turn presupposes a description). 'To give significance' is to perform a *correlation*. 'Description' and 'interpretation', therefore, are not *in principle different* cognitive modes, but two 'directions' – with different goals and specific methodologies – in which the cognitive process can tend. That they are both united and distinct means that the proof must undergo a *double* analysis: the structure of the text – and its function, that is, the structure of the vaster system in which it is integrated. The major merit of a sociology of literature is that it allows a multiplication of the mechanisms of control.

So to the hypotheses of this essay. The sociological hypotheses are that the detective story dispels from the consciousness of the masses the individualistic ethic of 'classic' bourgeois culture (that is, the culture described by Locke, Kant, Marx, and Weber); detective fiction creates an aesthetic model that implies the *impossibility of verifying* cultural forms, and thus overturns the experimental assumption that shaped early bourgeois 'public opinion'. The structural hypotheses are that the dominant cultural oppositions of detective fiction are between the individual (in the guise of the criminal) and the social organism (in the guise of the detective); its syntax consists in combining the same elements in two different ways so that the combination enacted in the *fabula* (that is, the solution) detracts all value from the combination proposed by the *sjužet*: in this way, detective fiction abandons the narrative form of the novel in favour of that of the short story. Finally, detective fiction is based on a *double system of meanings* – superficial and deep: the first is both the manifestation and the cover of the second. In what follows I shall shift between these hypotheses and, thus, from one field of investigation and methodology to another. A restless and disharmonic argument results: but it is the only way to depict this intersection of different planes, which is the focal point of this essay.

2. Baker Street and Surroundings

The criminal

A good rule in detective fiction is to have only one criminal. This is not because guilt isolates, but, on the contrary, because isolation breeds guilt. The criminal adheres to others only instrumentally: for him association is merely the expedient that allows him to attain his own interests. The metaphysics of the 'social pact' becomes his own and he takes it for what it is: pure form, a continuous pretence, which is not difficult to enact, because the world of detective fiction is crowded with stereotypes. The difference between innocence and guilt returns as the opposition between stereotype and individual. Innocence is conformity; individuality, guilt. It is, in fact, something irreducibly personal that betrays the individual: traces, signs that only he could have left behind. The perfect crime – the nightmare of detective fiction – is the featureless, deindividualized[6] crime that anyone could have committed because at this point everyone is the same. Such is the case of Robbe-Grillet's *Erasers*, where everyone has the same pistol, the same clothes, the same words: at the end, it is the detective who commits the crime. Detective fiction, however, exists expressly to dispel the doubt that guilt might be impersonal, and therefore collective and social. 'A typewriter', says Holmes, 'has really quite as much individuality as a man's handwriting' ('A Case of Identity'). As if to say: a guilty party can always be found.[7] *A* guilty party: crime is always presented as an exception, which by now the individual must be. His defeat is the victory and the purge of a society no longer conceived of as a 'contract' between *independent entities*, but rather as an organism or social *body*. The best known detective's assistant – Watson – is a doctor. And, as we shall see, so is Sherlock Holmes.

Holmes: 'Man, or at least criminal man, has lost all enterprise and originality' ('The Adventure of the Copper Beeches'). Spirit of initiative (enterprise, in particular, economic enterprise) and individuality: this is what Holmes wants to eliminate. He is not moved by pity for the victim, by moral or material horror at the crime, but by its *cultural quality*: by its *uniqueness* and its *mystery*. In detective fiction everything that is *repeatable* and *obvious* ceases to be criminal and is, therefore, unworthy of 'investigation': Agatha Christie's first book is set at the same time as the massacres of the Great War, yet the only murder of interest occurs on the second floor of Styles Court. Uniqueness and mystery: detective fiction treats every element of individual behaviour that desires secrecy as an offence, even if there is no trace of crime (for example, 'The Man with the Twisted Lip', 'The Yellow Face', 'A Scandal in Bohemia').[8] The idea that anything the individual desires to protect from the interference of society – the liberal 'freedom from' – favours or even coincides with crime is gradually insinuated, and is the source of the fascination with 'locked room mysteries'. The murderer and the victim are inside, society – innocent and weak – outside. The victim seeks refuge in a private sphere, and precisely there, he encounters death, which would not have struck him down in the crowd. The door was invented by the bourgeoisie to protect the individual; now it becomes a threat; one is advised never to turn the key. (Eliot, *The Waste Land*: 'I have heard the key/Turn in the door once and once only/We think of the key, each in his prison/Thinking of the key, each confirms a prison'.) This is the totalitarian aspiration towards a *transparent* society: 'My dear fellow', says Holmes to Watson, 'if we could fly out that great window hand in hand, hover over this great city, gently remove the roofs, and peep in at the queer things which are going on. . .' ('A Case of Identity'). Holmes exists because Peter Pan does not: it is not yet possible to fly through keyholes.

Murderer and victim meet in the locked room because fundamentally they are similar. In at least a third of Conan Doyle's stories, the criminal has been the victim of a preceding offence and vice versa. The victim, that is, has *asked for it*: because of his shady past and because he wanted to keep secrets, thus fending off society's 'assistance'; and finally because, exactly like the criminal, he is still devoted to the idea of *individual property*. Detective fiction originates at the same time as the trusts, the big banks, and monopolies: mechanisms that make wealth impersonal and separate capital and capitalist. The victim, on the other hand, is still attached to his small capital, like the criminal who covets it. They are betrayed by economic independence. Detective fiction enacts the antithesis between life and property and between life and individuality: to have one, it is necessary to give up the other. Kafka's inexorable law is already at work, but detective fiction cannot see the Castle that promulgates it.

The percentage of homicides in Conan Doyle's stories increases over the years. After him, they become the norm. Detective fiction *needs* death, on which it confers *archaic* features.[9] It is never a natural and universal event. On the contrary: it is always *voluntary*, always *individualized*. It is always a struggle (agony, antagonism). It is always the *punishment* of one who, wilfully or not, trespassed the boundaries of normality. He who distinguishes himself has his destiny marked out. To avoid death (and who wouldn't want to?) it is suggested that one conform to a stereotype: in this way, one will never be a victim or a criminal. It is, in effect, suggested that one never comes into the world, instead of yielding to what Freud called the death instinct: 'the expression of inertia inherent in organic life'.[10] And detective fiction's characters are inert indeed: they do not grow. In this way, detective fiction is radically anti-novelistic: the aim of the narration is no longer the character's development into autonomy, or a change from the initial situation, or the presentation of plot as a conflict and an evolutionary spiral, image of a developing world that it is difficult to draw to a close. On the contrary: detective fiction's object is to *return to the beginning*. The individual initiates the narration not because he lives – but because he *dies*. Detective fiction is rooted in a sacrificial rite. For the stereotypes to live, the individual must die, and then die a second time in the guise of the criminal. For the story to begin and the stereotypes to come alive, a victim is necessary: otherwise there would be *nothing to say*. 'Innocent' characters must, in fact, demonstrate only that they really are, were, and will be the stereotypes they seem to be: that is, that they *know no history*: '*It seems, then, that an instinct is an urge inherent in organic life to restore an earlier state of things* which the living entity has been obliged to abandon under the pressure of external disturbing forces. . .'.[11] Reinstate a preceding situation, return to the beginning, prove an alibi; declare oneself *elsewhere*, extraneous to the place where the disturbing forces broke loose; demonstrate, again, that one has always been the same: detective fiction's syntactic regression (from *sjužet* to *fabula*, from crime to prelude) duplicates the 'good-guys' compulsion to repeat. So it is too with the reader who, attracted *precisely* by the obsessively repetitive scheme, is 'unable' to stop until the cycle has closed and he has returned to the starting point. *Bildung*, expelled from within the narrative, is then evaporated by its relationship with the reader.

One reads only with the purpose of remaining as one already is: innocent. Detective fiction owes its success to the fact that it teaches nothing.

'The criminal who simply sets absolute store by self-preservation in reality has the weaker personality; the habitual criminal is an inadequate individual. . . . The ability to stand apart from the environment as an individual, and at the same time to enter into contact with that environment – and gain a foothold in it – through the approved forms of communication, was eroded in the criminal. He represented a trend which is deep-rooted in living beings, and whose elimination is a sign of all development: the trend to lose oneself in the environment instead of playing an active role in it; the tendency to let oneself go and sink back into nature. Freud called it the death instinct. . . . There is negation in the criminal which does not contain resistance.'[12] Detective fiction turns this image on its head. It is the innocent, not the criminal, who is defenceless and yielding. The criminal is the opposite of Raskolnikov, who *must* confess to his action, bare himself to the world, and demolish his individual shield *by himself*: whence the irrelevance of detection in *Crime and Punishment*. On the contrary, detective fiction always presents the criminal as a self-sufficient watertight consciousness wholly bent on an aim. For the sacrifice of the individual to be effective and 'educational', he must be endowed with all attributes. This reflects a new relationship with legal punishment: in the middle of the nineteenth century, the focus of attention shifts from *execution* to the *trial*. While the former underlines the individual's *weakness* by destroying his body, trials *exalt* individuality: they condemn it precisely because they have demonstrated its deadly greatness. The criminal is the person who always acts *consciously*. On this premiss, detective fiction detaches prose narration from historiography and relates it to the world of Law: 'Modern law is directed against the agent, not against the action. . . [and] enquires into subjective "guilt" whereas history, as long as it seeks to remain an empirical science, inquiries into the "objective" grounds of concrete events and the consequence of concrete "actions"; it does not seek to pass judgement on the agent.'[13] In detective fiction, as in law, history assumes importance only as *violation* and as such, must be ultimately repressed. Again, the ideal is for nothing to happen. But it is a *negative* ideal, based on a *lack* (as with the stereotypes and innocence), and in order to seem real, it has an obsessive need of its opposite.

I have insisted upon the individualistic ethic that detective fiction ascribes to the criminal. Reading Conan Doyle, however, one discovers that the criminals are *never* members of the bourgeoisie. Detective fiction separates individuality and bourgeoisie. The bourgeoisie is no longer the champion of risk, novelty, and imbalance, but of prudence, conservation, and stasis. The economic ideology of detective fiction rests entirely upon the idea that supply and demand tend quite naturally towards a perfect balance. Suspicion often originates from a violation of the law of exchange between equivalent values: anyone who pays more than a market price or accepts a low salary can only be spurred by criminal motives.[14] These 'excessive' expenses – which distinctly recall risky investments – underline and disconcert a world which maintains that the distribution of incomes has occurred once and for all, and the possibilities of social climbing have vanished (England at the end of the nineteenth century, which begins its parasitical decline on the dividends of the Empire). What, indeed, is theft if not a violent redistribution of social wealth? And is it truly an accident that it becomes a great cultural symbol in the first country to experience a strong trade union movement? But theft is crucial for yet another reason. Money is always the motive of crime in detective fiction, yet the genre is wholly silent about *production*: that unequal exchange between labour-power and wages which is the true source of social wealth. Like popular economics, detective fiction incites people to seek the secret of profit in the sphere of circulation, where it cannot be found – but in compensation, one finds thefts, con-jobs, frauds, false pretences, and so on. The indignation against what is rotten and immoral in the economy must concentrate on these phenomena. As for the factory – it is innocent, and thus free to carry on.

Let us return to the criminal who generally belongs to one of two major sociological types: the *noble* and the *upstart*. In the first case, he attempts to react to the thinning out of his wealth, to oppose the *natural* course of history. The detective's intervention aims precisely at assuring that the economy will follow its own logic, and will not be violated by what appears to be a revival of feudal arbitrary will. The upstart, on the other hand, aspires to a sudden social jump. The spectre of primitive accumulation materializes through him: capital as theft, and even as murder. By catching him, the detective annihilates a memory painful to his philistine audience: the original sin of nineteenth-century 'legality'. Just as this world will have no future, so its infected roots in the past must be eradicated.

There is also a third tenured criminal: the step-father, the adoptive father who steps in to seize the inheritance. This is perhaps the greatest obsession of detective fiction, as is to be expected in an economic imagination interested only in *perpetuating* the existing order, which is also a *legitimate* state of affairs, founded on the authority of the real father and sanctioned by the family tie, which moderates and spiritualizes individual egoism. The stepfather barges into this Victorian idyll, to break and degrade all ties for his exclusive gain. The stepfather is there to illustrate the difference between a 'father' (motivated by his children's well-being) and a 'private citizen' (who wants to rob them). Observing his wickedness, one is led to say: 'a father would never have done that'. Instead, this poor man does precisely what the real father did in more elegant forms. He wants to suppress those children – of whom there are too many – that the real fathers of the English middle bourgeoisie of the time (according to demographic studies) tried at all costs not to bring into the world. This particular economy was won through sexual abstention and coitus interruptus – at the price, presumably, of profound erotic frustration and lacerating emotional tensions, which were then projected on to the relationships with the children and, in particular, the *daughters*. Conan Doyle's adoptive fathers hide their stepdaughters from the eyes of the world, imprison them, or even seduce them under false pretences: all transparent manifestations of sexual jealousy. That is, the poor stepfather is a bit like the well-known 'uncle' evoked by early psychoanalysis: a mask for the father. Needless to say, Conan Doyle, unlike Freud, was not trying to make a sticky subject 'acceptable': had he suspected this, his pen would have frozen in his hand. Ideology – false consciousness – is not a lie, which always presupposes an awareness of the truth. Rather it is not a lie *a parte subjecti*, even if it is in fact. I shall return to this point.

These considerations bring us to a new problem. The fact that, in Conan Doyle's stories, the criminal possesses or excludes specific cultural attributes means that he is not simply the 'carrier' of the 'narrative function of crime'. He is not defined only by his syntactic position: he is bound also by several paradigmatic features. It would therefore seem that Lévi-Strauss's attack on Propp is completely justified: 'To his great credit, Propp discovered that the content of tales is *permutable*. But he too often concluded that it was *arbitrary*, and this is the reason for the difficulties he encountered, since even permutations conform to rules.'[15] Yet, if we turn to Agatha Christie, the situation is reversed. Her hundred-odd books have only one message: the criminal can be *anyone*: the narrator, 'the detective', the entire group of suspects, the most suspicious, the least suspicious, the most doting of lovers, the most infamous of scoundrels. That is, Agatha Christie abolishes all paradigmatic restrictions. The content becomes irrelevant: only the function specified by the formal mechanism of the syntax remains. Lévi-Strauss is wrong, Propp is right. Or rather, Propp's morphology offers the best approach to modern serialized narrative, which thrives upon paradox. It must tell ever-new stories because it moves within the culture of the novel, which always demands new content;[16] and at the same time it must reproduce a scheme which is always the same, not only because of 'productive' needs (serial production of works) but, more profoundly, because it incarnates a paralysis and a regression of the novel's cultural model. This is why detective fiction links a continuous novelty of content to a perennial fixity of the syntax. But this brings us far beyond Propp. The irrelevancy of the content is not an 'assumption' but a problematic datum, a fact which calls for explanation. And it is a *cultural* – not a syntactic – fact, which betrays the aspiration to a completely *formalized* and therefore *interchangeable* humanity: where what one 'is' is completely irrelevant, because the only thing that counts is what the social syntax compels one to do.[17]

The detective

Holmes: 'If I claim full justice for my art, it is because it is an impersonal thing – a thing beyond myself' ('The Adventure of the Copper Beeches'). Holmes lives to serve this impersonal thing, detection. He does not use it for personal gain: 'As to reward, my profession is its own reward' ('The Adventure of the Speckled Band'). He sacrifices his individuality to his work: his endless series of disguises, sleepless nights, and inability to eat during an investigation are all metaphors for this. Thus Holmes prefigures and legitimates the sacrifices of the other individuality – the criminal's. The detective abandons the individualistic ethic voluntarily, but still retains the memory of it. For this reason he can 'understand' the criminal (and, when necessary enact criminal deeds): potentially, he too was a criminal. In the figures of detective and criminal, a single renunciation, a sole sacrifice, is enacted, in different ways. This is seen in 'The Final Problem' when Holmes and Moriarty, 'locked in each other's arms', plunge into Reichenbach Falls.

This voluntary repression of the self is at one with Holmes's (and every other classic detective's) dilettantism. Dilettantism is not superficiality, but work done for the pleasure of work: 'To the man who loves art for its own sake . . . it is frequently in its least important and lowliest manifestations that the keenest pleasure is to be derived' ('The Adventure of the Copper Beeches'). Thus, Holmes is not a policeman, but a decadent intellectual (as is blatantly obvious from his escapes into music and cocaine). He is the intellectual who is no longer a person but a product: '[This case] saved me from ennui. . . . "L'homme c'est rien – l'oeuvre c'est tout", as Gustave Flaubert wrote to George Sands' ('The Red-Headed League'). He is the intellectual Max Weber and T. S. Eliot discuss: 'In the field of science only he who is devoted *solely* to the work at hand has "personality". And this holds not only for the field of science; we know of no great artist who has ever done anything but serve his work and only his work.'[18] 'The progress of an artist is a continual self-sacrifice, a continual extinction of personality. . . the more perfect the artist, the more completely separate in him will be the man who suffers and the mind which creates. . . . Poetry is not a turning loose of emotion, but an escape from emotion; it is not the expression of personality, but an escape from personality. . . . The emotion of art is impersonal. And the poet cannot reach this impersonality without surrendering himself

wholly to the work to be done.'[19] These words call for a redefinition of the concept of decadentism, in order to separate it from the
vague notion of 'decadence' and unite it to that of 'capitalist
development'. Decadent culture describes itself as an alienated
work process (Eliot: 'surrendering himself wholly to the work to
be done'; Weber: 'serve his work and only his work'). Art for art's
sake has its roots in production for production's sake.

To return to Holmes. He is not a policeman but a private detective: in him, detection is disengaged from the purposes of the law.
His is a *purely cultural* aim. It is preferable for a criminal to escape
(as, in fact, happens) and the detection to be complete – rather
than for him to be captured and the logical reconstruction be
pre-empted. But the corollary of this is that the cultural universe is
the most effective means of policing. Detective fiction is a hymn to
culture's coercive abilities: which prove more effective than pure
and simple institutional repression. Holmes's culture – just like
mass culture, which detective fiction helped found – will reach you
anywhere. This culture knows, orders, and defines all the significant data of individual existence as part of social existence. Every
story reiterates Bentham's Panopticon ideal: the model prison that
signals the metamorphosis of liberalism into total scrutability.[20]
Moreover, Holmes's culture resolves the deep anxiety of an
expanding society: the fear that development might liberate centrifugal energies and thus make effective social control impossible.
This problem emerges fully in the *metropolis*, where anonymity –
that is, impunity – potentially reigns and which is rapidly becoming
a tangled and inaccessible hiding place. We have seen detective
fiction's answer to the first problem: the guilty party can never
hide in the crowd. His tracks betray him as an individual, and
therefore a vulnerable, being. But detective fiction also offers
reassurance on the second point. All Holmes's investigations are
accompanied and supported by the new and perfect mechanisms of
transportation and communication. Carriages, trains, letters, telegrams, in Conan Doyles's world, are all crucial and *always* live up
to expectations. They are the tacit and indispensable support of
the arrest. Society expands and becomes more complicated: but it
creates a framework of control, a network of relationships, that
holds it more firmly together than ever before.

Let us, however, look more closely into the image of culture that detective fiction transmits. Since Poe, the detective has incarnated a *scientific* ideal: the detective discovers the causal links between events: to unravel the mystery is to trace them back to a *law*. The point is that – at the turn of the century – high bourgeois culture wavers in its conviction that it is possible to set the functioning of society into the framework of scientific – that is, objective – laws. Max Weber: 'We ask ... how in general is the attribution of a concrete effect to an individual "cause" possible and realizable in principle in view of the fact that in truth an *infinity* of causal factors have conditioned the occurrence of the individual "event" and that indeed absolutely all of those individual causal factors were indispensable for the occurrence of the effect in its concrete form. The possibility of selecting from among the infinity of determinants is conditioned, first, by the mode of our historical *interest*.'[21] According to Weber, then, social science can no longer produce *general agreement*. Just as there is no 'general interest' in economic and political life, so a common value system cannot exist. There are only values in the plural, each perennially in struggle with other ideals which are 'just as sacred to others as ours are to us.'[22] This picture is not completely convincing: there is a complex and surprising relationship between the conflictual partiality of the modern value system and its levelling and integrative potential. But we must return to detective fiction, which aims to keep the relationship between science and society *unproblematic*. What, indeed, does detective fiction do? It create's a problem, a 'concrete effect' – the crime – and declares a sole cause relevant: the criminal. It slights other causes (why is the criminal such?) and dispels the doubt that every choice is partial and subjective. But, then, discovering that unique cause means reunifying causality and objectivity and reinstating the idea of a general interest in society, which consists in solving *that* mystery and arresting *that* individual – and no one else. In finding one solution that is valid for all – detective fiction does not permit alternative readings – society posits its unity, and, again, declares itself innocent. If, in fact, detective fiction stems from a mystery, this is due to the absence of the *fabula*, the leading event, which only two characters could furnish: the criminal and the victim. Those who are unaware of the *fabula* – all the other characters of the detective story and, on the same plane, the reader – cannot, therefore, be actively or passively responsible for the crime. Because the crime is presented in the form of a mystery, society is absolved from the start: the solution of the mystery proves its innocence.

As we have seen with stereotypes, innocence, in the world of detective fiction, is lack of experience: stasis. Holmes's 'science' is also static. Its most striking features – the gratuitous 'revelations' for clients and friends ('You have been in Afghanistan, I perceive' – 'A Study in Scarlet' – are his first words to poor Watson) – owes its existence to the fact that Holmes knows all the possible causes of every single event. Thus the relevant causes are always a *finite* set. They are also fixed: they always produce the same effect.[23] Holmes cannot go wrong, because he possesses the stable code, at the root of every mysterious message – mysterious, that is, for the reader, who is kept in the dark with regard to the code, while Holmes takes in the only possible meaning of the various clues in a glance. Perhaps 'symptoms' is better than 'clues', for they are effects which are systematically and absolutely correlated to uni-vocal and stable causes, whereas Eco writes, 'As a matter of fact clues are seldom coded, and their interpretation is frequently a matter of complex inference rather than of sign-function recogni-tion, which makes criminal novels more interesting than the detec-tion of pneumonia.'[24] This is not true of the archetypal detective. Yet it detracts nothing from his fascination: for someone who feels ill, the doctor's diagnosis will always be spectacular, especially if reassuring. And Holmes is just that: the great *doctor* of the late Victorians, who convinces them that society is still a great *organ-ism*: a unitary and knowable body. His 'science' is none other than the ideology of this organism: it celebrates its triumph by instan-taneously connecting *work* and *exterior appearances* (body, clo-thing): in reinstating an idea of *status society* that is externalized, traditionalist, and easily controllable. In effect, Holmes embodies science as ideological common sense, 'common sense systemat-ized'. He degrades science: just as it had been humiliated by both the English productive structure and the education system at the turn of the century. But, at the same time, he exalts it. The need for a myth of science was felt precisely by the world that produced *less* of it. England did not attain the second industrial revolution: but it invented science fiction.

Clues, whether defined as such or as 'symptoms' or 'traces', are not facts, but verbal procedures – more exactly, *rhetorical figures*. Thus, the famous 'band' in a Holmes story, an excellent metaphor, is gradually deciphered as 'band', 'scarf', and finally 'snake'. As is to be expected, clues are more often metonymies: associations by contiguity (related to the past), for which the detective must furnish the missing term. The clue is, therefore, that particular element of the story in which the link between signifier and signified is altered. It is a signifier that always has several signifieds and thus produces *numerous* suspicions. 'This is significant', Poirot never tires of repeating: meaning that he finds himself before something that transcends the usual, literal meaning. This is also part of the criminal's guilt: he has created a situation of semantic ambiguity, thus questioning the usual forms of human communication and human interaction. In this way, he has composed an audacious *poetic work*. The detective, on the other hand, must dispel the entropy, the cultural equiprobability that is produced by and is a relevant aspect of the crime: he will have to reinstate the univocal links between signifiers and signifieds. In this way, he must carry out a scientific operation. In the terms of the Russian formalists, the criminal produces the *sjužet*, the detective the *fabula*. Again, the former embodies the literary pole, the latter the scientific. *Detective fiction* – I shall attempt to explain why in the conclusion – *is literature that desires to exorcise literature*.

Watson

Watson, poor fool. In detective fiction's oppositional system Watson has an uncertain role. He is not one of the 'innocents' to be acquitted. When he sides with Holmes, the latter transforms him into a puppet. When – rarely – he does something on his own ('The Adventure of the Solitary Cyclist'), he ends up by playing into the criminal's hands. And yet Watson (and all his reincarnations: the friends and helpers of the various detectives) is essential: as a *literary function* first of all. While the criminal opens the action and the detective closes it, Watson drags it out. His specific function is purely quantitative. A detective story can last ten or two hundred pages, and nothing changes: detective fiction always has the structure of the short story (according to the Russian formalists' definition, which seems the most accurate). When it assumes the dimensions and the name of novel, it is a novel only in the number of pages it takes up – that is, physically, not structurally. Yet Watson's function is quantatitive in a more profound way: he *accumulates useless details*. His descriptions furnish all – except the essential. He enters a room (in 'The Speckled Band') and for two pages describes its furnishings: but he does not even mention the false bell-pull which is the only clue. Thus, through the figure of Watson, detective fiction attacks naturalism. 'You see,' Holmes continuously repeats, 'but you do not observe' ('A Scandal in Bohemia'). Criminal reality no longer has a univocal and transparent meaning. With the alteration of the signifier/signified, surface/depth link, a poetics based on the mirror-image will always prove inadequate; Watson will never discover a single criminal. Finally, with its implicit criticism of naturalism, detective fiction reiterates the image of the criminal that it attempts to diffuse: the subject who *freely and consciously chooses*, and not the victim of that naturalist 'social milieu' which could explain and – worse yet – even justify his crimes.

Watson, c'est moi is what every reader of detective fiction might well say. Besides being the narrator, Watson is the *spectator* of Holmes's adventures. Holmes himself ascribes this role to him: 'Here he [the client] comes. Sit down in that armchair, doctor, and give us your best attention' ('A Scandal in Bohemia'). Detective fiction must create its reader. To do so it must snatch him from the 'world of affairs' and, in Poe's words, 'imprison him' in its plot. Thus Holmes with Watson: he drags him out of bed, away from his wife – away from work. 'A professional case of great activity was engaging my own attention at the time, and the whole of next day I was busy at the bedside of the sufferer. It was not until close upon six o'clock that I *found myself free*, and was able to *spring into a hansom* and drive to Baker Street, half afraid that I might be too late to assist at the *denouement* of that *little* mystery.' ('A Case of Identity'). This sentence heralds the devaluation of work that will characterize the new bourgeois ethic, and on which mass culture will thrive – both in its contents and in its self-justification.

Just as at a stylistic level, the naturalistic description is denounced as the wrong interpretation, so in the system of characters, Watson is the one who advances the wrong solutions. In this he is again the image of the reader who, indeed, competes with him – and is in this gratified: although we will never be as clever as the detective, we could never be as stupid as Watson. Detective fiction thus assigns the reader an intermediary role between the extremes of *passive reading* (Watson automatically records events that he does not understand) and of *writing* (Holmes, who narrates the *fabula*, emerges as the true author of the work: Poe affirmed that in writing short stories, one must always start from the solution). This potential transformation from reader into co-author is the 'challenge' of which detective fiction boasts, on the basis of the well-known formula 'the author is to the reader as the criminal to the detective'. Just as the detective 'rewrites' the story produced by the criminal, so the reader, furnished with all the necessary clues, can solve the mystery and thus 'write' the story that he is reading by himself. But this is not in reality a challenge to his intelligence. As reader, one is allowed to discover only what one would have found out anyway. To attempt to 'guess' is only to hide from oneself the fact that the rules are loaded, and to accept a situation in which the individual's brain might as well stop working. Detective fiction has created its reader.

3. Conclusion

In detective fiction, as in the short story, the weight gravitates towards the ending. Detective fiction's ending is its end indeed: its solution in the true sense. The *fabula* narrated by the detective in his reconstruction of the facts brings us back to the beginning; that is, it abolishes narration. Between the beginning and the end of the narration – between the absence and the presence of the *fabula* – there is no 'voyage', only a long *wait*. In this sense, detective fiction is anti-literary. It declares narration a mere deviation, a masking of that univocal meaning which is its raison d'être. And yet detective fiction's scientific loftiness *needs* literary 'deviation', even if it is only to destroy it: a solution without a mystery, a *fabula* without a *sjužet*, would be of no interest.[25] Not merely anti-literary, therefore, detective fiction expresses an ambivalent desire for the literary: literature is still desired but only to be mocked and relegated to useless memories.[26] Or, rather: it is still desired, but only if the text itself contains an explicit mechanism for the disambiguation of meaning. Detective fiction's 'solution' enacts an analogous function to the fable's 'moral'. It abolishes the Kantian 'finality without aim' and introduces an obligatory path for our reading of the work. The original function of 'autonomous art' – self-education, the *Bildung* which its fruition entailed – also declines. In detective fiction, reading is no longer investment, choice, experience and intellectual effort: it is waste, error, and 'giving into appearances'; it is only *distance* and *delay* with regard to the *revealed solution*. But something else must be added. I have defined detective fiction as 'scientific', and certainly it mimes the univocality of scientific language. Yet, unlike the assertions of the empirical sciences, the solutions of detective fiction are literary, and so non-referential. Detective fiction, therefore, furnishes only the sensation of scientific knowledge. It perfectly satisfies the aspiration to certainty, because it rigorously avoids the test of external reality. It is science become myth; and hence self-sufficient. Detective fiction empties the proto-bourgeois ideal of experimental culture by subordinating it to a literary structure that is anything but experimental. The cultural model it promulgates must not be coherent with external reality, but only with itself. This perfect self-referentiality ultimately defines detective fiction as a hyper-literary phenomenon. And it permits one to glean the true relationship between literary communication and ideology.

This entire essay is based on the hypothesis that there are two systems of meanings in detective fiction. The first is evident and literal: Doctor Roylott attempts to kill his niece by making a snake slither down a false bell-pull... I have attempted to reconstruct the second: the uncle, vicarious father and fallen noble, violates familial ties for money, leaving clues that the investigator decodes ... Of course, every literary text is built upon several levels of meaning, and criticism's first task always consists in establishing the basic and most abstract system which, through a series of transformations – whose procedures are, incidentally, far from clear – 'generates' the text as it presents itself. Detective fiction's distinctive feature is the *distance* between deep meaning and surface meaning. It is difficult to read *Hamlet* or *Eugene Onegin* without perceiving the existence of a host of meanings that become clearer with each reading; but it is possible (and common) to read Agatha Christie in the certainty that only the name of the murderer counts (who, in fact, ever 're-reads' a detective story?). While reading detective stories, one never thinks of the meanings dealt with in this essay. And yet they really exist, to the extent that they motivate all the laws of functioning of the surface structure – one guilty party, traces, the conflict between detective and police, the 'helper', scientific and objective deductions, and so on – rules that mystery writers themselves have always recognized (and even codified), but without ever having understood their 'necessity'. In other words, the surface construction of detective fiction depends on the cultural rules that form its deep structure. It is only through them that detective fiction acquires meaning and arouses interest. Yet this dependency is masked. Moreover, the refinement of the surface technique is at one with that of concealment: more complete in Christie or Van Dine or Queen than in Poe or Conan Doyle (whose work lends itself better to analysis). Mass success is inseparable from the refinement of concealment because it renders the deep cultural meaning unfathomable. This meaning continues to exist and act – but by now authors and readers are totally unaware of it. Mass culture is the culture of unawareness. It rests on iron premises and takes shape only through their consequences and effects, but the premisses never enter into the picture or become the object of discussion. Thus, mass culture avoids the most common form of ideological expression – the 'judgement on the world', of whatever nature – to diffuse a much more efficient one: the construction of a world. This world no longer appears 'true' against the backdrop of, or in comparison with, the outside world, but on the basis of the its coherence with its own internal laws. This brings us back to the argument of the preceding paragraph and to the connection between literature 'as such' and mass culture. Mass culture's non-referential world is no more than the extension of the literary universe. Therefore, literature is the most perfect form of ideological communication. If ideology is objectively false knowledge perceived as subjectively true,[27] literature, by definition, fulfils both conditions: it is subtracted from all external verification and at the same time presents itself to the subject with all the traits of real experience.[28]

The process of concealment of detective fiction's deep meaning is also the process of manifestation of its surface meaning. This two-sided process, enmeshed in the specific literary structure of detective fiction, presents an extraordinary analogy with the mechanism of capitalist production as Marx, in one of his many descriptions of ideology, describes it: 'This form *capital-interest* is precisely the form in which any mediation disappears, and capital is reduced to its most general formula, but for this reason also it is a form that is absurd and inexplicable in its own terms. . . . If capital originally appeared on the surface of circulation as the capital fetish, value-creating value, so it now presents itself once again in the figure of interest-bearing capital as its most estranged and peculiar form . . . since profit still retains a memory of its origin which in interest is not simply obliterated but actually placed in *a form diametrically opposed to this origin*.'[29] Commenting on this and other analogous passages, Nikolas Rose has observed how Marx discusses 'two realities and the distance between them. For the phenomenal forms are not *illusory* appearances, they are realities. *They are the form of the reality which capitalist relations of production* produce, a reality which is simultaneously the form of manifestation of these relations and the form of their concealment.'[30] This concept of two levels of reality – one superficial and obvious, the other deep and hidden, one the effect, the other the cause – has also been postulated by Lucio Colletti: '. . . there are *two realities* in capitalism: the reality expressed by Marx, and the reality expressed by the authors he criticizes. . . . The capitalist's eye, accustomed to synthesis and the overall view, does not deign to distinguish between the various things he has bought. From his point of view, wage labour is a *part* of capital. . . . But the important thing to understand is that more than a subjective point of view is involved: it is a point of view which corresponds in a certain sense to the actual courses of things. . . . Capital is produced by labour: labour is the cause, capital the effect; the one the origin, the other the outcome. And yet not only in the accounting of the enterprise, but in the real mechanism, the working class appears only as "variable capital" and as the wages fund; the "whole" has become the "part", and the part the whole.'[31] This discussion reveals that the most characteristic feature and the principal function of ideology consists in erasing the social process which produces those effects – that surface reality – which it places at the centre of the world: in rendering certain phenomena *absolute*. All of mass culture's great symbols and formal procedures emerge in precisely the same way. There is a cultural process which – through its deep structures – generates surface laws and symbols which then autonomously rescind the link with their roots. The deep and confused effect they universally provoke – the vampire as the vamp, suspense as the chase – depends precisely on the fact that basic cultural values are both present and missing, active and unrecognizable, in them. Mass culture is, in this way, a full-fledged example of *cultural fetishism*. This creates its capacity to function and to multiply the unawareness of producers and consumers. Fetishism is the transformation of a human capacity into an attribute of 'things': compositional laws, rhetorical procedures that now appear *obligatory, natural, and binding*. Their meaning can no longer be understood, precisely because they can be no longer *controlled*.

The autonomization of culture, its transformation into an objective form, capable of producing meanings basically independent of the consciousness and the will of its producers, is ideology's true core: its content can change with time, but its formal nature endures. Moreover, this is why ideology, strictly speaking, exists only in capitalism: only here, in fact, is the link between people – the social relationship – truly impersonal, abstract and formal. We thus return to the image of intellectual work sketched by Weber and Eliot; and, earlier and more rigorously, by Simmel. In an essay of 1911 – 'On the Concept and the Tragedy of Culture'[32] – Simmel had already written of 'the passionate dedication to the cause with its immanent laws demanding perfection, so that the creative individual becomes indifferent to himself and is extinguished. . . completely self negating devotion to an objective task.' In the production, as in the consumption of cultural work, the relationship between subject and object is in this way overturned: 'All these sequences [of cultural products] operate within the confines of purely internal laws. Whether and to what extent they can be subsumed in the development of subjective souls has nothing to do with its importance. . . .' The division of intellectual labour radically confirms culture's tendency towards autonomy: 'Through the cooperative effort of different persons, then, a cultural object often comes into existence which as a total unit is *without a producer*, since it did not spring forth from the total self of any individual. . . . If examined more closely, this appears as an extremely radical case of an otherwise general human-spiritual fate. Most products of our intellectual creation contain a certain quota which was not produced by ourselves. . . . The finished effort contains emphases, relationships, values which the worker did not intend.' And finally: 'The "fetishism" which Marx assigned to economic commodities represents only a special case of this general fate of contents of culture.' I shall leave aside the suggestions and objections evoked by such passages and stick to the central point. All seems to concur: the fetishism of commodities is duplicated in the fetishism of culture. The process of alienation governs the entire social framework. The reversal of subject and object determines even poetic inspiration. All seems to tally – and yet the problem originates precisely at this point. The attainment of autonomy by cultural forms implies – if the words have a meaning – that they develop according to their own specific logic and, therefore, cannot be predicted and deduced from analysis of other social spheres. If they are truly autonomous they can no longer be traced back to a central and unique 'cause-aim' which, in Marx, is the process of capitalist accumulation founded on the abstraction of work. They can no longer be deduced from it, nor do they reproduce it. They are not built upon, nor can they be explained by, the principle of homology or isomorphism. This, however, does not necessarily mean that the cultural forms develop as a constellation of fully independent and conflictual 'discourses', as a hierarchy of 'powers' always unstable and unpredictable and completely deprived of a centre and an aim. The centre – the process of accumulation – no longer exhausts the entirety of cultural and social production, in the sense that it no longer *assimilates* it – nonetheless, it can always control it on the basis of a principle of *functionality* which has nothing to do with the principle of homology. Functionality allows for both the *specialization* of different social activities and for their high index of *autonomy*. For the moment, however, this is simply a hypothesis: both because the existence and operational mode of the functionality principle remains to be fully demonstrated, and because it cannot be conceived of as something programmed, but as the purely objective result of a process of adjustment and integration of distinct structures. But it is clear that the opening argument of this essay is not merely methodological: the problematic theoretical correlation between distinct methodologies mirrors a correlation between diverse structures that has become problematic in reality.

This line of reasoning takes us beyond the classic Marxist framework where the emphasis always falls on radical levelling, the *reductio ad unum* which is implicit not in the 'economic structure' as such, but in the specific forms of capitalist accumulation. This gives rise to difficult questions: to what extent is this functional framework, which emerges towards the end of the nineteenth century as a product of capitalist development, really *congenial* to it? Is it theoretically conceivable that a process of accumulation and levelling can coexist with, and even create and strengthen, domains that resist and defy its 'incessant movement'? What is the present *symbolic* weight of capitalist accumulation in what we continue to call 'capitalist societies'? Is it perhaps perceived as society's *means* of existence, rather than its *aim*? But then how must we redefine the value system of this society, and reconsider its relationship to the economic sphere?

These problems go far beyond our subject, and have not yet found a satisfactory explanation. Until that time comes, any reflection on mass culture – which is a constituent part of this contradictory process – will be built on sand. The case of detective fiction does not help much, since it has played an ambivalent role in the formation of our brave new world. On one hand, it is an extreme example of liberal bourgeois ideology according to which society must 'self-regulate' on the basis of the impersonal and automatic mechanisms of the market economy. He who wants to submit these mechanisms to his arbitrary will is guilty of wanting civil society to regress to the natural state. The detective is the figure of the state in the guise of 'night watchman', who limits himself to assuring respect for laws – in particular, for economic laws. This is reflected in an image of culture (the detective's 'scientific system') as *extrema ratio*, the accumulation of data to be used only in the case of emergency – as an instrument of defence, not of social *development*. In this light, detective fiction is the swansong of the Manchester ideals. But on the other hand, detective fiction is liberalism's executioner, in all its fundamental meanings and especially because it promulgates a culture that is already a closed and self-referential system. In this sense – though the thought may seem offensive to some – it is a radical affirmation of culture's autonomy. With autonomy comes disenchantment. If you read a detective story, you read a detective story. It doesn't help you 'in life'; there is no *Bildung*. Life now also *consists in* reading detective fiction. The less the cultural form 'helps' – the less translatable, transformable, and useable it is – the more it *imposes itself*. Though 'useless', detective fiction, as we have seen, does have a meaning. But the meaning is hidden; it acts behind the reader's back; it has become uncontrollable. Detective fiction, through the detective, celebrates the man who gives the world a meaning. Yet, structurally, it embodies the opposite principle, which is to unfold fully in mass culture: a process which institutes a meaning – a culture – that disregards the active and conscious consensus of its members. It is the *sui generis* totalitarianism of contemporary capitalism: which, however, remains, in detective fiction, more a promise, so to speak, than a reality. The dates are illustrative: classic detective fiction is at its peak between 1890 and 1935. In the thirties, when Keynesian capitalism takes off and, at the same time, modern mass culture imposes itself, detective fiction becomes academic and manneristic. Its deep meaning has exhausted its historical function, which is eminently destructive, just as its pedagogy is strictly negative: innocence as inexperience, the ideal story as the absence of story, economic equilibrium as a renunciation of development, individual safety as de-individualization. Detective fiction does not found mass culture: it *prepares* it, by erasing the preceding hegemonic culture . It is here, and not in mass culture, that the 'dialectic of enlightenment' fulfils itself in overthrowing novelistic sensibility, in the paring down of European civilization that makes room for the American way of life. Mass culture could certainly not have come into being without this hecatomb, but it does not consist – as Horkheimer and Adorno seem to believe – merely in the continuous re-enactment of this 'sacrifice'. Rather, its true basis must be sought in the modern re-evaluation and reformulation of the mechanism of 'mythic thought'.

Kindergarten

Happy the times when Diderot could admit, without feeling in the least belittled, that he had wept profusely while reading a novel – happy and, in their own way, immodest times. Because for over a century European intellectuals have been ashamed to talk about tears. Laughter, yes: that stark display of power in which, as Canetti has said, one 'shows one's teeth' to someone else, it was permissible and useful to discuss. But not tears.

Yet, as is often the case, novels continued to be written which were designed to make people cry, and people continued to read them in order to cry. One says to oneself, this is a curious phenomenon, worth looking into more closely, and one soon discovers that although there are numerous theories of the comic, many of them sired by prestigious names, silence reigns over the 'moving'. At this point one hesitates. If more or less everybody studies laughter, and nobody studies crying, there must be some reason. . . . Yet, on inspection, this state of affairs by itself proves absolutely nothing. It can be claimed that the comic has been analysed and the 'moving' ignored because the former is important (for linguistic, narrative, psychological, aesthetic or other reasons) and the latter is not. Or we can elegantly invert this and claim that what is covered in silence is more significant – because secret, unmentionable – than what is comfortably discussed.

The second of these hypotheses would seem to be the one best suited to a study devoted precisely to 'moving' literature. But I would prefer to leave it in the background. Hierarchies interest me only up to a certain point, and anyway it can by no means be assumed that the comic and the moving are symmetrical phenomena. Let us recognize, rather, that the absence of a theoretical tradition makes the starting point of an investigation even more debatable and slippery than usual. A set of theories – even rival or largely erroneous ones – at least offers a basis on which critical reflection can rest, and then possibly abandon its initial hypotheses. One may consider all existing theories of tragedy or the novel to be totally wrong, but at least they usually allow two people to agree whether to classify a text as a tragedy or as a novel. And this initial operation, although obviously approximate, is in itself a judgement, an act that takes one towards the end result of the investigation.

In the case of 'moving' literature the preselection permitted by the existence of a theoretical context is not possible. One finds oneself faced with a continuum of texts in which one must make two cuts: from here to here, that is, 'moving' literature. But why precisely this group of texts and not others? Because – let theory addicts try to stay calm at this point – only these texts have made me cry.

There is no other way. If one wants to put forward a new 'object' for discussion one has to start from very empirical, subjective and crude premisses. One can only begin by asserting that the 'moving' is what makes one cry. (To be rigorous: what makes me and most – though not all – of the people I have consulted for the purpose cry). Having said this much, one must try to explain *how* the crying is brought on, and what could possibly be the *function* of texts able to generate this effect. The content of 'moving' literature becomes richer, its boundaries clearer; its procedures display a regularity that can be represented as a modest system of laws. If at the end of the research we know *more*, and *better*, about the texts we started from, and if our perception of the cultural system to which they belong also emerges modified, then there was a point in the operation – it was even, in its way, 'necessary'. At the present time it is good to remember that the real justification for *every* interpretation lies not in its being 'possible' ('we can interpret text x in the following way . . .') but in its being *necessary* in order better to understand things which, without interpretation, would appear obscure or contradictory. If it does not attain this end or, more modestly, if it is not motivated by this requirement, then the activity of interpretation is perfectly useless. And in the field of theory there is no accusation more damning than that.

But let us get on to the texts. The ones I shall concentrate on – *Heart*, *The Paul Street Boys* and, to a lesser extent, *Misunderstood*[1] – do not exhaust the field of 'moving' literature, but they clearly constitute a group. They are texts with 'boys' both as their protagonists and as their ideal readers. This fact allows – indeed compels – one to read them against the background of one of the main narrative currents of our civilization: that involving the ideal (although a hard one to define, as we shall see) of *Bildung*, and the narrative structures able to represent and promote it. The moving element as such is thus found to interact with one of the highest pedagogical aspirations expressed by the bourgeois world, and this will, perhaps, allow us to shed an unusual light on both aspects of the question.

1. Rhetoric of the Too Late

But Ferruccio spoke no more. The little hero, the saviour of his mother's mother, stabbed in the back, had rendered up his brave and beautiful soul to God. ('Romagnol Blood', in *Heart*)

And János Bóka, the general, broke in desperation into bitter, disconsolate tears. (*The Paul Street Boys*)

'In *yours*, father? you've always got Miles in yours. You never take *me* in your arms.' (*Misunderstood*)

One obviously starts crying at a particular point, and it is very likely that when they reach the three sentences quoted above, the vast majority of readers burst into tears. But it is certainly the case that not a single reader will have cried on seeing them printed here. The situation is paradoxical: precisely *that* sentence, made up of exactly those words, is necessary for one to cry, yet, on its own, the sentence is not enough.

Let us therefore put it back into context. We then discover that in all three cases, the same procedure has been adopted: the 'moving' sentence modifies the point of view that had directed our reading, organizing its expectations and judgements, in the pages immediately preceding. Before the disconsolate 'In *yours*, father?' with which the subjectivity of little Humphrey bursts forth, the narrative had been focused on the thoughts of his father, Sir Everard, who is convinced that Humphrey is not very interested in his attention. János Bóka, in the unforgettable battle episode, really has been presented as a 'general': and generals do not cry. As for Ferruccio, it is well known that De Amicis, through the grandmother's mouth, piles up pages upon pages of reproofs against him before sanctifying him in the final apotheosis.

The shift of perspective is sudden, but this does not make it new for the reader. The point of view that is re-established in the 'moving' sentence does retract the one prevailing in the section immediately before, but it does recall a point of view located even further back in the text, and which is in fact, by definition, the primary and unquestionable one, because it depends on the 'neutral' and 'impersonal' judgement of the narrator, not on the 'limited' and 'subjective' ones of the characters. Although Sir Everard is convinced of the opposite, we know right from the opening pages of *Misunderstood* that Humphrey wants his father's affection. The moving sentence dissipates Sir Everard's mistaken perception (which, for a number of pages, is also the one through which the reader is forced to follow events) by a short circuit that definitively re-establishes the original 'truth'. The same applies to Ferruccio ('He was not a bad-hearted boy, – quite the contrary' as De Amicis tells us straight away) and to Bóka, who is a boy like the others, forced by his friends' expectations to adopt prematurely a strenuous adult hard shell.[2]

We have moved another step forward but we are still not there. This mechanism of retraction and re-establishment of points of view has in fact always been familiar to literary theory under the name of 'agnition'. And agnition, in and by itself, is a neutral rhetorical procedure: it can serve just as readily to make the world collapse about Othello as to bring *Tom Jones* to a perfectly happy ending. What makes it produce a 'moving' effect is not the play of points of view in itself but rather the *moment* at which it occurs. Agnition is a 'moving' device when it comes *too late*. And to express the sense of being 'too late' the easiest course is obviously to prime the agnition for the moment when the character is on the point of dying.[3]

Death is an event in a class of its own, and I shall return shortly to its quite specific function in the chain of events that constitutes the narrative. First it is necessary to spell out what elements are involved in the belated 'agnition', and what reactions they induce in the reader. And since agnition has been defined as the resolution of a clash between opposing points of view, let us take an already classic statement of the problem of point of view, Lotman's *The Structure of the Artistic Text*: 'there are very few elements of artistic structure so directly related to the general task of constructing a picture of the world as the 'point of view' element. . . .a model of culture has its own orientation which is expressed in a certain scale of values, in relation to what is true and false, high and low. If we imagine a given culture's picture of the world as a text on a sufficiently abstract level, this orientation finds its expression in the point of view of the text. . . . The relation between creator and created is always a relation between text and point of view.[4]

Point of view is grounded in a symbolic hierarchy, and it therefore always expresses a *value* judgement. But artistic products, as is well known, enjoy the unusual privilege of themselves constructing the 'facts' against which the 'values' selected in each case are to be measured. What a 'creator' must do to corroborate a system of thought and scale of values is not show how they conform to already given facts but actually construct the facts that best accord with them. This operation is no 'easier' than the other, but it is different, and it means that the distinction between judgements of fact and of value – an extremely problematic one in any event – becomes institutionally impossible in the case of an aesthetic communication.[5] This situation makes literature the privileged vehicle of any ideology, if the aim of ideology is to make one accept value-postulates as facts and, inversely, charge what already exists with value.

But if all this is true, what has taken place in 'moving' literature? We start out with a first point of view, a 'higher'- order one, where judgements of fact and of value are fused. After a certain moment, *other* points of view – in accordance with the plurality of perspectives which Bakhtin, and later Lotman, have recognized as specific to modern fiction – intervene in the structure of the text. Facts and values no longer coincide. Indeed, the diversification of values starts up a mechanism of actions and reactions that quickly reaches a point of no return. Only then is the original truth-morality restored and the discrepancy in points of view reconciled. But it is too late. A universal consensus has been re-established, but to no avail. Even if everybody is now in a position to share the same values, nothing guarantees any longer that they can materialize in the world, that they can turn into facts. This state of affairs arises from what we have called the 'too late', and what could simply be called *time*. Every system of values is in fact inevitably driven, as a system, to want the flow of time to halt, or (what really amounts to the same thing) to proceed always according to predictable rhythms. But time does not stop, and it does not heed anyone's bidding. Still less does it turn back and allow us to use it differently. This is what the protagonist's death is for: to show that time is *irreversible*. And this irreversibility is perceived that much more clearly if there are no doubts about the *different direction* one would like to impose on the course of events.

This is what makes one cry. Tears are always the product of *powerlessness*. They presuppose two mutually opposed facts: that it is clear how the present state of things should be changed[6] – and that this change is *impossible*. They presuppose a definitive estrangement of facts from values, and thus the end of any relationship between the idea of *teleology* and that of *causality*. In this lies the second reason why death plays an indispensable part in 'moving' literature. The person who dies never appears as one who is carrying out an intention (these texts as a matter of principle do not permit suicide) but as one subjected to a chain of *causes* beyond his control – not as the artificer of his own desires, but as the victim of 'reality' in its most radical form.[7] And since there are few things as important, for the formation of human beings, as what is proposed to them as 'reality' when they are children, it is worth looking at the system of causal connections governing the world of 'moving' literature.

2. Crimes and Punishments

If we try to reconstruct why the protagonists of our novels die, we come upon the same procedure. Ferruccio is killed by the terrible robber Mozzoni. But if he had not come home 'at eleven o'clock, after staying out for many hours', by midnight he and his grand-mother would long since have been in bed, the robber could have gone peacefully about his work, which would have been completed without any need for knives thrust in the back. At the bottom of it all there is thus an element of 'guilt' on Ferruccio's part, which however receives a decidedly disproportionate punishment. As for Nemecsek, he dies of pneumonia contracted after going to spy on a 'council of war' among his enemies, the Botanical Gardens Gang. On revealing himself, he is tossed into a pond (where he had already fallen some time before through carelessness, getting 'a filthy cold'). He might just pull through. But on the day of the battle, he escapes his mother's surveillance, runs to the field and signs his own death warrant. Another transgression 'punished' with extreme measures: Humphrey dies after falling from a tree he had been told expressly, and more than once, not to climb. The moral is the same as in the two previous cases. One could multiply the examples. Thus when, in *Love Story*, Oliver and Jenny con-travene the unwritten laws of the Barrett family, one senses some-thing must happen: but leukemia really seems excessive. Or again, in a splendid science-fiction story by Tom Godwin. 'The Cold Equations', a young girl stows away in a spaceship. When she is discovered, she comes out with a candid 'All right – I give up. I'm guilty, so what happens to me now? Do I pay a fine, or what?' – and instead, because of complicated ratios of fuel, weight and destination (the 'cold equations' which constitute an 'inexorable physical law') she must be jettisoned into space in shirt and jeans.

Now, in itself and by itself, the transgression-punishment se-quence is extremely common. One might say that there is not a single text of fiction where it does not appear in one form or another. It is not the sequence as such, then, but the element of *disproportion* that is specific to 'moving' literature – and, we can add, to the modern world, to Western bourgeois democracy. Although the idea that the punishment must be proportionate to the crime is to be found here and there in more remote times as well, it has only become definitively established in the last two hundred years. Only in this intellectual-historical context has disproportionality become clearly visible, and felt as something unjust and painful, something that 'ought not to happen' (but does happen neverthe-less: it is the same contrast between facts and ideals that occurs in the agnition on the point of dying).

Guilt, punishment, disproportion: let us pursue the investigation of these three elements. It emerges that the first two are sharply distinct from the third. The representatives of guilt and punish-ment in the story are always human characters: Ferruccio and his grandmother, Humphrey and Sir Everard, Nemecsek and Ferenc Ács, Oliver-Jenny and Mr Barrett, the girl and the pilot in 'The Cold Equations'. But the element of disproportion does not derive from this first conflict. *Two* forms, or degrees, of punishment are in fact present in the text. The first comes entirely from 'human' authority: the reproaches of Ferruccio's grandmother, Hum-phrey's father and the spaceship pilot, the laughter and the bath decreed by Ferenc Acs, the financial cutting-off by Mr Barrett. But the second type of punishment – the excessive one – is always due to other causes. There is always a third element (or actant) which comes into play, and which generally does not possess 'human' characteristics: a cold that turns into pneumonia, a branch that breaks, leukemia, the technical 'laws' of astronautics. An exception to this rule is Mozzoni in 'Romagnol Blood', yet De Amicis presents him as supremely inhuman,[8] a fact that enables us to introduce a further distinction. The third element is always that which it is *impossible to live with*: a fatal illness, deceitful nature, the iron laws of physics, Vito Mozzoni, the Austrians who kill the little Lombard scout. In a word, the *enemy*. The first two elements, on the other hand, always appear as a *potential community* that has not worked out: the family in the case of *Heart*, *Misunderstood* and *Love Story*; the peer group or the crew in Molnár and Godwin.

At its highest level of abstraction, 'moving' literature thus invites us to *shift* our gaze, to see the conflict not in the institutions (family, school, peer group) which are the direct product of socio-historical equilibria, but in oppositions that overhang them in the name of a more primitive and elementary threat: the opposition between 'friend' and 'enemy', and the really definitive one be-tween 'human' and 'natural'. We are in the presence of what Beniamino Placido has called, with reference to *Uncle Tom's Cabin*, the 'lightning-conductor strategy': everything negative and

contemptible is gathered at one pole, so as to reflect back innocence and charm the world as it is. I shall return to this procedure
as it features in 'moving' literature. At this point, the primary task
is to avoid the trap and concentrate our critical inquiry on precisely
those elements for which the text requests (wrongly, as we shall
see) acquittal on grounds of insufficient evidence.

3. Fathers and Sons

On opening *Heart* the opposition between friend and enemy
comes to mind again. Parades, medals, mayors, flags, little martyrs
of Italian Independence and Good Kings wink at us from every
page. De Amicis's patriotism is explicit, crude, and above all vigil-
ant. Its aim is not persuasion or enthusiasm but surveillance. It
wants to keep an eye open and to constrain, not to convince. An
introverted patriotism, it aspires not to the foundation of the
Fatherland but, more modestly, to that of the School: its principal
theme and its principal means of diffusion. By definition a compul-
sory state institution, the school is a place where one learns to
assimilate the values presented not out of any inner conviction
(which may even be present, but is inessential and superfluous) but
through sheer fear of authority.[9]

In fact the diary framework of *Heart* is a great panopticon open
to the rigorous gaze of authority.[10] Enrico Bottini – the children's
Dr Watson, in his irredeemable mediocrity – cannot even make a
move without running into someone who puts him back on the
straight and narrow with a good talking to. The real aim of the
book is ruthlessly to emphasize the protagonist's sense of moral
inferiority, and I would not be surprised if the infamous Franti and
the odious Nobis were only there to show that Enrico is not the
worst creature on this earth. Even so, Enrico comes off badly, for
the simple reason that *Heart* is a book where the fathers (and
teachers) never die. Garrone's mother dies, as does Enrico's
former teacher (a woman): both at school and in the family the
pole of 'affection' is shown to be vulnerable to time. But not so the
pole of 'duty': Enrico's *father's* teacher (to whom one of the
longest chapters in the book is devoted) is still alive and endowed

with great moral authority. Furthermore, Enrico's father is also, and above all, a 'teacher' of life, and the teacher, conversely, is a 'father' to his pupils. Family and school are superimposed in a single, escape-proof disciplinary structure. Even games nearly always take place under adult supervision. All this might seem strange and vaguely unreal, but it becomes crystal-clear if one sees *Heart* as a book which, contrary to appearances, does not aim to depict and stimulate growth but to exorcise it.[11] At the end of the year, Enrico has not changed a bit: what is required of him, rather, is that he should remain a permanent minor.

The narrative organization of Enrico's diary confirms this. It is made up entirely of anecdotes – a form of story-telling whose sententious brevity imposes a clear and irrefutable moral – and of characters who are all summed up *in a single trait* (Stardi's clenched fists, Franti's laughter, Garrone's bread-chewing) and who never deviate from the identity pinned on them at the beginning. *Heart* is a gallery of caricatures and stunted limbs: and if De Amicis is continually saying that in the boy (in the *fixity* of the boy would be more exact) one can already 'read the man', this evidently means that between the boy and the man there will be neither change nor growth.

Opposed to this on almost every count, and a hundred times more intelligent, is Molnár's strategy in *The Paul Street Boys*. Here collective ideals are no longer a duty to which one is called by the fanfare of the Fatherland's authorities, but a *choice*. The places where values are formed and come into conflict is not the school but the *game*: the most 'free' and 'private' thing a boy has, a game – the war between the two gangs – so innervated with rules, chivalry and loyalties that it becomes the only true measure of human behaviour. It can, if necessary, overturn the verdicts of the teachers: the Franti of *The Paul Street Boys* (expelled from his school with a black mark) is Ferenc Ács, and he is a shining example of courage and honesty – whereas the swot Geréb is a little scoundrel. The real prize of the game, moreover, is not to conquer the field of Paul Street but rather – as the ethics of the duel require – to show (primarily to oneself) one's mettle, to prove whether one is up to one's own standard, one's own ideal, whether one is capable, literally, of 'growing'.

This brings us to the nub of the matter. Unlike *Heart*, *The Paul Street Boys* is a *novel*: it narrates, parallel to Nemecsek's death, the story of Bóka's growth to maturity. It is a real growth because here nobody is prescribing the path to follow. The relations between fathers and sons in *The Paul Street Boys* are the reverse of those in *Heart*. In the latter, the adult world represented those moral ideals to which the son's narcissistic egoism needed constantly to be recalled. In Molnár, however, the boys are guided by values beyond their direct interest, while the adults – or the other substitute figures in whom authority is sometimes embodied – have eyes only for their own self-interest. Molnár assembles a little gallery of these egocentric adults: the sweet-vendor outside the school, whose only aim is to make money; the caretaker János, who is open to any kind of corruption for a box of cigars; the teachers, only good for giving a ticking-off for some trivial matter; Geréb's father, stupid, big-headed, and ready to lash out against Nemecsek in his absence; the customer at old Nemecsek the tailor's, who, confronted with a dying child, can do nothing better than get annoyed that his jacket is not ready yet. And lastly, there is the unforgettable penultimate page of the book:

'On Monday the workers are coming; they are going to dig all round the field to lay the foundations . . . and build the cellars. . .'

'What?' – Bóka shouted this time. 'They are going to build a house here?'

'A house, a house', the Slovak replied impassively, 'a block of flats . . . three floors. . . It's the owner of the building land. . . He is having it built'.

This, then, is the adult world. It should be realized that, apart from the extreme case of Nemecsek's customer, these are not monsters. They are simply adults, some worse and some (Nemecsek's neighbours, the doctor) better. The point is, rather, that whether bad, good or indifferent *they have nothing more to teach* the boys. Because their lives have no other aim in view than to conserve what exists inasmuch as it *exists*, not because it has a meaning;[12] in other words, they can no longer point towards aims or promote ideals. The adult has nothing left to say to the boy, or he to the adult. This breakdown in dialogue constitutes an essential step towards the catastrophe. Let us go back briefly to the beginning of the narrative sequence, to the 'crime' (of disobedience, inattention or incautiousness) committed by the young protagonists – and let us add that the text always makes it understood that this crime can easily be remedied. Ferruccio comes home late: but if he performed a certain action his grandmother would stop telling him off, they would go to bed and be safe. Nemecsek reveals himself to the Botanical Gardens Gang and later disobeys the orders of the Putty Club: but he too has a surefire means of avoiding an icy ducking or a demotion. Humphrey could easily vanquish his father's severity, and thus no longer need to vent his bitterness by climbing trees, if only . . .

If only he would speak. All three are done for because, at a crucial turn in the story, they keep silent: or rather, it is precisely their silence and that alone which makes this moment decisive. They only need to say: 'I've got a cold'; 'Let me go, I'm on the trail of a traitor'; 'But look, father, it's not true that I do not love you'; 'Yes, grandmother, I did wrong to stay out late, forgive me', and everything would be fine. But all three keep their mouths shut. They may be 'generous, good, daring, patient, brave', but they are also 'obdurate, sullen, stubborn, proud, pig-headed'. Silent pride is perhaps their real crime. But where do this pride and this silence originate from? A passage from Walter Benjamin will help put the problem in focus: 'in tragedy, pagan man becomes aware that he is better than his god, but the realization robs him of speech, remains unspoken. Without declaring itself, it seeks secretly to gather its forces. Guilt and atonement it does not measure justly in the balance, but mixes indiscriminately. There is no question of the 'moral world order' being restored; instead, the moral hero, still dumb, not yet of age – as such he is called a hero – wishes to raise himself by shaking that tormented world. The paradox of the birth of genius in moral speechlessness, moral infantility, is the sublimity of tragedy.'[13] Of course, Nemecsek is not Orestes, nor Humphrey Oedipus. But that terrifying discovery – that one is better than one's gods – recurs practically identically in these boy heroes. They are better than their own fathers, or those figures who stand in for the father in constituting authority. This is why they stay silent: to speak – admitting to a misdemeanour or a minor weakness – would mean restoring to the pettiness of adults a superiority they no longer deserve.

But perhaps there is an even more substantial reason for the silence: it has become impossible to communicate because boys and adults now speak, deep down, two different languages. If the boys, in Molnár, are better than their fathers, this is not because they are 'younger' but because, unlike the adults, they are guided not by 'interest' but by 'conscience'. They do not organize their lives according to the 'reality principle' but according to the super-ego. Bóka and Nemecsek do follow the moral code of the Paul Street gang not for any advantage they may gain from it, but because it makes them feel satisfied with themselves – a satisfaction that derives from having established a norm, an ideal of life, and shown they match up to it.

What drives them to this is not the fear of punishment, as in the authoritarian world of Enrico Bottini. It is something that sinks its roots much further back, in the break-up of what Weber called 'societies based on tradition', the consequences of which can be summarily put thus: society no longer prescribes by authority to individuals what their role shall be, and thus the *meaning* of their lives. This meaning is no longer to be recognized and accepted; it is, rather, to be created by a risky individual choice. Hence the need for 'values' (in the plural, inevitably), and for a period of 'formation and self-formation' of the individual: and hence the emergence of the ideal of *Bildung*.[14] The Paul Street boys cannot wait to get away from school or from home and meet in *their* field, to play by *their* rules. Only there, for them, can life acquire a meaning. Nobody has anything to teach them. They are alone. They themselves must build a hierarchy, a possible world, and take responsibility for it.

They do: with traumatic results. And the trauma lies not just in the fact that Nemecsek (like Humphrey or Ferruccio) dies. It is above all in the discovery that between the super-ego – those laws, those values which regulate individual existence – and the laws on whose basis reality functions *there is no relation*, just as there is no relation between the Father on whom one had formed one's own ideal and flesh-and-blood fathers. When psychoanalytic theory has dealt with 'civilization and its discontents', with the sacrifices it imposes on the individual, it has always concentrated exclusively on the giving up of the 'pleasure' principle: an event that it locates in the very first stages of human life. But there is a second sacrifice, perhaps even more painful than the first, since it takes place at a conscious age, and this is *the giving up* (or at least the silencing) *of one's own super-ego* – which is like giving up what has come closest – in the whole course of human history – to the ideal of *individual autonomy*. Although the super-ego is not of course really 'free' (it is itself the product of a violent imposition and it draws its strength from the fact that it stays essentially unconscious), it is nevertheless in its process of formation and unfolding that Riesman, Marcuse and, better than anyone, Adorno, have recognised that faint and ephemeral glimmer of the free individual, able autonomously to formulate laws and to strive to obey them: 'psychoanalysis, which once set out to break the power of the father image, firmly takes the side of the fathers, who either smile at the children's high-falutin ideas with a droop at the corner of their mouth or else rely on life to teach them what's what, and to consider it more important to earn money than get silly ideas into one's head. The attitude of mind that distances itself from the realm of immediate ends and means, and is given the chance to do so during the brief years in which it is its own master before being absorbed and dulled by the necessity to earn a living, is slandered as mere narcissism. The powerlessness and fallibility of those who still believe in other possibilities is made out to be their own vain fault; what is blamed on their own inadequacies is much more the fault of a social order that constantly denies them the possible and breaks what potential people possess.'[15]

It is symptomatic that Adorno is talking here about the adolescent: a term rarely met in the literature of psychoanalysis, yet which is at the centre of the great nineteenth-century European novel. The writer's obsessive theme is, always, whether it is possible to reconcile the demands of the super-ego with those of reality, and if so, how. In *The Paul Street Boys* (not in *Heart*: a world of father-teachers has no need of a super-ego) the final echo of this question still reverberates, simplified and rendered more drastic by the so obviously 'premature' age of its protagonists: values that are 'taken too seriously', lived ingenuously 'to the limit', become inevitably *dangerous*. Growing up, as we shall see, means getting rid of this excessive sense of 'obligation', which must be banished as a risky illusion. Fine: but at least there was a time when one could act in the conviction that an aim was being pursued, when the world seemed permeable to values. Whoever read *The Paul Street Boys* as a boy realized that he would have to give up his own hopes. But whoever read *Heart* never knew what hope means.

4. Phenomenology of Resignation

Let us start once again from the relation between boys and adults. We can now add that the latter are always, without exception, characterized by a form of blindness. Sir Everard understands nothing about Humphrey, the grandmother understands nothing about Ferruccio, the teachers in the Budapest school understand nothing about what their pupils are up to, not to mention the father of the little Florentine scribe or the captain of the Sardinian drummer, who, when the boy is hit by the bullets which will cost him an amputated leg, can do nothing better than shout: 'Ah, the infamous poltroon has sat down!'. Every time the boy stubbornly insists on being faithful to his own personality, the adult, blindly, sees only a deliberate sneer directed at him. He therefore reacts, managing only to intensify the other's obstinacy in a spiral which necessarily ends in the death of the weaker party. And why does it come to this? Because on both sides, obstinacy and blindness have triumphed. Or to put it in more classical terms, Pride and Prejudice.

Naturally: in order to understand the place of 'moving' literature in the typology of modern fiction there is no better counter-work than Jane Austen's novel. If Lukács had known English literature there is no doubt that *Pride and Prejudice* would have stood alongside *Wilhelm Meister's Apprenticeship* as an unparalleled example of the *Bildungsroman*. In reading it we witness the complete success of a 'compromise' as Lukács understood it in the *Theory of the Novel*: the founding of a relationship, a community, which neither exhausts nor radically modifies reality, and yet is invested with an intersubjective sense: the family, formed on the basis of the eighteenth-century sense of complimentariness, of sympathy. And this becomes possible because Pride and Prejudice have been dispelled, because the two protagonists become willing to explain themselves and understand one another: to speak and listen. *Conversation* is the most carefully tended part, as it were the summit, of Jane Austen's work. Attention to language, and the ability to use it and decode it with *propriety*, is in her world the highest guarantee of ethicality. It indicates respect for and command of the *social mediation par excellence*, a perfect sense of the community and its multiple nuances.

It is the other way round in 'moving' literature, where the catastrophe germinates in the interruption of communication, in the collapse of that dimension which can connect the antagonists and thereby neutralize their antagonism. In the last section I tried to show that there are deep-seated reasons for this interruption. The boy's silence arises from the discovery that the demands of the super-ego are not given any importance by the world. The adult's verbose blindness is the reverse of this: it arises from the fact that those who lose their own super-ego along the way can no longer even 'see it' in others. Here are two modes of existence that must inevitably clash: the recurrent theme of 'incomprehension' – of not speaking the same language – is a consequence of this state of affairs.

'Moving' literature, however, inverts this sequence of cause and effect. It does not present obstinacy and blindness as simple manifestations of two opposite forms of life, but as the unfathomable source from which everything else springs. The point of the repeated, obsessive insistence on these traits of 'character' is not to make us understand better but to deter our attempt to do so, presenting the effort as wholly superfluous. At bottom, indeed, the aim is to make the conflict itself appear superfluous. It is presented as a simple misunderstanding which – not being resolved in time, like that of *Pride and Prejudice*, with a wealth of letters and conversations – ends up festering and literally *degenerating* into tragedy. The great final 'recognitions' demonstrate precisely that if the understanding had come earlier, the tragedy would have been easily avoided.

Incomprehension, consequently, is not presented as the *manifes-*

tation of a specific conflict but as its true *cause*: if this cause had been discovered the division would never have occurred. The image of interpersonal conflict presented by 'moving' literature is thus very different both from that implicit in classical tragedy and that typical of the eighteenth-century 'tear-jerker'. In *Antigone* or *Emilia Galotti*, for example, there is no misunderstanding at all. Everything is clear as day. The catastrophe is precipitated because in these works two systems of values, or laws, coexist with no possibility of conciliation between them. The texts make it clear that one or the other must succumb. Hence one is not 'moved' over the fate of Antigone or Emilia – *one is angered* (or else – it is all a question of point of view – gladdened). The unravelling of the story accentuates the division, deepens and legitimates the one-sidedness of the contending parties. One can – one must – be on one side or the other. There is no possibility of finding a common ground or bringing about a mediation or a compromise.

In the works we are concerned with here this pattern is turned on its head. Being moved – and crying, which is its most complete manifestation – is the exact opposite of being angry. Anger divides; tears *unite*. But *to whom* do they unite us? Not to the protagonist-victim. It is not to Nemecsek or Humphrey that our tears draw us. Our identification slides, imperceptibly yet inexorably, towards the others, the survivors. As at a funeral, the death of the protagonist manages to rebuild the community of those who remain. Through communal weeping, all rancour, all injustice, all blame is abolished. It is a ritual of reciprocal collective absolution. In this it expresses a constituent aspiration of the modern world, and of the narrative form of the novel: the aspiration to *compromise*. To be moved to tears is a typically *novelistic* reaction to a tragic situation. It is in this interweaving of levels – and not in the tragic situation proper, where in fact from the Renaissance onwards it is no longer to be found – that the only form of catharsis possible in the modern world is to be sought. It is, however, a catharsis that implies a definite *disavowal* of the tragic: the understanding so fully reached on the deathbed undoes the legitimacy of the behaviour that led there. It does not bring tragedy nearer but irrevocably distances it, branding it as an inapposite exaggeration.

This mechanism whereby tragic one-sidedness is downgraded by the superimposition of the novelistic capacity for conciliation seems to be made for inculcating, at a tender age, the greatest respect for Hegel's cynical reflections on the destiny of the free subjectivity that wants to be faithful to itself alone. Although the attributes of the historical-ideal 'types' constructed by Hegel have an unpleasant tendency to become reciprocally overlaid and confused, the salient moments of that journey, from the *Phenomenology* and the *Aesthetics*, can reasonably be reconstructed thus:

'But once [the single consciousness] has arrived at this idea [of being a pure individuality on his own account], as he must, then this *immediate* unity with the Spirit [in other words the original community], the [mere] *being* of himself in Spirit, his trust, is lost. Isolated and on his own, it is he who is now the essence, no longer the universal Spirit. . . .

In thus establishing himself . . . the individual has thereby placed himself in opposition to the laws and customs. These are regarded as mere ideas, having no absolute essentiality, an abstract theory without any reality, while he as this particular "I" is his own living truth. . . .

[For the rational self-consciousness this] is the beginning of the ethical substance . . . The ethical substance has sunk to the level of a predicate devoid of self, whose living subjects are individuals who themselves have to provide the filling for their universality and to fulfil their essential nature through their own efforts. . . .

The law, therefore, which is immediately self-consciousness's own law, or a heart which, however, has within it a law, is the *End* which self-consciousness proceeds to realize. . . . [But] this heart is confronted by a real world. . ., a law by which the particular individuality is oppressed, a violent ordering of the world which contradicts the law of the heart. . .'.[16]

So far we have followed the widening division between 'individual' and 'way of the world'. Now these two entities must measure up in a direct confrontation. And at this point, Hegel continues, one discovers that 'the law of the heart' is nothing other than the 'delirium of self-conceit': it puts 'the way of the world' on trial, attributing – in the 'ravings of an insane self-conceit' – all responsibility for it to the machinations of 'fanatical priests, gluttonous despots'. Whereas in reality the opposite is the case: it is the law of the heart that is 'something merely *intended* which, unlike the established order, has not stood the test of time, but rather when thus tested is overthrown.'[17] And likewise thrown overboard, in a famous section of the *Aesthetics*, are both the concept of 'love'[18] and that of 'honour'.[19] In each case, Hegel criticizes and derides what seem to him to be mere *exaggerations of the imagination* deaf and blind to the true shape of the existing order.

However, such realism does not mean *knowing reality better* but rather – and there is quite a difference – *recognizing in it an intrinsic rationality and ethicality*: so that there is not the slightest reason for the individual to 'understand', still less try to change, the existing order of things. The realism Hegel looks towards does not consist in clarifying one's knowledge and subjective aims, but in doing away with them as mere *illusions*. In the end we find that the lone journey of the 'free subjectivity' has been utterly useless, and Hegel makes no mystery about treating it as little more than a necessary evil, an infantile disorder:

'consciousness drops like a discarded cloak its idea of a good that exists [only] in principle, but has as yet no actual experience. In its conflict it has learnt by experience that the "way of the world" is not as bad as it looked; for its reality is the reality of the universal. . . . The individuality [reintroduced into] the "way of the world" may well imagine that it acts only for *itself* or in its own interest. It is better than it thinks, for its action is at the same time implicitly universal action. When it acts in its own interest, it simply does not know what it is doing; and when it avers that everyone acts in his own interest, it is merely asserting that no one knows what action is.'[20]

'But in the modern world these fights are nothing more than "apprenticeship", the education of the individual into the realities of the present, and thereby they acquire their true significance. For the end of such apprenticeship consists in this, that the subject sows his wild oats, builds himself with his wishes and opinions into harmony with subsisting relationships and their rationality, enters the concatenation of the world, and acquires for himself an appropriate attitude to it. However much he may have quarrelled with the world, or been pushed about in it, in most cases at last he gets his girl and some sort of position, marries her, and becomes as good a Philistine as others. The woman takes charge of the household management, children arrive, the adored wife, at first unique, an angel, behaves pretty much as all other wives do; the man's profession provides work and vexations, marriage brings domestic affliction – so here we have all the headaches of the rest of married folk. – We see here the like character of adventurousness except that now it finds its right significance, wherein the fantastic element must experience the necessary corrective.'[21]

This should not be considered a superfluous digression. 'Moving' interests me because it is a literary structure that intervenes in its own way in the process of formation and self-formation of consciousness, because it is one of the various points at which the problem of the theory of the novel intersects with that of *Bildung*. The work of Hegel is the ineradicable basis of both these questions.[22] The reader will already have made certain obvious correlations between the argument of the last section and the texts under examination. *The Paul Street Boys*, *Misunderstood* and the monthly stories in *Heart* tell of those whose downfall is brought about by excessive commitment to their own still uncertain law of the heart, in other words by an excessive desire for *one-sidedness* – the sin of sins, in the Hegelian system.[23] They have refused to recognize in the world as it is (the 'uncritical positivism' that Marx pinpointed in Hegel) not so much a reality everyone must inevitably come to terms with as *reality itself*, one and unquestionable; not so much the fact that it certainly has its own rationality as that it is innervated by a *universal* and *objective* rationality, in the face of which it is stupid or suicidal to voice doubts or demands.

If *Bildung* consists in finally abandoning one's own values as deceptive chimeras in order to insert oneself happily into the existing world and find fullness of meaning there, then 'moving' literature tells the story of a *Bildung* that has failed to occur. But we must go carefully. We need not assume that the (inevitable) education of the individual into the laws of reality must follow all three moments of the idyllic Hegelian waltz, that it must try to convince us the world is *alright* as it is. It only has to say it is *like this*, and that it is *strong* enough to bend anyone who tries to oppose it. This would also appear to be the meaning of a passage in *Civilization and its Discontents*: 'Another procedure operates more energetically and more thoroughly [than the search in art for the fulfilment of wishes that are difficult to carry out]. It regards reality as the sole enemy and as the source of all suffering, with which it is impossible to live, so that one must break off all relations with it if one is to be in any way happy ... [One] can try to re-create the world, to build up in its stead another world in which its most unbearable features are eliminated and replaced by others that are in conformity with one's own wishes. But whoever, in desperate defiance, sets out upon this path to happiness will as a rule attain nothing. Reality is too strong for him. He becomes a madman, who for the most part finds no one to help him in carrying through his delusion.'[24]

We seem to be back in the world of the *Phenomenology*. But there is a basic difference: Freud says the world is *stronger*, not more moral or more rational than the 'delirium' of the individual. We find something very similar in the conceptual framework of early nineteenth-century criminal psychology, reconstructed by Foucault in *Histoire de la folie*: 'This region of madness and frenzy in which the criminal gesture arises does not declare it innocent except in so far as it does not have a rigorous moral neutrality, but acquires a precise function: to exalt a value which society recognizes without permitting its realization. One prescribes marriage but one is obliged to close one's eyes to infidelity. Madness will have a power of justification if it reveals jealousy, obstinacy, fidelity: even at the price of revenge. Psychology must install itself within a guilty conscience, in the relation between recognized values and claimed values. Then, and only then, can it dissolve the reality of the crime and declare it unpunishable, by a sort of quixotism of impracticable virtues. ... One is innocent in the immediate and violent transition from one morality to another, from a prescribed morality that one hardly dares to recognize to an exalted morality which, for the greater common good, one refuses to practise.'[25]

In both Freud and Foucault it is clear that the 'delirium of self-conceit' is not – as it was for Hegel – the *cause* of the individual's downfall but its *consequence*. It is only *after being defeated* that the individual aspiration becomes a 'delirium'. Its 'madness' lies in the weakness of its forces, not in the moral exertion as such. The game is played entirely on the morally 'neutral' field of power relations. Growing no longer means learning to recognize in the world the unrivalled intelligence of the Hegelian Spirit, but rather learning to fear the power of the world. And this is really the kind of *Bildung* (if it is still legitimate to call it that) that a world founded upon and geared to power relations, and not to moral ends or rational models, needs if it is to work. But this civilization, if it wants to be consistent, must also give up the Hegelian consolation that surreptitiously reintroduces values into the world. This is not because these values do not exist – even the most prosaic world is full of them. It is because *its legitimacy does not depend on their presence*, but rather, primarily, on the sheer force of what is.

This is the discovery to which the second main character of *The Paul Street Boys*, János Bóka, is driven:

'And the following day, at school, when everyone was seated at their places, and the teacher Rácz, amid a religious silence, walked up to his desk with slow, grave steps to remember in a subdued voice Ernest Nemecsek, after which he invited the whole class to gather at three o'clock the next day in black or at least dark clothes in Rakós Street, János Bóka gazed pensively ahead. And for the first time in his pure and simple soul there flashed the idea of what this life really is. A life which compels us to fight as if we were at its command, at times placidly, it is true, but at times with great sadness.'

This is the last paragraph of Molnár's novel. For the first time, Bóka is formulating a judgement on the world. And everything that has happened has not in the least enabled him to *understand any better* what 'this life' is, nor to find a *higher meaning* in it. Rather, it has destroyed what few certainties he had and dispelled all hope. All that Bóka can see in the *strength* of the world, 'which compels us to fight as if we were at its command'. Behind him we can already catch a glimpse of Törless, Dedalus and Rossmann, with whose enigmatic bewilderment the curtain will fall once and for all on the organic optimism of the *Bildungsroman*.

5. Beyond Tears

Let us return a last time to the ultimate effect of 'moving' literature: tears. And this time, instead of asking '*Why* does one cry?',
let us ask '*What happens* when one cries?' What happens is that a
curtain drops between us and the world. Crying enables us *not to
see*. It is a way of distracting us from the sight of what has upset us,
or rather of making it disappear. Crying never simply coincides
with distress: it is not its immediate and inevitable effect. It is
above all a *reaction* to distress – the most infantile reaction, one
might say: the reaction of someone who, faced with a world that
thwarts, no longer wants to look and to reason, but performs the
equivalent of a magic gesture aimed at making it go away.

To reason, or to confide in a 'magic' act: what adult would
hesitate between these two attitudes? Yet things are a little more
complex than this. 'Reasoning' can in fact have two diametrically
opposed meanings. It can indicate an operation that attempts to
trace the *causal connections* of an event, or one that aims to make
a *plan* for future events. No dialectic could ever heal this laceration
which constitutes the human subject, suspended and torn between
the two poles of causality and teleology, reality and desire –
equally necessary to his existence, but which *never* balance. It is at
a specific moment in the relationship between the two poles that
crying is 'triggered': the moment when the tension finally drops
because desire and teleology are shown to be futile, unattainable.
Hence the contradictory sensation of crying: definitive sadness,
because the loss is definitive; and at the same time relief, because,
if nothing else, all inner conflict has ceased.

But there is another, still more significant, duality in the act of
crying as induced by these texts, exemplified literally in a splendid
passage of *The Paul Street Boys* and implicitly in the final 'agni-
tions' of all the moving texts. Tears render the ultimate homage,
the honours of war, to the realm of ends, the super-ego, happiness.
At the same time, in crying, one takes definitive leave of it:
because tears bind us to (by making us behave in the same way as)
Mr Barrett, Sir Everard Duncombe and Geréb – not to Jenny,
Humphrey or Nemecsek. Clearly we encounter here two very different, in a sense even opposed, emotional movements. It should
not therefore surprise us that crying is often considered to be

something hypocritical. To a large extent it really is. It is a surrender to reality which at the same time pays blatant homage to that ideal which tried to wage war on it. It is the way of appeasing one's conscience that is typical of *false* consciousness; and indeed it is good to be suspicious of someone who is too prone to tears. But someone who never cries is worse still, because when one cries one is at least admitting that, in the reconciliation with the world, something important has been lost – that it is thus not a true reconciliation, more a defeat. And one can at least hope that the person who admits – if only through tears – the reality of defeat has not entirely extinguished the desire for revenge, and may one day decide against resignation to a mutilated human condition.

Not to resign oneself means, of course, to go on nurturing *illusions*, to plan new chimeras which dissolve in new tears: because human happiness 'is not foreseen' either in the plans of Creation, as Freud observed, or in that of any society we have known so far. Yet this tension is the principal virtue of the human animal. To try to relax it is base. One must rather try to press it to the limit, not budging from one's own ideals, and then, at the moment of tears, the moment when facts start mocking values, opening one's eyes wider still to understand their logic. This is how a scientific attitude commences. To know can only mean to know something that is *different from us*, and this becomes possible only when 'we' – our ideals, our desires – encounter something that compels us to perceive its difference by rejecting and offending us.

Contrary to a theory currently in vogue, the origin of this scientific attitude is not of a piece with the 'will to power'. Knowledge arises always and only from the perception of otherness. And the most clear-cut, and realistic, sensation of otherness is pain, which tells us that, even though knowledge may attain its end and finally 'comprehend' the object of its investigation, that object is still not going to bend to our will. And while there may be nothing wrong with this in the case of the objects of nature, which rightly maintain an adamantine indifference to talking bipeds, things are quite different where human aggregations are concerned. That the social relations binding people together should – all of them – tighten with the cold indifference to ends that is typical of the laws of nature: this *must* continue to strike us as painful. Whoever does not feel this is not going to understand anything about the world. To aspire to happiness is sacrosanct, but to believe one has attained it in our world is a symptom not of happiness but of stupidity – and this is not a quality suited to intellectual labour. It is true enough that until there is proof to the contrary, this state of affairs must be considered unalterable. I would simply like to be clear that what is unalterable contains in itself a *necessity* but not a *purpose*. One can and must 'accept' it, but to 'defend' it is absurd. That is all.

And so we come back, and really for the last time, to our books. Only one real charge can be laid at their doors: that they do not trace the origin of pain to where it is obscene that it should exist – in relations among people – but where it is inevitable: in nature. This is why death by strictly natural causes is the one crucial topos of 'moving' literature, and its one great lie. The lie does not consist, obviously, in emphasizing the irreparable sadness of every death, but in projecting onto that death a sense of injustice and injury (a young person's death is always felt to be 'unjust') whose only legitimate place is within the human community. Nature is demonized in order to absolve society by showing its sad powerlessness. In this, its ultimate end, 'moving' literature consumes and repudiates that potential for knowledge which, by placing us in the presence of pain, it had managed to arouse.

The Long Goodbye:
Ulysses and the End of Liberal
Capitalism

1. Portrait of a Crisis

Ulysses caused a deep split within the development of European literature and, particularly, of the novel: this much was immediately clear. Less clear was – and still is – the link between this split and the rupture that occurred in the functioning of capitalist societies at the turn of the century. The mutual indifference of socio-historical research and literary research has perhaps even intensified with time to the disadvantage of both. This essay is an attempt to reconnect the two sides of the problem. The instruments used are not new: the only innovation is the attempt to integrate them systematically. This simple operation, however, compels one to read *Ulysses* from a very different viewpoint.

There is a deep attraction between the two terms, '*Ulysses*' and 'crisis'. Yet, in current critical use, the meaning of the second has been assimilated to a hazy image of the end of the world, values, literature – of the bourgeoisie, as, with the logic of folly, students never tire of repeating. It is as though *Ulysses* bewitched readers to such an extent as to make them forget that more than half a century has passed since 1922 and that in the meantime the world, values, literature, and, indubitably, the bourgeoisie, have continued to thrive. Thus, it is necessary to set down the boundaries of this crisis and this *Ulysses*: to define them as historical events, which will never come back to life.

Desirous of moving from the Crisis to the crisis, literary criticism almost always resorts to one single and specific event: the war. There, in the summer of 1914 the break came. There lie the roots of the crisis and of the literature of crisis – of *Ulysses* and *The Trial*, *The Magic Mountain*, *The Waste Land* and *The Man Without Qualities*. Yet, among the few things these works have in common is exactly the opposite certainty: the war is not the *cause* of the crisis, but only its violent and conspicuous manifestation. The investigation shifts to the years preceding the war (with Mann and Musil, less directly with Joyce), or even cancels it from the picture (Kafka), or finally (with Eliot), treats it as a mere variant of a mythically constant history. Such a shift of analysis is a drastic choice, bristling with consequences: in making it, this 'great bourgeois' literature rejects the spontaneous ideology of Europe's dominant class of the period – that 'conservatism of the twenties' which so strongly linked the war and the crisis and which, for that very reason, lasted no more than a decade.[1]

The roots of the split are, therefore, pre-war: they lie according to the main hypothesis of Polanyi's study, in the definitive decline of the 'self-regulating market'. This, in turn, entails the decline of the liberal form of bourgeois society, to which the free market guaranteed rational functioning, automatically regulating its conflictual, irrational, and private foundations. Although fleetingly, Asor Rosa perceived the cultural dimension of the problem in writing of the 'discovery . . . that the real is not rational. And by the real, one means exactly the *capitalist real* to which this culture directly refers itself and which, in order to retrieve a form of co-ordination, regulation and participation for intellectual activity, requires the use of a more formal universe of concepts and values than in the past, and such as to contain within itself the capacity for rational ordering which proves capable of "arranging" something which instead manifests itself in its substance as disjointed, random, and often unjustifiably unjust.'[2]

Thus, in the first decades of the century, society no longer seems endowed with an intrinsic rationality; it is no longer an organic system of relations capable of holding all its elements together and of giving them a *function* and a *meaning*. According to two of the most cogent semiological analyses, *Ulysses* shows precisely the same lack of internal cohesion:

'These heterogeneous materials have no value of unity of meaning in Joyce's writing. . . . The value lies precisely in its heterogeneity, in the very distance between the different elements which the writing covers in an incessant play of relations and correspondences, on the basis of which every element becomes the simulation of another. . . . What is built in this game of mutual relations is a discontinuity in progress, a continual displacement from one fiction to another. The negativity of Joyce's writing emerges because of this discontinuity.'[3]

Just as *Dubliners* expressed a situation of "paralysis", *Ulysses* expresses a lack of relationships. . . . The situation expresses a total dissociation. This dissociated world recognizes itself as such but is incapable of finding internal patterns or organization. This is why Joyce resorts to an external pattern and turns his story into a muddled allegory of the Trinitarian mystery.'[4]

For the time being, let us lay aside the literary and ideological issues raised by *Ulysses*'s use of 'external patterns of organization', and try to conclude this first point by examining the tie between the *general* form of the capitalist crisis and that peculiar historical crisis caused by the disappearance of the self-regulating market. As Colletti writes: 'The general form in which the capitalist crisis manifests itself consists, according to Marx, in the interruption of the process of circulation of commodities: the result of this interruption is that the two instances of "buying" and "selling" separate, and enter into a contradictory relationship. . . . The consequence is that "civilized" form of economic crisis – peculiar to capitalist conditions. . . – known as the crisis of *overproduction*: that is, the seemingly paradoxical condition of the coexistence, on the one hand, of unsold goods, and on the other, of unsatisfied needs.'[5]

The capitalist crisis, therefore, is characterized by this *separation* of elements which should, rather, compose a unitary system – by the 'forcible separation from each other of processes which in essence are one', according to an epigraph from Marx.[6] It is, however, precisely because of such a separation of 'supply' and 'demand', products and producers, that the crisis cannot be seen as an 'irregularity' in the normal development of capitalism. On the contrary it expresses in a conspicuous form that same split which, in an obscure form, characterizes this society's most specific product: the commodity itself. According to a famous passage of *Capital*, the commodity form already contains within itself the 'potentiality' of the crisis: 'Thus the mystery of the commodity form is simply this, that it mirrors for men the social character of their own labour, mirrors it as an objective character attaching to the labour products themselves, mirrors it as a social natural property of these things. Consequently the social relation of the producers to the sum total of their own labour, presents itself to them as a social relation, not between themselves, but between the products of their labour. . . . To find an analogy, we must enter the nebulous world of religion. In that world, the products of the human mind become independent shapes, endowed with lives of their own, and able to enter into relations with men and women. The products of the human hand do the same thing in the world of commodities.'[7] Even within the sphere of production (that is, in a 'non-critical' situation *par excellence*), the product is an extraneous and separate entity, and cannot be controlled by the producer: crisis, therefore, originates *along with* capitalist social relationships: it is not an exception, but their full and patent expression.

Although the crisis is ingrained in production, it nonetheless manifests itself within the sphere of circulation: it is in the market that it becomes visible. Joyce wrote in a historical phase which, though it did not encounter a general economic crisis for approximately thirty years, experienced something even more significant: the crisis of the market *as such*, as an automatic mechanism of social equilibrium. This means that the crisis had become a *permanent* feature of capitalist society as it was then known. In Joyce, the typical phenomena of the crisis are no longer sudden and exceptional catastrophes: rather, they are the ordinary conditions of social relationships. This allows him to immerse himself into the 'arcane' depths of capitalist society and give us, in the 'Circe' chapter, what is still the unsurpassed literary representation of commodity fetishism. *Ulysses*'s particularity – its historical and, as we shall see, geographical 'limitedness' – is, therefore, the most stable pedestal on which to rest its 'universality': as the poet of the crisis of classical capitalism in its classical area of development, Joyce offers us a monumental autopsy of an entire social formation.

2. The Strange Death of Liberal England

In Britain, the crisis of the political, economical, and ideological structures of liberal capitalism had a very particular development and outcome. During the crucial decades, the dominant class proved both resistant to and incapable of enacting those basic transformations which, elsewhere, were to permit the move into a new phase of capitalist development, whose leading power was to emerge – emblematically – from the conflict between Germany and the United States.

Decade after decade, the British crisis dragged on with monotonous regularity: a full-fledged *decadence*, without sudden tensions or traumas (the example of 1929, when the international crash had relatively mild consequences for the British economy, is illustrative), but also without any innovative steps. An inkling of the forthcoming decline had already emerged during the depression of the last quarter of the nineteenth century, which, according to Hobsbawm, revealed 'that Britain was not ready for all but one of the possible methods of dealing with [the new] situation. Unlike other countries ... Britain held firmly to free trade. She was equally disinclined to take the path of systematic economic concentration – the formation of trusts, cartels, syndicates, and so on – which was so characteristic of Germany and the USA in the 1880s. She was too deeply committed to the technology and business organization of the first phase of industrialization, which had served her so well, to advance enthusiastically into the field of the new and revolutionary technology and industrial management which came to the fore in the 1890s. This left her with only one major way out ... imperialism. Britain had escaped from the Great Depression (1873–96) – the first international challenge – not by modernizing her economy, but by exploiting the remaining possibilities of her traditional situation."[8]

The secular stability of liberal practice and ideology and with the monopoly of the world market, the two great resources of nineteenth-century British capitalism, were now suffocating it. To continue to adhere to that model implied – as Hobsbawm rightly observes – what would prove an irretrievable delay in the new forms of capitalist organization which were both a logical consequence and a drastic denial of the free market. The delay was apparent in the absence of economic concentration and of convergence between industrial and financial capital,[9] which were so typical of German and American development at the turn of the century, and which formed the true theoretical core of Lenin's study on imperialism. Just as crucial was the absence of the instrument which proved decisive for capitalism's new course: the systematic use of the state to regulate, redefine, and, ultimately, to expand capitalist accumulation. Stuart Woolf, among others, has observed that 'The role of the state in the economic development of those nations which came to industrialization relatively late – in Germany and Belgium, as in Russia and Italy – was always more prominent than in England, the mother country of free-trade.'[10]

This further disjuncture – between state and society, politics and economy – was probably something more than a simple delay. It does not so much reflect the inability of the English dominant class to 'update' itself (which still holds true, however) as the inability to organize from within and assert itself to the outside world as just that: the dominant and hegemonic class of the period that saw the decline of liberal non-interference. Since the close of the era of great statesmen, the English ruling class has produced, over the last century, only mediocre bureaucratic administrators as its political representatives: and this in the face of ever more uncontrollable events. To this phenomenon Joyce dedicated one of the central chapters of *Ulysses*, 'The Wandering Rocks', which is a splendid miniature of the overall structure of the novel. It is impossible to restore organization and dynamism to the social fabric on the basis of the existing forms of power ('spiritual' and 'temporal' – ideological and political), but it is also unthinkable for Joyce to envisage reality except on the basis of these forms – by now lethargic and lifeless – of power and consciousness: a vicious circle which will return, at its highest level, in the use of 'myth'.

But let us now move on to another macroscopic parallel between the decline of English society and the social universe in *Ulysses*. In *Imperialism*, Lenin does not pass up the opportunity of flogging the 'putrefaction' of English capitalism and the growing diversion of resources from productive activity towards conspicuous consumption, recreation, sports, fox-hunting, and so on. This same 'mark of parasitism' – on a less genteel level, obviously enough – is one of *Ulysses*'s most evident social references: '[In *Ulysses*] we see people eating, drinking, making love, arguing; they go after money . . . and all this is felt as happening simultaneously. But there is no sign of the productive activity without which none of this could happen. . . . there is not a worker in the book. . . His selection of the social relations to be described is that of the consumer.'[11]

This is both precise and naive. Precise, because this is exactly the state of affairs in *Ulysses* (although a closer analysis shows that consumption can by now occur only at the level of mere survival – eating and drinking – and for the rest Joyce shows us the *unsatisfied* aspiration to consumption, especially in Bloom). Naive, since Joyce enlarges this aspect of reality and renders it 'absolute', not because he is unaware of or scorns the rest of the picture (as West's elementary realism would have it), but because of a deliberate cultural choice: seen in this light, *Ulysses* sets out to be a cynical portrait of how Victorian society will end if it follows its deepest inclinations. Joyce is so confident that the situation will take precisely that course, he feels so deeply involved in this parasitical decline, that he does not offer the British ruling class some sort of 'solution' – as Eliot will strive to do in his overzealous and speculative way – but only the hideous caricature of itself and its world. A few lines from Bloom's nocturnal reflections in 'Eumaeus' will suffice:

'Intellectual stimulation as such was, he felt, from time to time, a first rate tonic for the mind. Added to which was the coincidence of meeting, discussion, dance, row, old salt, of the here today and gone tomorrow type, night loafers, the whole galaxy of events, all went to make up a miniature cameo of the world we live in, especially as the lives of the submerged tenth, viz., coalminers, divers, scavengers, etc., were very much under the microscope lately.'[12]

Here Joyce gives voice to the petty-bourgeois philistine who sees himself and his occasional table-mates as a 'miniature of the world', and who nonchalantly liquidates all productive activities with the commonplaces of the dominant culture ('submerged tenth', 'under the microscope'), automatically ('viz.', 'etc.'), to the extent that he seems unaware of the very reality of the workers, whose existence he must 'deduce' with an uproarious literal interpretation of the metaphor of the 'submerged tenth': 'coalminers, divers, scavengers'!

It is true then: in *Ulysses*, social relationships appear only through the prism of consumption. Yet, this occurs because the novel's sole field of investigation, its starting point and its finishing point, is the dominant and spontaneous ideological consciousness of the first decades of the decline of English society. And what has been said about the accusation of paying too much attention to consumption also holds true for that 'Marxist' criticism which attacked *Ulysses* for the *stasis* and *mediocrity* of its world (even Lukács was to do so in *The Meaning of Contemporary Realism*: '*Ulysses* is static. It is more like Cheops than Magnitostroy', wrote Mirsky in 1933, and Radek, the following year asked, 'What is the basic feature in Joyce? His basic feature is the conviction that there is nothing big in life – no big events, no big people, no big ideas; and the writer can give a picture of life by just taking "any given hero on any given day" . . . '[13]

Ulysses is indeed static, and in its world nothing – absolutely nothing – is great. But this is not due to any technical or ideal shortcoming on Joyce's part, but rather to his subjection to English society: for Joyce, it is certainly the only society imaginable, although he just as certainly condemns it, through a hyperbolic presentation of its worst features, to a future of paralysed mediocrity (a future that Joyce, with a stroke of genius, places in the past, as if to underline his consummate scepticism: one can always hope never to reach the negative utopias of science fiction, but if a negative utopia came into being twenty years ago, and no one realized it, then the die is truly cast . . .). Joyce's writing is not 'revolutionary' in any reasonable sense of the word – and yet, no Marxist, novelist or otherwise, has ever been able to perceive the end of the liberal century with such intelligence or with such fury.

Before moving on to *Ulysses* once and for all, a brief explanation is in order. I have dealt – and shall continue to deal – with Joyce and *Ulysses* as expressions of English society and culture. Of course, it is a well-known fact that Joyce is Irish and that *Ulysses* takes place in Dublin. But if Joyce were an Irish *writer*, comprehensible and containable without any loose threads within Irish culture, he would no longer be Joyce; if the city of *Ulysses* were the real Dublin of the turn of the century, it would not be the literary image *par excellence* of the modern metropolis. Cultural phenomena cannot be explained in the light of their *genesis* (what ever has emerged from the studies that interpreted Joyce on the basis of Ireland?); what counts is their objective *function*. And there is no doubt that *Ulysses* fully belongs to a critical turning point of international bourgeois culture – a status it would not have achieved in the investigation of Ireland's peripheral and backward form of capitalism (which was, moreover, dependent on the destiny of British capitalism: yet another reason to move from the effect to the cause).

The hypothesis of this study, then, is that a 'structural homology' exists between the specific social nature of the British crisis and the specific literary structure of *Ulysses*: if they appear as mutually integrative of each other, the question of Ireland is no longer pertinent. Or, rather, it gives birth to a different problem: why is the most cogent and involved interpreter of the British crisis not English? We face here the vaster question of 'immigrant culture'. Virtually all the protagonists of twentieth-century British culture (the most notable exceptions being Keynes and Leavis), have been immigrants.[14] Just as British society has been unable to produce a ruling class worthy of the name, so it has been incapable of producing a hegemonic culture by itself. Only those who had not been moulded by its moribund value system could have any awareness of the crisis and of the possible ways out: only those who saw Britain from afar were truly capable of understanding it. And Joyce, an Irishman (this is the only legitimate domain of the 'genetic' approach) had every reason and every means to probe deeply in the entrails of British society. The ruthless acumen he shows in describing its degeneration originates here – as also does the impossibility of *opposing* anything whatever to that degeneration. Joyce's precocious scepticism concerning the political and cultural choices of the Irish national movements was to be reconfirmed by the search for sheltered environments (Trieste, Switzerland, the expatriate circles of Paris) at the edge of both storm and renewal. Joyce's ideological position is structurally ambiguous:

neither an 'apology' for nor a 'criticism' of classical capitalism, it is a position that desecrates it and at the same time 'has no other gods before it'; that raises it to universal heights, but in this way renders the condemnation universal. Here again is the image of the vicious circle.

3. *Ulysses*, Disorder, and Myth

From what has been said above, it should be clear that the root of the capitalist crisis lies in the inability of the market's economic mechanisms to assure society's organic functioning. This also produced the crisis of nineteenth-century ideology, both in its *contents* and in the awareness of its social *function*. In literature, this cultural crisis and the attempts to overcome it are manifest with singular clarity, because the concept of aesthetic 'form' is directly involved. If social reality proves incapable of attaining a rational and full form by itself (Asor Rosa: 'the real is no longer rational'), culture and art can no longer have the 'mirror image' as their formal ideal, since that choice would imply the loss of their internal coherence and their possible hegemonic function. On the contrary, art and culture must autonomously contribute to restoring a form to society: but they must, so to speak, count only on themselves, and work on the basis of their peculiar formal mechanisms. They will be able to accomplish their task only by postulating a radical autonomy, a formal self-determination that accentuates to the utmost the distance and the heterogeneity of their foundations, which attempt to be organic, from the non-organic reality of everyday social relationships.

The process by which art creates its form offers itself as an *example* to society at large, and hence claims the right to logical and historical anticipation of all transformation (hence, the common denominator of idealism of twentieth-century poetics). Eliot's discussion of the 'mythical method' in the well-known essay *'Ulysses*, Order, and Myth' (*The Dial*, 1923), is among the most explicit examples of this mode of reasoning: 'The novel, instead of being a form, was simply the expression of an age which had not sufficiently lost all form to feel the need of something stricter.' But things have changed: '[The mythical method] is simply a way of controlling, or ordering, of giving a shape and a significance to the immense panorama of futility and anarchy which is contemporary history.'

Control, order, giving shape and significance – concentration, intervention, redefinition of the social order and its functions: Eliot's quest (as becomes clearer and clearer) expresses in a metaphorical and, later, religious guise, the basic needs of a new phase of capitalist development. Cancelling out futility and anarchy means forcing the course of history in one direction only, and paving the way for a regulatable and controllable future. But it also means cancelling out *Ulysses*, willingly ignoring its monumental stasis and irregularity.[15] A discussion of the mythical method helps us to understand Eliot, not Joyce. Free at last from the interlinear Homer-Joyce homework, it is no longer possible to doubt that Joyce uses myth only to desecrate it, and through it to desecrate contemporary history: to parody Bloom with Ulysses, and Ulysses with Bloom; to create an order which gives greater relief to the absence of order, a nucleus gone haywire with irony and distortions. In Eliot, there is a clear distinction: on the one hand myth ('controlling, ordering, giving a shape and a significance'), on the other, history ('immense panorama of futility and anarchy'). Myth must mould history: it is the active agent of the pair, *form* to history's *content*.[16] In Joyce, myth and history are *complementary*: they presuppose and neutralize each other, and it is impossible to establish a formal or ideological hierarchy between the two. In Joyce, myth is not identified with the aesthetic *form* (as in Eliot), and therefore cannot be the starting point for a new *cultural hegemony*.

It is worth examining these two myths – *The Waste Land*'s and *Ulysses*'s – more closely. The first is truly a myth with all its anthropological requirements in order: it is the myth of the Fisher King.[17] But what *Ulysses* is based on is *not* a myth: There is no 'myth of Ulysses': Ulysses is precisely he who avoids myths: he triumphs over them and relegates them to the past. *The Dialectic of Enlightenment* – which is also, like *Ulysses*, a long reflection on the end of the liberal era – contains exemplary judgements on the symbolic and ideological function of the *Odyssey*: '*if it does not already presuppose a universality of language, the Homeric narrative effects one*... The venerable cosmos of the meaningful Homeric world is shown to be the achievement of regulative reason, *which destroys myth by virtue of the same rational order in which it reflects it* ... The myths have been transformed in the various layers of the Homer narrative. But the account given of them there, the unity wrested from the diffuse sagas, is also *a description of the retreat of the individual from the mythic powers* ... The opposition of enlightenment to myth is expressed in the opposition of the surviving individual ego to multifarious fate.... The prehistoric world is secularized as the space whose measure the self must take; and the old demons inhabit the distant bounds and islands of the civilized Mediterranean, *forced back into the forms of rock and cavern* ... *The behaviour of Odysseus the wanderer is reminiscent of that of the casual barterer*. In the pathetic image of the beggar, *feudal man retains the features of the oriental merchant, who returns with unheard-of riches* because for the first time, and contrary to tradition, he has stepped outside the milieu of a domestic economy, and 'embarked for other lands' ... *the Odyssey is already a Robinsonade.'* [18]

If, with Ulysses, trade emerged as a stimulus to knowing the world, giving it an internal order as well as external boundaries, creating a 'universal' language, and defeating superstition, by now, with Bloom, the *same* social function sails in an uncontrollable and unknowable world, reducing attempts at universality to flat banalities (Bloom's 'philosophy') and falling prey to thousands of new superstitions. It is worth remembering that Joyce insists on the fact that Bloom is an advertising agent. And advertising – as Baran and Sweezy observe in their 'Theses on Advertising' [19] – becomes an indispensable aid to modern trade precisely at the time of *Ulysses*, because of the definitive crisis of the automatic balance between supply and demand. But advertising (here again Joyce is blind to those contemporary phenomena which already disclose the mechanisms of the future) does not confer – unlike trade in the *Odyssey* – any unity on *Ulysses*, just as it assures the protagonist no social identity or self-awareness.

Joyce, therefore, uses Ulysses, indeed he *has* to use him, because Ulysses is the *first* symbolic figure of the cultural era of which Joyce is the ultimate offspring. But Ulysses no longer controls the surrounding world, and thus becomes Bloom. His symbolic value becomes dialectical and ambiguous: what saved Ulysses now condemns Bloom, what was universal no longer makes sense. Confronted with the crisis of liberal capitalism, Joyce looks for its causes in the very foundations of that society's and that culture's 'good working order'.

4. Myth, Stream of Consciousness, Advertising

While Ulysses had tamed the myths *because* he had established the rational order of trade and free individuality, Bloom is the product of the dissolution of that order and of that individuality, and there is nothing odd in his succumbing to myths once again. The question of myth returns to the centre of *Ulysses*, but in a completely different way from that in which Eliot posited it: not as a metahistoric image of a fable and several typical characters, but as a relationship between subjective intellectual consciousness and intuition of objective reality; not as a metaphoric pattern for the narration, but as its technique. In his study of the linguistic expression of myth Cassirer maintains that '[In mythic thought] the ego is spending all its energy on this single object, lives in it, *loses itself in it. . . .* For in this mode, thought does not dispose freely over the data of intuition, in order to relate and compare them to each other, but *is captivated and enthralled by the intuition which suddenly confronts it.*'[20]

What is striking, in this outline, is that it coincides in all essential points with Umberto Eco's analysis of stream of consciousness (especially, but not only, of Bloom's): 'Remaining within the conscious facts – all recorded with absolute fidelity as so many equivalents – *personal identity itself is questioned.* In the flow of overlapping perceptions during Bloom's walk through Dublin, the boundaries between "inside" and "outside", between how Bloom endures Dublin and how Dublin acts on him, become very indistinct.'[21] Stream of consciousness is, then, the linguistic expression of the loss of individual identity: the exact opposite of what it was in Dujardin who used it as an instrument of self-control and redemption of the character of the individual. Dujardin's true heir is Proust, not Joyce, who overturned him in the same way as Eliot did Laforgue. In *Ulysses*'s stream of consciousness the individual is split, and expresses himself as such. The illusion that he could be an autonomous and independent subject collapses. Far from being the expression of an 'interior freedom' (as Zeraffa would have it with his thesis of the 'revolution of the novel'), stream of consciousness indicates that the individual is enslaved by arcane and uncontrollable forces: stream of *un*consciousness would be a better definition, and though this technique does *not* coincide with the psychic domain that Freud defined as 'unconscious', it is clear that both enact the function of emphasizing a discontinuity within the individual psyche.[22]

Stream of consciousness and crisis of the ideology of the free individual meet under the ensign of advertising. This is the new 'myth' to which Bloom – advertising agent and victim of advertising – succumbs with increasing regularity. And this is so because advertising is the myth of the commodity – commodity transformed into myth, into a fetish that parades, instead of hiding, its 'arcane' features. While nineteenth-century advertising described the use-value of a product, hence reproducing the mental acts that any purchaser would spontaneously perform in the market, modern advertising, as we have seen, originates in the paradoxical and 'critical' situation of a perennial imbalance between supply and demand. But this paradox is none other than the patent manifestation of the alienated relationship between producers and products. 'Thanks to' advertising this relationship is no longer hidden and denied, but rather accepted – albeit, as we shall see, unconsciously – as something obvious and permanent. Advertising, therefore, is not so much the exhibition of 'a' commodity as of *commodity fetishism*: it boosts the product by making a fetish of it. It is no accident that one of advertising's favourite rhetorical figures is a metaphor in which – pathetic fallacy indeed – the product emerges as a 'force of nature'. The commodity must visibly take on independent, natural, and even human properties:

'We're a capital couple are Bloom and I;
He brightens the earth, I polish the sky.'

So sings Bloom's notorious soap, rising as the sun in the 'Circe' chapter.

To diffuse its essential content, advertising aims at a form of persuasion based on unawareness, rapid and deep because capable of circumventing all intellectual resistance. Advertising then becomes part of stream of consciousness to the point of dominating its mechanisms and organizing to its own advantage Cassirer's 'loss of self' and Eco's absence of boundaries between 'inside and outside'. If this attempt works, then it is true that 'advertising campaigns if sufficiently large, persistent and unscrupulous (availing themselves of such methods as subliminal suggestion and the like) can sell to the customer "almost anything".'[23] To be able to sell anything, that is, to spread out over the entire social universe; 'All kinds of places are good for ads' Bloom reflects, in a passage which is exemplary for the mulplying and centrifugal effect of an ad on his stream of consciousness.

But advertising is not just one of *Ulysses's* most original leitmotifs: in at least two cases, in 'Ithaca', Joyce himself relates it to the stream of consciousness technique:

'What were habitually his final meditations?
'Of some one sole unique advertisement to cause passers to stop in wonder, a poster novelty, with all extraneous accretions excluded, reduced to its simplest and most efficient terms not exceeding the span of casual vision and congruous with the velocity of modern life.'

. . .

'What also stimulated him in his cogitations?
'. . . the infinite possibilities hitherto unexploited of the modern art of advertisement if condensed in triliteral monoideal symbols, vertically of maximum visibility (divined), horizontally of maximum legibility (deciphered) and of magnetizing efficacy to arrest involuntary attention, to interest, to convince, to decide'.

'The span of casual vision', 'congruous with the velocity of modern life', 'magnetizing efficacy', 'to arrest involuntary attention, to interest, to convince, to decide'. Here we find precisely the randomness, rapidity, discontinuity, uncontrollability and depth of the stream of consciousness. And these passages demonstrate that the associations of stream of consciousness are by no means 'free'. They have a cause, a driving force, which is *outside* the individual consciousness: even syntactically, the subject of the last passage quoted is advertising: the individual psyche is only the necessary buttress of its effectiveness.

It is, therefore, completely logical that stream of consciousness is eminently paratatic: the absence of internal order and of hierarchies indicates its reproduction of a form of consciousness which is subjugated to the principle of the *equivalence of commodities*. It indicates that the use-values – the concrete qualities of any given commodity – are by now perceived as secondary (and indeed advertising never 'describes' the product, and its very ideal – 'to sell *anything*' – presupposes that every product can become an exchangeable and abstract entity). What is left to fire the imagination and inflame desire is only the overall attraction of this chaotic and unattainable collection of commodities: here lies, perhaps the reason for that continual 'shift and metamorphosis' of sense that Heath observes in *Ulysses*: no concrete and univocal meaning can be attributed to a world of abstract and interchangeable objects. Here again, Cassirer's analysis of mythical thought proves useful: 'If we see [the world] as a whole, this whole nevertheless consists of clearly distinguishable units, which do not melt into each other, but preserve their identity that sets them definitely apart from the identity of others. But for the mythmaking consciousness these separate elements are not thus separately given . . . For this reason the mythic state of mind has been called the "complex" state . . .'[24]

Thus far I have based my argument on Bloom's stream of consciousness. Yet, it works, with due precautions made, for Molly and Stephen as well. This is immediately clear with Molly because, in her stream of consciousness, we find ourselves before the full realization of the tendency towards parataxis and loss of identity, reproduced in the continual fluctuation between 'me' and 'I'. This can cause no surprise, given that in *Ulysses* Molly is unconditionally posited as the quintessential representative of consumerism. But the argument holds true for Stephen, too. It is essential, in this respect, that his early theory of epiphanies – the attempt to penetrate the underlying and unalterable meaning of things, people, situations – no longer works. 'Signatures of all things I am here to read': Stephen still holds to this idea at the beginning of the third chapter, 'Proteus'. But this 'signature' is no longer the sign of a univocal transcendent order, just as 'the soul' – consciousness – is no longer the 'form of forms'. If in Stephen's stream of consciousness in the first chapter images appear which could lead to an epiphanic moment, this moment does *not* arrive, and the images remain undeciphered. Even the doctrine of incarnation, at the end of the third chapter, succumbs to a grotesque sequence of metamorphoses ('God becomes man becomes fish becomes barnacle goose becomes featherbed mountain') that deprives it of all intrinsic or teleological meaning. Certainly, unlike Bloom's and, to a greater extent, unlike Molly's, Stephen's stream of consciousness is still the mirror of a *conflict* between the attempt to dominate the world rationally and the world's mute or equivocal substance. But the latter triumphs, just as, at the level of plot, *hazard* drives Stephen back and forth during the day and night. The only character who, throughout *Ulysses*, undergoes a transformation can do so only because he has remained artificially extraneous ('backward', so to speak) with regard to the dominant social conditions.

5. Bloom

The symbolic function of Ulysses and the narrative use of stream of consciousness are two of *Ulysses*'s cardinal points. Within this general framework I wish now to indicate a more tangible example of the sociological hypothesis of this study. If *Ulysses* expresses the cultural dialectics of liberal capitalism in agony, then it will necessarily linger upon the dissolution of the figure of the petty bourgeois – the free producer, economically independent and intellectually proud of his own autonomy – so relevant within the Anglo-Saxon ideological system in the eighteenth and nineteenth centuries.

Clearly, Bloom is the key. He is a socially ambiguous figure from the start, neither completely independent nor completely dependent. But he has already betrayed his father's religion – that

Hebraism which prefigured the bourgeois-puritan ethic – and with it the practical ideal of *innerweltliche Askesis*. His father – or, rather, the image of him produced by Bloom's sense of guilt – admonishes him in 'Circe' for both:

'RUDOLPH: Second halfcrown waste money today. I told you not go with drunken goy ever. So. You catch no money. [. . .] Are you not my son Leopold, the grandson of Leopold? Are you not my dear son Leopold who left the house of his father and left the gods of his fathers Abraham and Jacob? . . . One night they bring you home drunk after spend your good money.'

Bloom has no social future (yet another reason for compressing *Ulysses* into twenty-four hours), and this is why Joyce concedes him a genealogy, but no male descendent: Bloom's son manages to come into the world, but he does not quite manage to survive, just as Bloom's father, not wanting to abandon the heroic ethic of the free market, is thrashed by it and kills himself. Bloom's life is suspended between these two deaths: by now, he is an accident, a historical relic. And his is indeed an ethic of pure and simple survival: the balance between debit and credit, at the end of the day, is perfectly even. Savings – one of the first things he associates with the memory of his father: 'commercial advice (having taken care of pence, the pounds having taken care of themselves)', – this secular symbol of economic freedom, this guarantee of the future, has somehow become impossible and none of the characters in the novel can even aspire to saving any more, as one of the meanest characters in *Ulysses*, Mr Deasy, complains to Stephen in 'Nestor'. In Joyce's novel one truly lives day by day – and yet, tomorrow is not another day.

If Bloom feels the precariousness of his position, and his only raison d'être is to manage to preserve it, then the most frightening thing becomes the unusual, the different, the irregular. Thus Bloom to Stephen in 'Eumaeus':

'Mr Bloom, who at all events, was in complete possession of his faculties, never more so, in fact disgustingly sober, spoke a word of caution *re* the dangers ot nighttown, women of ill fame and swell mobsmen, which, barely permissible once in a while, though not as a habitual practice, was of the nature of a regular deathtrap for young fellows of his age.'

And in 'Nausicaa', the philistine eulogy of masturbation compared to coitus is unforgettable: one runs fewer risks when alone. And a short passage in 'Ithaca' raises the issue of risk again:

'His mood?
'He had not risked, he did not expect, he had not been disappointed, he was satisfied.
'What satisfied him?
'To have sustained no positive loss.

The relevance of these last lines goes beyond their immediate meaning. Here, in fact, Bloom is thinking of the horse Throwaway, the unexpected winner of the Gold Cup: this is a minute episode, which Joyce does not even describe directly, but extends throughout *Ulysses* as a perfect metaphor for what is at this point the illusory character of free competition. Throwaway, in fact, does what Bloom has always failed and always will fail to do: it suddenly passes, with a lash of the whip (or a stroke of genius, like the thoroughbred which convinces Ulrich, in *The Man Without Qualities*, to change his way of life?), from anonymity to fame, from precariousness to wealth. At this point, only horses can play the free market: no longer self-made men (as Bloom still deludes himself of becoming with his 'inventions' – in the age that saw the birth of industrial laboratories . . .) but only self-made horses. (Here, incidentally, is the secret of the resurrection of sport in the modern world [the first Olympics were held in 1896]: the extraordinary increase in *real* inequality, due to the concentration of economic and political power, makes a conspicuous *formal* reproposal – not accidentally, under the ensign of the most puritan dilettantism – of the sacred idol of 'competition among equals' all the more desirable.) Throwaway could certainly have been Bloom's lucky strike, the great surprise – but luck and surprise are by now true exceptions, and serve only to show how firm the rule is.

Clearly, Bloom is prey to this social rule without understanding it. His awareness is partial and distorted. The great corporations undermine his social identity, but Bloom can grasp this phenomenon only by thinking . . . of the Roman Catholic Church:

'Wonderful organization certainly, goes like clockwork. . . . Square-headed chaps those must be in Rome: they work the whole show. And don't they rake in the money too?

.   .   .

'Mass seems to be over. Could hear them all at it. Pray for us. And pray for us. And pray for us. Good idea the repetition. Same thing with ads. Buy from us. And buy from us.'

Bloom's consciousness, finally, epitomizes and exalts itself in the commonplace. A parody of the reasoning illuminist, Bloom is capable of coming up with commonplaces on any subject: from the concept of nation to relations between the sexes, from the appeal to generosity to social programmes, he believes – by remaining faithful to the letter of liberal orthodoxy – that he can understand and control a world with which he has permanently lost contact. In this light, as Della Volpe has written, *Ulysses* '. . . is a summation and judgement of our humanitarian bourgeois civilization in the sense that the justification of that civilization is reduced to the terms of its now *lifeless commonplaces*.'[25] Thus, Joyce's relentless satire is aimed at Bloom because, through him, it can aim higher. And, once more, Joyce's historical judgement is imprisoned between two terms that ridicule and yet implicate each other. Hence the peculiar nature of Joyce's irony, which has none of the 'detachment' indicated by his contemporary Thomas Mann as the price paid in order to understand, judge, and preach, but which, on the contrary, comes from the inside of a system of unresolvable contradictions.

6. Useless Wealth

So far we have seen how *Ulysses* presents some social phenomena typical of the crisis of liberal capitalism. What is perhaps the most important element remains to be seen: what effects does this crisis have on culture and on literature? What social function does Joyce assign to them and how does it emerge in *Ulysses*'s structure?

Joyce's answer is radical and defines itself on two distinct planes. The first and more elementary concerns the way the novel's characters use – or do not use – culture. Stephen is the most representative figure in this respect. He is the intellectual as intellectual worker: in him, culture and work are one and the same. Consequently, in Stephen culture undergoes the same destiny to which the capitalist crisis condemns every type of work: under-use, if not out and out waste. And, in fact, from the very first pages, Stephen refuses to communicate and to put his accumulated knowledge into circulation, not out of intellectual pride, but because he is obscurely convinced that the effort would have no outcome. That Stephen's culture is a culture of 'opposition' – anti-British and anti-Catholic – certainly contributes to his silence: yet, we must add that the most radical doubt about his own function assails Stephen on the completely calm and neutral territory of teaching ancient history to children. At school, in the second chapter, Stephen is forced to live on two planes intellectually: on the private one of his own reflections and on the socially acknowledged one of teaching. But between these two areas there is no relationship any more, so that Stephen's intellectual wealth hinders him in carrying out his job regularly. At the end of the chapter, with faultless logic, Stephen quits; in the following chapter, 'Proteus', that culture, already socially useless, also reveals itself to him as intrinsically fragile and precarious. Gradually, in the course of the novel, he relegates his knowledge further and further towards a limbo: when he uses it, it is merely to astonish (who could take his interpretation of *Hamlet* seriously?). In 'Eumaeus', he exasperatedly denies Bloom any access to it.

One might think that this occurs because Stephen's culture is obsolete and Thomist. But this explains only the definitive, mute dismissal that it encounters. What seems to me central – that knowledge has been laboriously 'accumulated' and then proves unusable – is valid also for Bloom, although in a different way because his social function is different. Stephen scandalizes him because 'after all the money expended on [his] education' he is unable to 'recoup [himself] and command [his] full price', Bloom reaches the point of racking his brains to find a way to use the young man's culture to his personal advantage, and then moves on to dreaming of profiting from his own infantile homemade know-how, or from his wife's canorous abilities, or a thousand different small follies. This is an important aspect of Bloom's 'intellectual physiognomy': his desperate managerial vocation, his effort to capitalize on every little thing in view of its potential economic usefulness.

As such, Bloom is the relentless parody of the 'spirit of capital-ism' of a Benjamin Franklin (all the more so – as has been seen – because when it comes down to it, even the most modest savings are impossible for him); just as his aspirations towards an omni-lateral culture are the parody of the *Encyclopédie*. Bloom's library, described at length in 'Ithaca', is a masterpiece of randomness and uselessness, and its key is furnished in 'The Wandering Rocks'. A scene closes with Lenehan's line to M'Coy:

'He's a cultured allroundman, Bloom is, he said seriously. He's not one of your common or garden ... you know. ... There's touch of the artist about old Bloom.'

The scene immediately following opens icily:

'Mr Bloom turned over idly pages of *The Awful Disclosure of Maria Monk*, then of Aristotle's *Masterpiece.* ... He laid both books aside and glanced at the third: *Tales of the Ghetto*, by Leopold von Sacher Masoch. ... Mr Bloom, alone, looked at the titles. *Fair Tyrants* by James Lovebirch. ... *Sweets of Sin*'.

Bloom's library, and his culture, are thus the library and culture of a second-hand bookstore: both show the same absence of order and hierarchies. The levelling logic of the culture market inte-grates with the stagnant passivity of the overall social mechanism. The accumulation of knowledge has become gigantic and has knocked down the barriers of time and space, but, finding no purpose, lies in disuse on the shelves and in the head of an adver-tising agent.

These last remarks bring us to that aspect of *Ulysses* in which the idea of culture's 'unproductivity' manifests itself both in the most specific and the most ostentatious ways. We enter, that is, the field of *Ulysses*'s aesthetic forms. The most peculiar aspect of Joyce's novel is that it uses a plurality of aesthetic forms that lie at opposite extremes. To notice the phenomenon is not difficult: to interpret it is another matter, especially since this feature of *Ulysses* has for a long time been the hunting grounds of a critical trend that is satisfied with recognizing and cataloging its stylistic procedures, and which, in so doing, becomes inebriated, and in its euphoria extols the novel's 'wealth', and reads and describes it as an unorthodox but magnificent summary of the history of literature and of rhetoric. It is as if that professor of professors, Ernst Robert Curtius, had not written with bitter awareness, in 1929: 'Joyce's work comes from the revolt of the spirit and leads to the destruction of the world. With an inexorable logic there appears in Joyce's Walpurgis-night, amid larvae and lemures, the vision of the end of the world. A metaphysical nihilism is the substance of Joyce's work.... This entire wealth of philosophical and theological knowledge, this power of psychological and aesthetic analysis, this culture of the mind educated in all the literatures of the world, this ratiocination which is so far above all positivistic platitudes – all this is finally nullified, refutes itself in a world of conflagration, in a sprinkling of metallically iridescent flames. What remains? Odour of ashes, horror of death, apostate melancholy, tortures of conscience...'[26]

Curtius is right. The mechanics and meaning of this 'destruction of the world' remain to be understood. For the great bourgeois culture of the beginning of the century, the destruction of the world is a corollary and consequence of the destruction of the world of culture – since only culture can posit itself as system, hierarchy, and order. In *Ulysses*, then, the world goes to pieces not because it is a text prolific in apocalyptic visions, but, rather, because in it every idea of cultural system goes awry. Stuart Gilbert, in *James Joyce's 'Ulysses'*, observes that 'All facts of any kind, mental or material, sublime or ludicrous, have an equivalence of value for the artist.' This principle of equivalence which establishes itself in Joyce's novel is irreducibly opposed to the hierarchical principles of the great bourgeois culture of his time.

By rendering any 'organic' pretension of the work of art vain, Joyce also declares the impossibility of 'deducing' from it an idea of a cultural system capable of restoring order to society.

Joyce dismantles the ideology of 'organic' art: but not in the ways suggested by Robert Musil when he writes that 'another characteristic of Joyce and the whole tendency is dissolution. He gives into the contemporary state of dissolution and reproduces it through a sort of "free association", whereas he supposedly practices a "heroic conception of art".'[27] According to Musil, *Ulysses*'s dissolution derives from art's 'surrender' to reality, from the collapse of a selective aesthetic order and its substitution by 'free association' (to which, in fact, it is not possible to reduce the style of *Ulysses*). Exactly the opposite is true. Dissolution is possible and effective only because of an extremely controlled formal involvement. But this formal involvement – here is the decisive innovation – now aims completely at showing that every style is arbitrary and therefore irrelevant.

The idea of an arbitrary literary style – that would dominate and determine its subject, and would not be simply its transparent and 'sensitive' representation – already belonged to the 'decadent' reaction to Hegelian aesthetics. Artistic and theoretical research, at the time of *Ulysses*, continued to centre on this problem. But in this tradition the concept of 'arbitrariness' is functional to the foundation of a new cultural *Koiné*: it is an attempt to reformulate at one and the same time the ideological consciousness of the elite and individual artistic techniques. Experimentalism strives towards the completion of cultural control. This is why Nietzsche attacks Wagner, and Eliot the Edwardian poets: not for giving in to the current taste *per se*, but in so far as this concession precludes a future hegemony. But an arbitrary convention, to be hegemonic, must put itself forward as the only possibility: Nietzsche's allegory, which finds in Kafka its sinister realization. To propose two or more conventions for the same 'object', on the contrary, is to invalidate them all and renounce all hegemonic pretentions. This is exactly what happens in *Ulysses*.

I have said that *Ulysses* is built upon a plurality of styles. This procedure has nothing to do with James's or Conrad's differential point of view, where the diversity of styles is *motivated* by the diverse psychology of their characters. In Joyce, when one episode is presented in two or three or fifty different styles, the procedure is not based on any codified literary motivation. It is pure technical exploration (and the 'everyday' quality of the subject also serves to intensify the metaliterary quality of the novel). The exploration, however, does not lead to a choice. The various styles – and the ideological forms they embody – are all perfectly equivalent: all equally arbitrary, all equally incapable of imposing themselves. All, therefore, are equally *irrelevant* as interpretations of reality or formalizations of literary language. While they detract meaning from each other, none becomes its privileged vehicle.[28] In *Ulysses*, there are no 'trustworthy' styles, capable of 'explaining' reality, and 'false' ones, intent on 'masking' it – just as there is no qualitative distinction between 'elite' and 'mass' culture: the 'titles' of 'Aeolus' are neither 'truer' nor 'more false' than the colloquial dialogue that surrounds them; Gerty's 'novelettish' style is neither truer nor more false than Bloom's philistine monologue or the narrator's impersonal style; the same holds good for the alternation of epic hyperbole and colloquial naturalism in 'The Cyclops', and above all for the plethora of styles used in 'Oxen of the Sun'.

Joyce's indifference to any criterion of functionality or truth in cultural forms brings him close to Dada. However, the Dadaist collage was limited to declaring the equivalence of ready-made, finished products. Joyce goes further: his extraordinary mimetism attempts to indicate that even compositional procedures – literary 'means of production' – are equivalent, interchangeable: lacking any definite social function, and not worthy of a future. *Ulysses* is a mad clearance-sale of literary styles; and it is no accident that Joyce does not found a school, and that those who use him as a model and imitate one of *Ulysses*'s many styles betray the fundamental intention of his novel: the systematic refusal to assume *one* style as the privileged vehicle of expression.

What has been said for style is also true of ideology in *Ulysses*. There is nothing *but* ideology in this novel: it is the universe of false consciousness. This is immediately clear if one recalls the clogged consciousness of its characters, who are incapable of understanding what is happening, or even their own actions, unless by producing grotesque reasons that the course of events destroys and resuscitates in different but equally sterile forms (one need only remember the thousands of problems Bloom faces, considers, and fails to solve during the course of the day). While Lukács's theory of the novel postulated a tension between the hero's 'spiritual world' and the 'second nature' of the outside world, Joyce levels this tension and reduces it to meaningless and aimless habits: ideology is no longer a tool – partial and perhaps ineffectual, but 'heroic' – to attempt to mould the world, but a fatuous routine that outlives its function.

Ulysses is an ideological universe though, mainly because of its treatment of style. In general, every stylistic choice 'translates' or preannounces an ideological choice within the literary sphere, thereby ramifying its social influence. And yet, as soon as a stylistic choice reaches its final literary objectification – as soon as 'it resolves itself completely into poetry' as Croce would have said – its ideological function, which has just been achieved, seems to vanish and the style puts itself forward as a purely literary operation, an 'intrinsic' necessity of artistic development. Such 'innocent' embodiment of ideology in literature is Eliot's great effort, from the theory of the 'objective correlative' to the writings on the politics of culture. Joyce, on the other hand, lets the mask drop. *Ulysses* denies literary exploration all 'objectivity' and all 'naturalness', because it presents all stylistic choices as partial, arbitrary, and subjective. In so doing, Joyce demonstrates the persistently ideological nature of all styles.

This does not, however, mean that *Ulysses* should be read as a *criticism* of ideologies, even less of ideology in the abstract, as the specific form of consciousness of capitalist alienation. In *Ulysses*, Joyce presents styles and ideologies as purely formal entities, products of an experiment lacking any motivation and purpose.[29] In other words, Joyce can give us a grand representation of ideological and literary phenomena because, at the same time, he implicitly declares these phenomena neither necessary nor functional to the society from which they issue. His criticism of ideologies is itself based on an ideology: the ideology of culture's social *superfluity*, which is a typical product of the common consciousness of classical capitalism, for which cultural 'superstructures' were, indeed, superfluous to the regular operation of society – Polanyi's self-regulating market, itself a mechanism typically independent of all cultural values and aims, took care of that.

The conviction of culture's superfluity is so deeply ingrained in Joyce that he considers the aesthetic sphere incapable of being either an example to, or a compensation for, the state of the world. Eco observed that the aim of *Ulysses* (and even more so, of *Finnegans Wake*) is to offer a linguistic duplication of the real: this is true, and is a declaration of total superfluity. Armed with this certainty, Joyce had only to reproduce, in the literary sphere, the same deranged mechanisms which governed society. And this is what he did with *Ulysses*: a novel both eminently 'literary' and eminently 'social', and which forces criticism to switch incessantly from semiology to sociology and vice versa.

I have often underlined the historical determination of Joyce's work. The idea that ideological and aesthetic phenomena are socially redundant and unproductive also belong to the past: the history of our century has demonstrated that the opposite is true. Yet this decidedly obsolete idea furnished Joyce with a cultural cynicism that made of him a prophet of the cynicism to follow. The mutual in-difference of cultural values and expressive techniques, the multiplication and equivalence of ideological fashions, the false freedom of choice: the substance of *Ulysses* is the substance of the contemporary cultural system. The dismantling of cultural hierarchies, Curtius's 'destruction of the world', is nothing other than the abolition of the fixed and hierarchical limits that held back the expansion of the 'cultural market' and towards which Joyce acted as true radical leveller. The integral coincidence of culture and society, of value choices and everyday life: this is the story of the fifties. But is it really so absurd to think that contemporary capitalism is also the parody of its liberal past?

From *The Waste Land*
to the Artificial Paradise

This essay has as its starting point several problems related to Eliot's *The Waste Land*, which appeared in its final form in 1922. *The Waste Land* belongs to that extraordinary concentration of literary masterpieces around the First World War. 'Extraordinary' because of its quantity, as even the roughest list shows (Joyce and Valery, Rilke and Kafka, Svevo and Proust, Hofmannsthal and Musil, Apollinaire, Mayakovsky), but even more than extraordinary because that abundance of works (as is by now clear, after more than half a century) constituted the last *literary season* of Western culture. Within a few years European literature gave its utmost and seemed on the verge of opening new and boundless horizons: instead, it died. A few isolated icebergs, and many imitators: but nothing comparable to the past.

Eliot's work – and *The Waste Land* in particular – takes on its fullest meaning precisely in the light of this exhaustion of literature's *raison d'être* and its historical function within Western culture. There is, in fact, no doubt that the poem of 1922 constitutes an exemplary and disquieting 'borderline' product: in it is the last echo of the *Bildungsroman* and of the tradition of the decadent lyric, the coldness of religious allegory and the instability of parody, the erudite historical quotation and the will to build a cultural microsystem based on mythic arrangement. There is, in effect, a bit of everything; and it is difficult to understand how all this can hold together.

There is, of course, a very simple, and thus very common, way of explaining such a state of affairs: one need only resort to the idea –

suggested in various places by Eliot himself[1] – of 'all-inclusive' and synthetic poetry. This is an evasion, however. For historico-literary analysis, this 'all-inclusiveness' (as we shall continue to call it for the time being) should indeed constitute a *problem*, requiring elucidation as regards its historical necessity and mode of operation. To transform it magically into the *solution* of the problem explains everything because it explains nothing. It leads one to believe that Eliot thereby laid the groundwork for a new 'era' in the development of literature; whereas, when sober, one realizes that exactly the opposite is true.

I shall attempt to develop a different line of reasoning here. The hypothesis is that *The Waste Land* and the mythic arrangement (the nature of which will be specified) that constitutes its skeleton,[2] are decidedly provisional, unstable, and approximate cultural products. The reason is that with *The Waste Land* Eliot attempted to solve in the literary domain problems that instead required the institution of new aesthetic and cultural systems. That is, Eliot tried to obtain with poetry results that would be attained only with *mass culture*, and which, obviously, in this new symbolic system, would also take on different connotations. Indeed, the third section of this essay endeavours to trace some of these developments and transformations. Although this is, formally, the end-point of the investigation, these pages are extremely hypothetical: they aim mainly to suggest that – in the case of several key works of the twentieth century – literary analysis can 'conclude' only outside its 'proper' domain. As, in fact, some of the functions traditionally absolved by literature pass over to other cultural activities, so literary criticism must 'tail' them and strive to fathom the meaning of this metamorphosis. I realize that one runs the risk – which I am not sure I have not incurred – of losing all methodological specificity and evaporating into a hazy 'omnology'. But with contemporary culture, slippery and protean as it is, this is a risk worth running.

1. Towards myth

'[The mythical method] is simply a way of controlling, of ordering, of giving a shape and a significance to the immense panorama of futility and anarchy which is contemporary history.'[3] This is one of Eliot's most famous critical statements, the theoretical formula which endeavours to indicate the common deep structure of *Ulysses* and *The Waste Land*. The first thing worth noticing is that Eliot believes the mythical method necessary – so much so that he attributes to it 'the importance of a scientific discovery', compares Joyce with Einstein and maintains that 'Mr. Joyce is pursuing a method which others must pursue after him' – because the modern world can no longer be represented in the form of the *novel*: 'If [*Ulysses*] is not a novel, that is simply because the novel is a form which will no longer serve. . .' This is a casual remark – almost a parenthesis: yet it is a crucial juncture which illuminates the ambition and cynicism with which Eliot, in the early twenties, looked upon the major trends of Western literature. Cynicism: the novel is liquidated once and for all with the icy observation that it 'will no longer serve'; in the following decades Eliot the critic – and few critics were as omnivorous and versatile as he – will devote to it an insignificant part of his meditations. And ambition: this is a man who reasons in terms of historical 'eras' and who, sensing that he is at the beginning of a new phase, has no qualms about abandoning the most exemplary form of two centuries of European civilization.

But why has the novel become 'useless'? '[I]t is because the novel', Eliot continues – 'instead of being a form, was simply the expression of an age which had not sufficiently lost all form to feel the need of something stricter.' Let us clarify. The novel has entered its final crisis ('The novel ended with Flaubert and with James,' concludes Eliot, three lines later) not for reasons inherent in *literary* evolution, but because the *era* that made it possible is undergoing a crisis and has been transformed into a 'panorama of futility and anarchy'. Eliot does not do much to help us understand the characteristics of this era which has now succumbed, yet the one thing he says is quite clear: *'which had not sufficiently lost all form'*, an era that was able to give itself a form – an order – without having to resort to literary products as models of organization. It is not accidental that the novel is defined as 'the expression of the age': the emanation of an order of another nature, not form strictly speaking, but the *manifestation* of an underlying form.

Here a possible frame of reference for Eliot's argument begins to emerge. His judgement on nineteenth-century civilization coincides on an essential point with the hypothesis that will find its classic formulation only twenty years later in Karl Polanyi's *Origins of Our Time*. The nineteenth century sees the realization of the idea that society can function in a rational and coherent way due to the existence of a *purely economic* mechanism, the 'self-regulating market': a mechanism, that is, which seeks strictly economic and quantitative finalities and is, therefore, free from any restriction issuing from *symbolic* and *cultural* values. Society in this theoretical model functions *independently of* the culture it is able to assume: consequently – and here we return to Eliot – the structuration of the cultural universe may remain relatively elastic, and give way to such scarcely formalized phenomena as the novel.

This is not the place to establish whether such a hypothesis is well founded or not. What is important here is to observe how, in the first decades of the century, a theoretical picture akin to Polanyi's in more or less explicit forms upholds the research of numerous European intellectuals. To return to the years of *The Waste Land*, the analogy between some of Eliot's premises and the investigation carried out a few years earlier by Lukác's in *The Theory of the Novel* cannot pass unobserved. Like Eliot, Lukács maintains that the novel has an extremely uncertain formal status: drama 'can . . ., *in its formal a priori nature*, find a world that is perhaps problematic but which still is all-embracing and closed within itself. But this is impossible for the great epic.' Yet, is it meaningful to speak of a 'form' if not 'a priori' – 'free' with respect to the material on which it exercises its ordering faculties? Lukács seems to think not; and in fact he continues: 'For the epic, *the world at any given moment is an ultimate principle*; it is *empirical* at its deepest, most decisive, all-determining transcendental base . . . it can *never, while remaining epic, transcend* the breadth and depth, the rounded, sensual, richly ordered nature of *life as historically given*. . . . The epic and the novel, these two major forms of great epic literature, differ from one another not by their authors' fundamental intentions *but by the given historico-philosophical realities* with which the authors were confronted.'[4]

Such passages abound in Lukác's text. And although *The Theory of the Novel* is an extremely contradictory piece of writing, and pervaded by a desperate, formative stoicism ('We have invented the productivity of the spirit . . . We have invented the creation of forms. . .', there is no doubt that Lukác's believes that the curse of 'the necessarily inseparable relationship with concrete historic contingency' has been cast on the novelist's formal attempt: and this inevitably frustrates all effective realization. Lukács and Eliot meet therefore on at least one essential point: the form of the novel depends on, and declines with, the form of the 'epoch'. When, in the last pages of *The Theory of the Novel* Dostoevsky is indicated as the possible herald of a 'new world', Lukács is compelled by the logic of his reasoning to affirm exactly that 'Dostoevsky did not write novels': an assertion that one must evidently take lightly as far as Dostoevsky is concerned, but which is highly symptomatic of Lukác's aspirations. If one wants to enter into a new epoch it is necessary to abandon the novel. The problem now is to understand what literary form will take its place, with what means, and to what ends.

Let us now pick up the statement of 1923 again: '[The mythical method] is simply a way of controlling, or ordering, of giving a shape and a significance to the immense panorama of futility and anarchy which is contemporary history'. Here, finally, is the 'a priori form': on the one hand, a non-organic and meaningless world – on the other, a method that 'controls', 'orders', assigns 'a shape and significance'. The relationship between epoch and culture that had characterized the age of the novel has been overturned: here the epoch is completely formless, and culture is *only* form, abstract ordering ability.

Eliot, however, does not limit himself – as do Worringer and Hulme – to underlining the *abstract* character of aesthetic form: 'a way of controlling, or ordering, of giving shape and a significance . . .' The last term is, perhaps, the keyword of Eliot's poetic project. It is important that the word is *significance* and not *meaning*. Significance is a bivalent word that contains the idea of meaning, but links and subordinates it to that of 'importance', 'relevance', and 'value'.

This short circuit between 'meaning' and 'value' places Eliot's research right in the middle of one of the most exciting conceptual tangles tackled by European culture at the turn of the century. We shall start from 1892 when the logician Gottlob Frege published an essay which was destined to fame: 'Über Sinn und Bedeutung'. Frege intended to assert a double distinction: the first, which was to be followed up in linguistics, between referent (*Bedeutung*: the object to which the sign 'refers') and sense (*Sinn*: the 'mode of presentation' of the object); thus 'the reference of "evening star" would be the same as that of "morning star", but not the sense.'[5]

Although Frege's name is usually associated only with this first distinction, his argument does not stop here:

'The reference and sense of a sign are to be distinguished from the associated idea. If the reference of a sign is an object perceivable by the senses, my idea of it is an internal image, arising from memories of sense impressions which I have had and acts, both internal and external, which I have performed. Such an idea is often saturated with feeling; the clarity of its separate parts varies and oscillates. The same sense is not always connected, even in the same man, with the same idea. The idea is subjective: one man's idea is not that of another. There result, as a matter of course, a variety of differences in the ideas associated with the same sense. A painter, a horseman, and a zoologist will probably connect different ideas with the name 'Bucephalus'. This constitutes an essential distinction between the idea and the sign's sense, which may be the common property of many and therefore is not a part of a mode of the individual mind. For one can hardly deny that mankind has a common store of thoughts which is transmitted from one generation to another.

In the light of this, one need have no scruples in speaking simply of *the* sense, whereas in the case of an idea one must, strictly speaking, add to whom it belongs and to what time. It might perhaps be said: Just as one man connects this idea, and another that idea, with the same word, so also one man can associate this sense and another that sense. But there still remains a difference in the mode of connection. They are not prevented from grasping the same sense; but they cannot have the same idea. *Si duo idem faciunt, non est idem.*[6]

These sentences posit the essential terms of the problem. Not only does all natural coincidence between sense and referent, that is between language and reality, disappear, but the linguistic–cultural universe itself splits between the relative stability and certainty of meanings and the absolute randomness of what Frege calls 'ideas' – what Max Weber, following a similar line of reasoning in a different sphere a few years later, is to call 'values'. The situation outlined can be confronted in two perfectly symmetrical ways. On the one hand, meaning and idea-value may appear *too close together and confused*, so making the field of meaning – which aspires to scientific certainty – difficult to distinguish from that of values – which have completely different principles and aims. On the other hand, between sense – which for Frege is fundamentally intersubjective – and value – which instead embraces the most profound individual motivations – the relationship is no longer *sufficiently tight and univocal*, and can no longer assure any cultural cohesion and continuity: whether on the social or on the individual plane: 'The same sense is not always connected, even in the same man, with the same idea.'

Max Weber approached the first side of the question. It is necessary to recognize that the subjectivity of values guides all intellectual activity and cannot be eliminated: it is therefore inevitable that our ideals enter 'in the struggle with other ideals which are just as sacred to others as ours are to us'.[7] But if this is true, culture's duty consists in recognizing that 'there is and always will be . . . an unbridgeable distinction [between] . . . those arguments which appeal to our capacity to become enthusiastic about and our feeling for concrete practical aims or cultural forms and values . . . and . . . those arguments which appeal to our capacity and need for *analytically ordering* empirical reality in a manner which lays claim to *validity* as an empirical truth.'[8]

As is well known, Weber's research, while recognizing that all socio-historical analysis is motivated by our 'interests' or 'values', delves into the second site of the problem, and define those criteria which can guarantee scientific arguments *'validity* as empirical truth'.[9] Weber aims, that is, to specify the *separation* between the field of meaning and that of values. But just two years before his essay, Hugo von Hofmannsthal had explored the other side of the problem. 'The Letter of Lord Chandos' follows Frege's reasoning point by point, but in a melancholic tone called forth by lost unity:

'My case, in short, is this: I have lost completely the ability to think or speak of anything coherently.

At first I grew by degrees incapable of discussing a loftier or more general subject in terms of which everyone, fluently and without hesitation, is wont to avail himself. I experienced an inexplicable distaste for so much as uttering the words *spirit*, *soul*, or *body*. . . . the abstract terms of which the tongue must avail itself as a matter of course in order to voice a judgement – these terms crumbled in my mouth like mouldy fungi. . . .

It filled me with an inexplicable anger which I could conceal only with effort, to hear such things as: This affair has turned out well or ill for this or that person; Sheriff N. is a bad person, Parson T. a good man; Farmer M. is to be pitied, his sons are wasters; another is to be envied because his daughters are thrifty; one family is rising in the world, another is on the downward path. All this seemed as indemonstrable, as mendacious and hollow as could be. My mind compelled me to view all things occurring in such conversations from an uncanny closeness. . . . I no longer succeeded in comprehending [human beings and their actions] with the simplifying eye of habit. For me everything disintegrated into parts; no longer would anything let itself be encompassed by one idea. Single words floated round me; they congealed into eyes which stared at me and into which I was forced to stare back – whirlpools which gave me vertigo and, reeling incessantly, led into the void.

I tried to rescue myself from this plight by seeking refuge in the spiritual world of the Ancients. . . . Through the harmony of their clearly defined and orderly ideas I hoped to regain my health. But I was unable to find my way to them. These ideas, I understood them well: I saw their wonderful interplay rise before me like magnificent fountains upon which played golden balls. I could hover around them and watch how they played, one with the other; but they were concerned only with each other, and the most profound, most personal quality of my thinking remained excluded from this magic circle. In their company I was overcome by a terrible sense of loneliness; I felt like someone locked in a garden surrounded by eyeless statues.'[10]

Here are the phases of Chandos's annihilation: first language loses all spontaneity for the user; then one becomes aware of its 'mendacious and hollow' nature compared with reality; finally, and this is the decisive step, the conceptual coherence, while considered valid in its sphere and with respect to its aims, by now appears unable to be one with 'the most profound, most personal quality of my thinking'. It can no longer *produce values*: promote an attitude towards the world, *within* the world. This situation will return ten years later, in the first of *The Duino Elegies*:

> True, it is strange to live no longer on earth,
> and to practice no longer customs scarcely acquired;
> roses, and other expressly promising things,
> not to give them the meaning of human future;
> what in endlessly anxious hands one used to be,
> to be this no more, and even one's own name
> to lay aside, like a toy that is broken.
> Strange, not to go on with one's wishes. Strange
> to see all relations go loosely
> fluttering in space. And it is tiresome to be dead. . .[11]

Whereas for Weber the problem consisted in keeping the omnivorous and all-pervasive nature of 'values' under control, for Hofmannsthal and Rilke exactly the opposite is true. It is not the omnipotence of man's symbolic activity which dismays them but its *absence*: 'Look, the trees *exist*; and the houses/we live in – still stand. But we pass them by/like an exchange of breath.' (*The Duino Elegies*, II, lines 39–41). The concepts intertwine 'their wonderful interplay' but this no longer helps Chandos *give a significance* to the world. This is the matrix of the extraordinary 'restraint' of the Austrian literary world at the turn of the century:[12] the reserve of one who has understood how futile it is to project the reassuring shadow of one's own desires on to the world. This world may well have a meaning, but not meaning *for us*: that correspondence between values and reality is irreparably lost. 'One feels inclined to say,' Freud observes in *Civilization and its Discontents*, 'that the intention that man should be "happy" is not included in the plan of "Creation".'[13]

It is against the background of these radical acknowledgements of the 'disenchantment' of the human world that Eliot's attempt assumes its full meaning. Eliot wants his reader to feel 'at home' once more: to fill the gap between meaning and values, values and reality. This is the aim of the theory of the 'objective correlative', another of the strongholds of his thought: 'The only way of expressing emotion in the form of art is by finding an ";objective correlative"; in other words, a set of objects, a situation, a chain of events which shall be the formula of that *particular* emotion; such that when the external facts, which must terminate in sensory experiences, are given, the *emotion is immediately evoked*.'[14]

Here, although stated in Eliot's incorrigibly elusive critical language, the intention is clear: the artistic form is the means that reconnects expression and emotion, social objective meaning and subjective value. It is not accidental that most of Eliot's early poetry represents the attempt – for the time being, unsuccessful – to enact that connection. 'It is impossible to say just what I mean'; 'And I must borrow every changing shape/To find expression'; 'After such knowledge, what forgiveness?'.[15] These lines are clues to a permanent stalemate – until 1922, Eliot still uses the typically lyric function of 'the individual voice'. Even if this voice – from Prufrock to the anonymous narrator of the 'Portrait' and 'Gerontion' – becomes gradually disembodied and loses individuality, it still continues, from the point of view of grammar and culture, to be an 'I': only one of the *many* subjects who can use language. It is an element, that is, which still has a partial and casual relationship with the universes of meaning and value, and which therefore cannot aspire to become the vehicle of that connection which is *valid for all* and which Eliot – in his essay on *Hamlet* as in the one on *Ulysses* – means to institute between these two fields. To attain this aim he had to reach *The Waste Land*, and that mythic scaffolding which is at its base.

The Waste Land has often been defined as an 'all-inclusive work': almost as if it were capable of containing every kind of heterogenous material, of talking about everything in existence without any longer making distinctions between 'styles' or levels. It seems quite clear to me that this is a naive apology: but if one manages to translate it into more rigorous critical terms, it contains, as we shall see, a nucleus of truth. *The Waste Land* transmits the sensation of being 'all-inclusive' not because it contains 'everything', but because all its elements possess, besides their more or less 'ordinary' meaning – on the basis of which we can only consider them heterogenous and lacking in reciprocal relationships – a second figurative meaning which derives from the poem's deep semantic structure, where, on the contrary, they are consequently perfectly *homogenous* and *connected.* In other words: in *The Waste Land* there is a code that allows for the *assimilation* of elements taken from different codes: the 'all-inclusiveness' that appears on the poem's surface is the consequence of this deep formal procedure: and this, in turn, functions substantially as a *mythic system*: 'The semantic function of myth consists essentially in the link which it sets up between the different levels, in the multiple parallelisms which it institutes between the various spheres of human experience. . . It seems worthwhile to specify the semantic peculiarity of myth in its ability to attest that between different orders (for example, the cosmic order, the cultural, zoological, meteorological, social. . .) there is a precise isomorphism. . . Each myth . . . must be considered as a veritable *intercode* destined to permit a reciprocal convertibility between the different levels.'[16]

This, then, is the first manifestation of the famous 'mythical method': in *The Waste Land* a veritable *system* of semantic analogies is created, which is completely different from the metaphors (in some ways perhaps even more 'audacious') of the first poems, which were purely *occasional*, and, therefore, incapable of imposing a unitary meaning on the different components of the text. But this is not all. Exactly because capable of instituting regular connections between different levels of human experience, the mythic system also resolves the problematic relationship between expression and emotion, meanings and values, description and evaluation: 'the symbols of the *savage mind* enact a connection between two distinct planes: that is, that of the images of natural beings and their sensitive qualities on one hand, and that, on the other, of the meanings which each symbolic code attributes to the diverse elements of the natural world . . . This particularity also produces that sort of ideological equivocation which plays a central role in mythic thought. . . It is easy to be led to believe, in the case of myth, that meanings are *by nature* inherent in things, and that they are therefore independent from all will and all interference of man.'[17]

In a summarizing formula of Lévi-Strauss's: 'Savage thought does not distinguish the moment of observation and that of interpretation . . .'.[18] And here the first part of the argument may be considered closed. The use of the mythic system allows Eliot to develop a poetic programme aimed at healing the split between factual judgements and value-judgements, to establish in its place a form of communication and perception in which the two instances are indistinguishable. This also permits the solution of the basic problem of Lukác's *Theory of the Novel*: how to reconstruct an image of the world as a 'concrete totality' in which full 'immanence of meaning' is given anew: in which, that is, the individual no longer perceives a discrepancy between the world 'as it is', empirically given, and his own 'ideals'. The two planes, in fact, are now correlated *ab origine*: the ideals are already ingrained in the structure of the world as it presents itself to perception, since the literary text prescribes an interpretive route in which 'objective comprehension' is at one with ideal consensus – the 'subjective satisfaction' of the reader.[19]

By going one step backwards, myth ensures that culture is no longer a mere superstructure in relation to the symbolic 'neutrality' – and therefore potential disorder – of historical existence: rather, it presents itself as that value-system which pervades and ascribes 'significance', and hence humanizes all manifestations of that existence. Indeed, we shall see that the relationship between history and values, time and myth, constitutes the corner stone of *The Waste Land*.

2. On Madame Sosostris's table

One of the first things that strikes one when reading *The Waste Land* is its enormous freight of literary reference. Whether such references are actual quotations, graphically presented as such (the italics or the notes which indicate lines taken from other works, and are not usually attributed to any one of the poem's 'voices'); or verbatim but now assimilated to a different context from the original (like the line from *The Tempest* pronounced by Madame Sosostris or Ophelia's farewell which concludes the second section of the poem); or 'modified' and implicit, patiently dug up after decades of critical work (as in the case of the first thirty lines of the second section, one thing is certain: without this literary scaffolding *The Waste Land* would be absolutely unthinkable.

Criticism has interpreted Eliot's recourse to the fragment extracted from literary tradition in a great variety of ways. As far as I know, however, no one has ever noticed in it one of the most typical – or, rather, obligatory – procedures of the famous mythical method. The first chapter of *The Savage Mind* is in this respect illuminating; and the analogy between mythic construction and *bricolage* can reasonably be extended to *The Waste Land*. Like the *bricoleur*, Eliot extracts certain elements (generally sentences or lines) from organized wholes of various nature, and chooses precisely those elements which are capable of performing a new function, more or less distanced from the original, in the new structure, *The Waste Land*. 'Mythical thought, that "bricoleur", builds up structures by fitting together events, or rather the remains of events. . . fossilized evidence of the history of an individual or a society.'[20] Here Lévi-Strauss uses a term – 'remains' – that critics of Eliot have used assiduously and with like vagueness. Perhaps the analysis in *The Savage Mind* can help clarify its meaning: developing Lévi-Strauss's train of thought, one comes to realize that the 'fragment' used by mythic discourse (and *The Waste Land*) is a two-sided entity. One may call it a 'fragment' – and thereby underline its incompleteness and the difficulty of deciphering it – if one looks towards its original context: in this case, what leaps to the eye is the *loss* of meaning, the amputation undergone by the element in question. If, however, one looks at its *new* context, one encounters a completely different state of affairs. The 'fragment' has become a *function*: what is striking is no longer that it is dislocated and mangled , but that it possesses a precise meaning and role, and that it contributes effectively towards the composition of a new organized whole.

The Waste Land's construction materials, therefore, reveal themselves in a double and complementary light: as 'fragments' and 'incomplete meanings' when judged with reference to literary tradition; as 'functions' and 'adequate signifiers' when attention is shifted to the poem, or to myth. *The Waste Land*'s construction therefore involves the reader in two simultaneous evaluations: on one hand, it makes history seem an accumulation of debris, a centrifugal and unintelligible process; on the other, it presents mythic structure as a point of suspension and reorganization of this endless fugue. Sense of history and faith in myth appear as inversely proportioned criteria for evaluation: the more senseless and directionless the past seems, the more will the eternal present of the myth be able to absorb every signifying capacity within itself. '. . . [I]t is always earlier ends', observes Lévi-Strauss, 'which are called upon to play the part of means: the signified changes into the signifying. . .'[21] In a word: if the Western world – unlike the 'savage mind' – has developed a culture of history, to Eliot's eyes this retains value only in so far as it can be disintegrated, and its remains used to build a myth.[22]

This is a radical devaluation of history, and Eliot's conservative tendencies do not tell the whole story. *The Waste Land*'s true aim is not the idealization of any particular past epoch in order to disparage the present or any of its features. Something else is at stake: it is a question of overturning the very way in which Western civilization has considered the historical process. History must no longer be seen as irreversible as regards the past, and mainly unpredictable as regards the future, but as a cyclical mechanism, which is, therefore, fundamentally static: it lacks a truly temporal dimension. This 'timeless' history then will have a very different meaning from that usually attributed to it. It will not be the territory where various values originate, confront each other, and disappear in an incessant struggle whose outcome is impossible to predict. It will no longer be the patent manifestation of how partial, provisional, and conflictual every culture is. It will be, on the contrary, the place where a single and immutable structure of values, with negligible variants, establishes itself. And it will also be 'objective', in the same way as the mythic structure is: in this structure, every possible human action possesses its own a priori and single meaning, universally recognized and accepted as such.

To 'stop' history is, therefore, only the first step, the necessary means towards the realization of a much more ambitious project: to reinstate a single, unified, and, so to speak, definitive culture.

'There is thus a sort of fundamental antipathy between history and systems of classification. This perhaps explains what one is tempted to call the 'totemic void', for within the bounds of the great civilizations of Europe and Asia there is a remarkable absence of anything that might have reference to totemism, even in the form of remains. The reason is surely that the latter have elected to explain themselves by history and that this undertaking is incompatible with that classifying things and beings (natural and social) by means of finite groups. All societies are in history and change. But societies react to this common condition in very different ways. Some accept it, with good or bad grace, and its consequences (for themselves and other societies) assume immense proportions through their attention to it. Others (which we call primitive for this reason) want to deny it and try, with a dexterity we underestimate, to make the states of their development they consider 'prior' as permanent as possible.'[23]

In post-war London, T. S. Eliot sets out precisely to subvert this aspect of Western civilization. If, turned towards the past, myth disarranges the course of history to the point of making it unrecognizable, when turned towards the future it is the ideal instrument for preselecting historical events, and therefore ridding them of all unpredictability. In no way is Eliot subject to the fascination of the 'appeal of the new': it is here, incidentally, that his distance from the avant-gardes – about which he always maintained absolute silence – can be fully measured. The 'new' can be accepted only if inserted in a symbolic framework that assigns it a position and a meaning a priori, thus neutralizing its novelty in the strong sense.

Eliot was certainly not the only one to take this path. The image of history – of the past, as of the future – implicit in *The Waste Land*'s deep structure had, several years previously, already found its pharaonic realization precisely in a historiographical work: Oswald Spengler's *Decline of the West*. '[R]eal historical vision. . .', writes Spengler, 'belongs to the domain of significances [the English translator uses the same bivalent term as Eliot in his review of *Ulysses*], in which the crucial words are not "correct" and "erroneous", but "deep" and "shallow". . . . Nature is to be handled scientifically, History poetically.'[24] And the configurations of values return – unchanged and unchangeable – in every historical epoch: the great ambition of *The Decline of the West* consists in 'show[ing] that without exception all great creations and forms in religion, art, politics, social life, economy and science appear, fulfil themselves and die down *contemporaneously* ['I designate as contemporary two historical facts in exactly the same – relative – positions in their respective Cultures, and therefore possess exactly equivalent importance.'] in all the Cultures; that the inner structure of one corresponds strictly with that all of the others . . .'.[25]

The most interesting aspect of this line of reasoning is that the principle of causality – that is, the very base of all historiography with any scientific ambition – disappears without a trace. In the outline drawn by Spengler and Eliot, in fact, no event will ever be able to constitute a 'problem' that must be resolved by specifying its causes, for the good reason that all events are already foreknown, all effects prescribed. It is an enchanted world: nothing happens there. It was precisely this immobility that bestowed such fascination on these images of 'history'. 'And this', Lucien Febvre has remarked, 'is what gave Spengler success. It is not the success of a historian who analyses and deduces, but of a prophet, a magician, a visionary. . . The average reader was flattered in his individual self-love and in his current self-love. A Prussian or Saxon petty bourgeois, he certainly did not possess a Faustian soul; but he longed for it and imagined he had it . . .'.[26]

Thus, Spengler and Eliot offer their reader the opportunity of participating in the monumental and petrified return of the centuries. One feels once more immersed in an atmosphere pervaded by destiny: all freedom has been lost, no doubt, but existence has regained a symbolic and meaningful aura that seemed irretrievably lost. Thirst for destiny is the starting point of what is perhaps *The Waste Land*'s most famous passage, Madame Sosostris's fortune-telling (lines 43–59). On the fortune-teller's table, the ideal of a cyclical history takes on an exemplary form. Characters, situations,

developments find themselves existing in a configuration dominated by *simultaneity*: one card under another, or next to another.
This disposition recalls the way of ordering mythic materials
elaborated by Lévi-Strauss to explain the temporal paradox inherent in myth, 'both reversible and non-reversible, synchronic and
diachronic'.[27] The paradox can be unraveled only by 'translating'
the temporal flow into spatial terms, that is, into that dimension
which *knows no temporality*. 'Time, my son, here becomes space':
perhaps it is not accidental that this line is to be found in Wagner's
Parsifal which, forty years before *The Waste Land*, also centres on
the myth of the Grail.

Madame Sosostris's table is the centre of *The Waste Land*. Like
the thousands of civilizations of cyclical philosophies of history
or the finite and isomorphic series of mythic thought, the constel-
lations of the Zodiac and the symbols of the tarot cards manifest
themselves with unchangeable regularity, within an order both
majestic and familiar. Adorno has observed: 'Inasmuch as the
social system is the "fate" of most individuals independent of their
will and interest, it is projected upon the stars in order thus to
obtain a higher degree of dignity and justification in which the
individuals hope to participate themselves.'[28] To *reconsecrate*, as
far as possible, everyday experience: this is the common pursuit of
all the forms of thought so far examined. The fact that, in *The
Waste Land*, this aspiration is revealed through a charlatan's
empty words must not mislead: in spite of the surface irony, as
Cléanth Brooks has observed with great precision: '. . . all the
central symbols of the poem head up here. . . and the "fortune-
telling", which is taken ironically by a twentieth-century audience,
becomes *true* as the poem develops . . .'.[29] When all is said, in *The
Waste Land* superstition comes true.

The Madame Sosostris passage throws light on another of *The
Waste Land*'s crucial motifs: the treatment given to the literary
'character' or, more precisely, the dissolution of this convention
within Eliot's poem. The modern 'character' – which is, substantially, the character of the novel – becomes possible when the
attributes that define him, the values of which he is the more or
less conscious bearer, gradually *change* as the narration proceeds.

He demands, that is, a structure in which the syntagmatic axis – the temporal dimension – is not limited to revealing the paradigmatic oppositions from which it started, but contributes to modifying them and producing new ones. Once the original fixity of the *picaro* is broken, the novel's hero finds himself right in the middle of the process: if Nestor always remains the wise Nestor, a Wilhelm Meister will let others 'educate' him to values greatly different from the ones he started from, and, with due modifications, a Rastignac will follow an analogous trajectory.

The character of the novel, in other words, emerges as such to the degree in which he frees himself of the limitations inherent in the 'roles' – social before literary – that characterize all forms of status society. The 'role' pinpoints a number of restricted, homogenous, and unchangeable functions: the 'character', on the contrary, develops as a heterogenous and changeable entity. In accordance with the overall structure of *The Waste Land*, Eliot brusquely turns around on this point as well. That all the characters of the poem are already 'contained' in the deck of tarot cards (as, to dispel any doubt, Eliot himself points out in the note to line 46) means, quite simply, that their attributes and their possible relationships have been prescribed and established once and for all. The cards, in effect, are nothing more than a symbolic representation of certain socio-cultural roles that are considered particularly significant: and *The Waste Land*'s characters exist only to reincarnate these roles and confirm their validity. They are not so much characters as *exempla*: mere manifestations of a pre-established order. It is not an accident that – unlike Prufock, the narrator in the 'Portrait', Gerontion – in *The Waste Land*, no one any longer reflects about himself: when the meaning of existence has already been ingrained in the individual's objective position, the subjective dimension of doubt or curiosity simply become superfluous – with no regrets.[30]

Eliot's radical *anti-individualism* emerges here.[31] Even the Quest, the solitary course *par excellence* of the search for the Grail, can come to a conclusion only if its subject disappears: in the last two sections of *The Waste Land* not only is it no longer possible to recognize any 'character', but the first person pronoun itself hardly ever occurs.[32] Therefore, just as the 'mythical method' helped diminish the role of individual interpretation, substituting for it the 'immediate' perception of the universal 'objective' correlatives, so *within* the poem itself, it eliminates the individualizing convention of the literary character by flattening it on to the impersonal symbol of the tarot card.

It is the 'sacrifice' of individuality that is necessary to establish the post-liberal world: the sacrifice which opens *Le Sacre du Printemps* and closes *The Trial*. *The Waste Land*'s sacrifice is bloodless, but nonetheless drastic and effective. Eliot, having prefigured it at the beginning of the first section of the Madame Sosostris passage (the *contemporary* seer), reiterates it, with a grand sense of symmetry, towards the end of the third section, in the Tiresias episode (the *ancient* seer) and in the note that accompanies it: 'Tiresias, although a mere spectator and not indeed a "character", is yet the most important personage[33] in the poem, uniting all the rest. Just as the one-eyed merchant, seller of currants, melts into the Phoenician Sailor, and the latter is not wholly distinct from Ferdinand Prince of Naples, so all the women are one woman, and the two sexes meet in Tiresias. What Tiresias *sees*, in fact, is the substance of the poem.'

These words faithfully mirror the process in train in *The Waste Land*, the lessening of all *principium individuationis*: 'The primordial fear of losing one's own name is realized.'[34], and the individual sinks into a 'totality' from which he will never extricate himself. This is a tendency that will be confirmed in Eliot's other works, from the 'Suffer me not to be separated' which closes *Ash Wednesday*, to St. John of the Cross's maxim placed as epigraph to *Sweeny Agonistes*, to the terribly orthodox. 'In my beginning is my end' and 'In my end is my beginning', which open and close 'East Coker'. It need only be added that this highly mythic reabsorption by a binding totality is, for Eliot, the only historical process worthy of being upheld. Here one can gauge his proximity to more vociferous totalitarian philosophies, which is confirmed by the fact that, from the middle twenties, Eliot gave his best as an *ideologue*: not as a poet, even less as a dramatist, nor even as a critic, but in those writings dealing with cultural systems that are by definition totalizing: the religion of *After Strange Gods* and *Idea of a Christian Society*, and the even more all-pervasive 'culture' of *Notes Towards a Definition of Culture*.

It must be added, however, that Eliot remained at the edges of the totalitarian wave; and while his solemn Jesuitical caution, strengthed by his conversion to Anglo-Catholicism, must have played some role, the more cogent reason for this reserve seems to reside elsewhere. The fact is that *The Waste Land* – in spite of the icy simplicity of its framework – contained several 'flaws', so to speak, which hindered Eliot's myth from transforming itself, like others, into a confident and compact instrument of death. It is to such flaws in Eliot's work that we must now turn.

3. 'Signs are taken for wonders'

So far we have seen what motivated the renewed interest in mythic thought, and the traits that *The Waste Land* shares with myth as an archaic cultural structure. It is, however, inconceivable that myth be reborn with all its original purity: such a Second Coming in the twentieth century would be simply absurd. Thus, we must now turn to that compromise – that mutual adjustment which took place between the demands of the mythic structure and the diversified cultural situation, assymetrical and founded on heterogenous aims, typical of our century.

First of all, it must be observed that – compared to myth in the narrow sense – *The Waste Land* is articulated in an irremediably approximate way. Lévi-Strauss has shown that any minor transformation of mythic structure is buttressed by an iron logic; in *The Waste Land*, this is not the case. While the literary citations, the 'characters', the historical parallels, the metaphors which appear on the poem's surface structure can, indeed, be traced back to a system of homologies similar to that on which mythic thought was based, they can no longer *be deduced* from it. The various levels or codes of mythic thought consisted of a *finite* and *limited* number of elements which correspond exactly to the other elements in other codes. Only *those* elements could be used, and this permitted – or, rather, *compelled* – all narration to follow an extremely rigorous combinatory logic. Between this situation and the present, however, several millennia of development and cultural diversification have intervened – quickening decisively from the seventeenth century on. Entire codes have disappeared, completely new ones have arisen, and, above all, each code has substantially followed its own path, transforming and multiplying its elements and no longer caring whether a rigid parallelism between the different cultural spheres continues to exist: that is, no longer caring whether that system of systems distinguished by an absolute isomorphism – myth – continues to exist.

Therefore, when Eliot embarked upon his project of revivifying the fascination of mythic thought, his undertaking could only emerge as some sort of compromise between the demands of the mythic *structure* and its constituent *materials*. *The Waste Land*'s irony – what little there is – consists precisely in recognizing that the purity of the mythic project can never be fully realized. Only to a certain extent do things tally in *The Waste Land*: all connections are questionable, all homologies transmute into analogies. The function of that particular line from Baudelaire or Dante could easily be carried out by *another*, similar, line; the woman in the pub and the typist could be replaced by many other characters (as Eliot himself admits in a note); the Punic Wars or Elizabeth's London are historical *exempla* that can be metamorphosed with relative liberty.

I am not pointing out a 'flaw' in *The Waste Land*. The poem might appear imperfect to the anthropologist attempting to treat it as myth in a narrow sense, or to the literary critic who sees the North Star in the *mot juste* and in the unsurpassable precision of every single image. But, viewed from a different perspective, the poem's approximations prefigure the secret of our everyday mythology: a mythology no longer based on taboo, on the forbidden, but on the *permitted*.[35] The primitive world was a universe of prohibitions: myth had to exclude or realign everything that did not fit into a specific cultural arrangement, and for precisely this reason it had to resort to an inflexible logic. The Western twentieth century is, on the other hand, the paradise of liberties, and its mythology is based on the premiss that *everything* may be admitted, connected, and absorbed: the rhetoric of duty is supplanted by that of 'right'.

Dada (and to a lesser extent, Surrealism) forged further ahead on this path than Eliot: one need only recall how it 'solved', so to speak, the problem of metaphor, that most 'mythic' of rhetorical figures, since its task consists in establishing ever new connections between different semantic spheres. If Baroque poetry – the first literary movement that had to deal with the tumultuous, non-organic multiplication of ever more independent cultural codes – spread the conviction that the more 'surprising' a metaphor, the more 'poetical' it was (so that its value increases with the distance that cultural conventions place between the two related terms), with Dada this tendency undergoes a *qualitative* change. Any Dadaist poem or manifesto shows that what is being proposed is no longer the validity – that is, the intersubjective 'meaning' – of a *specific* connection, but the sneering affirmation that *any* connection can be accepted, and therefore, none is more valid than any other.

For Dada everything is possible indeed: *The Waste Land*, which follows it by a few years, tends to restore balance. Eliot belongs more to the Baroque than to the avant-garde: he always attempts to 'naturalize' even the most audacious and 'free' associations, by linking them to semantic fields, however wide and hazy. Dada's radicalism dissolves – it becomes, if you will, more banal and takes on what the Formalists would have called 'motivations'. But history proved Eliot the classicist right and Tzara the anarchist wrong. The mythology that surrounds us does not originate from the *levelling out* of all intersubjective meaning, but, rather, from its unending metamorphosis into thousands of different and equally unsatisfactory forms. In this universe, where everything seems possible, it is *imprecision* that reigns, not arbitrary will.[36]

Hence, the importance of *redundancy* both in *The Waste Land* and, later, in mass culture. If the connection between the image and its deep meaning has become hopelessly elusive and uncertain, the only way to convey the desired meaning consists in continuously circling round it and taking for granted that the attempt will never work permanently: it is no longer a question of finding the 'right' word, but simply a better one. And this also explains – to return to a point dealt with in the first section of this essay – that the 'feeling at home' granted by modern myth will necessarily be different, not only from what happened in primitive myth, but also from the model elaborated in one of the great 'synthetic' moments of bourgeois civilization, in Goethe's *Bildungsroman*. At the end of *Wilhelm Meister's Years of Apprenticeship* everything – episodes, characters, values – finds an unambiguous arrangement within an organic totality. Wilhelm Meister's *Bildung* – and, through him, the reader's – consists precisely in *recognizing* this state of affairs; in feeling integrated and finally finding one's peace there: '. . . I have attained a happiness which I don't deserve and *which I would not like to exchange for anything in the world.*'

But this is no longer possible for Eliot's reader. In *The Waste Land*, there is no process through which the mythic totality develops, finally to reveal itself. It always remains the same: evident and obscure; omnipresent and at the same time difficult to perceive; fundamentally poor – like Barthes's 'concept' of the modern myth – and at the same time sumptuously, but parasitically, rich: it takes hold of one image after another, but it can never fully dominate them, because it always connects them through an inevitably narrow minimum common denominator.

Eliot's reader, like the city-driver or the television-watcher, is in a truly strange position. Everything seen, read, or heard makes sense only in so far as it is connected to some underlying 'totality': but the effect, the fascination of the message, consists precisely in the fact that its code can never be traced with certainty nor its totality uncovered; rather, it is preserved in a hazy and undefinable state. Contrary to the hypotheses advanced in *Dialectic of Enlightenment*, mass culture does *not* 'mockingly satisf[y] the concept of a unified culture . . . ',[37] because it no longer possesses that full and warm transparency which constitutes the basis of every organic system. Mass culture does not find its rhetorical dimension in Goethe's 'symbol', or substitute for it the 'allegory' as studied by Benjamin and De Man. The oppositions traditionally associated with symbol and allegory (natural/artificial, synchronic/diachronic, organic/fragmentary, reassuring/ironic, and so on) in the case of mass culture lose all explanatory power: a hint, and not the least important, of its historically unheard-of character.

A rhetoric of mass culture (which would inevitably modify the existing classification) will perhaps permit decisive progress in this field. Meantime, the most intelligent attempt to interpret this terribly elusive aspect of the contemporary world is Roland Barthes's brief discussion of the 'structure of the news item': '*The event is fully experienced as a sign whose content is however uncertain. . .*

The [news item's] role is probably that of preserving within contemporary society the ambiguity of the rational and irrational, the comprehensible and unfathomable; and this ambiguity is historically necessary as man still needs signs (which reassure him), but also signs which are uncertain in content (which make him irresponsible) . . .'.[38]

This is a twilight condition of consciousness: neither high noon nor tender night. And precisely for this reason our relationship with mass culture is in itself interminable. There can be no conclusion or certainty, where the very structure of communication has founded the reign of perplexity, of dissociation, of procrastination. 'The consumer's relation with the real world, with politics, history, and culture is not one of interest, investment, or engaged responsibility – nor is it any longer one of complete indifference – rather, it is one of curiosity . . . One must try *everything*: in fact man in consumer society is tormented by the fear of "missing" something, any enjoyment whatsoever . . . It is no longer desire or even taste or specific inclination that is in play, it is a generalized curiosity motivated by a widespread anxiety'[39] – the all-pervasive anxiety of Riesman's radar-man, always ready to pick up signals from the outside world and, especially, always uncertain as regards their decipherment. This is no longer the 'anxiety' described in *Beyond the Pleasure Principle*, which was motivated by the fear of trauma, that is, by the conviction that the outside world is fundamentally hostile to the individual. It is no longer the state of mind of one who lives in the constant expectation of *danger*: it is the anxiety of always feeling on the verge of – but only on the verge of – finally grasping the object of desire, the meaning of life, the rules of the game. Instead, one has only changed position on the boundless chessboard of the modern world – and must, therefore, repeat this same act incessantly.[40]

How was all this possible? The question is not so much 'what image of the world does mass culture convey?', but rather, 'what kind of world is this that lets itself be pervaded by such a value system?' Before we try to answer, a new element must be brought into the picture.

At a certain point in his essay 'Über Sinn und Bedeutung', Frege wonders whether it is possible 'that a sentence as a whole has only a sense, but no reference'. The answer is yes:

'The sentence "Odysseus was set ashore at Ithaca while sound asleep" obviously has a sense. But since it is doubtful whether the name "Odysseus", occuring therein, has reference, it is also doubtful whether the whole sentence has one. . . . The thought remains the same whether "Odysseus" has reference or not. The fact that we concern ourselves at all about the reference of a part of the sentence indicates that we generally recognize and expect a reference for the sentence itself. The thought loses value for us as soon as we recognize that the reference of one of its parts is missing . . . But now why do we want every proper name to have not only a sense, but also a reference? Why is the thought not enough for us? Because, and to the extent that, we are concerned with its truth value. This is not always the case. In hearing an epic poem, for instance . . . we are interested only in the sense of the sentences and the images and feelings thereby aroused. The question of truth would cause us to abandon aesthetic delight for an attitude of scientific investigation. Hence it is a matter of no concern to us whether the name "Odysseus", for instance, has reference, so long as we accept the poem as a work of art.'[41]

Here Frege describes that very particular semantic situation which distinguishes literature and makes it a form of communication *beyond true and false*. This is a relatively modern way of judging literary and artistic manifestations: it appears in the *Critique of Judgement*, and was probably motivated by the necessity of 'justifying' aesthetic activity on the basis of principles no longer strictly cognitive: if such were the case, the development of empirical sciences in the seventeenth and eighteenth centuries would, ultimately, condemn art to a limbo of 'imperfect knowledge' – inferior and second-rate.[42]

Art emancipates itself from knowledge and ethics, then, and through this process becomes the only field in which – as Freud observes in the third section of *Totem and Taboo* – the principle of the 'omnipotence of thought', which had gradually been banished from other sectors of human culture, still remained effective. I believe that one of the most startling traits of our century consists in a radical inversion of this process. An ever-growing number of cultural activities has loosened or dissolved all referential ties to the advantage of an essentially aesthetic dimension, concerned only with the double plane of cultural meanings and values. To find instances of this change is anything but difficult. Political life offers perhaps the most blatent examples, and if this is even too evident in the case of the totalitarian ideologies of the first half of the century, by now it is clear that the same logic – although less virulent in tone – dominates in our time as well. Some of the most interesting parts of *One Dimensional Man* are dedicated to the self-contradictory character of post-war political rhetoric and conclude with the apparently paradoxical affirmation that '[t]o a mind not yet sufficiently conditioned, much of the public speaking and printing appears utterly surrealistic.'[43] Following a completely different line of reasoning, Roman Jakobson arrives at the same conclusion when, in a famous essay, he shows how the success – the *political* success – of the 'I like Ike' slogan can be explained only on the basis of its 'poetic' appeal.

Thus, the 'rational' and 'experimental' aspirations that presided over the birth of the bourgeois public sphere disappear, just as they disappear from what was its principal instrument, the newspaper. There is a truly mythical paradox at the root of modern journalism: the 'fact', the news item, which every single day manages to produce in one way or another, can be accepted within the newspaper only if inserted into a system of expectations which not only must not be corroded by it, but must, if possible, be reinforced and strengthened. The true aim of the daily newspaper does not consist in following history step by step in its unpredictability, but in slyly sauntering along in order to show that nothing that happens requires that our ideas truly change. Far from being enslaved to the 'cult of fact', the newspaper transforms every event into the support of a value system. It is not, nor can it be, interested in a news item's 'truth value', but only in its symbolic effectiveness.

We thus come to the last classical example of the loss of the referent: advertising. Advertising – as the Latin etym of the word (*publicitas*) indicates – makes objects 'public', but in such a way that their truly 'social' qualities no longer have anything to do with the objects themselves, but only with the meanings and the values we associate with their possession. Advertising is never, therefore, advertisement of an *object*, but of the symbolic contents of which the object has become – like the fact in relation to opinion in journalism – the mere vehicle. 'Rather than going towards the world through the mediation of the image, the image turns back upon itself through the world', Baudrillard writes. And he adds, 'The truth is that advertising (and the same holds true for the other mass-media) doesn't trick us: *it is beyond true and false*.'[44]

Beyond true and false: mass culture's most typical products lead us back to the proposition that founded, in its time, the autonomy of art, but with the decisive difference that while literature's non-referential character was evident and recognized as such, thus limiting the pretensions and the range of action of this particular use of language – mass culture, instead, spreads this semantic artifice *over the entire range of cultural activities* – except for science and technology – thus transforming self-referentiality from the borderline case it used to be into the *normal* praxis of communication.

In the twentieth century, therefore, a formidable *aestheticizing of culture* has taken place. And it is perhaps precisely for this reason, as was remarked at the start of this essay, that at the beginning of the century what is probably the most exemplary artistic form of bourgeois civilization – written literature – has passed into an unarrestable decline: what at one time had been its *specific* function has now moved and transformed itself into a constellation of cultural practices, rendering the existence of an activity exclusively dedicated to this end almost superfluous.

This explains Eliot's recourse to myth and also its failure, the abandonment of the experiment after a few hundred lines. If one wants to keep literature alive in a situation in which it is gradually losing all specificity, it will be necessary to try to make it, precisely, 'mythic': to endow it with an intercultural function, posit it as the instance capable of harmonizing and reconnecting the different symbolic spheres.[45] But if the mythic attempt succeeds – and in *The Waste Land*, even with the variations we have seen, it succeeds – we have a product that is no longer 'literature', but precisely 'myth'. On one point, Eliot was indeed mistaken: the mythical system is not a 'method', but a classificatory whole aiming at completeness and self-sufficiency, and which cannot recognize the existence of *other* symbolic systems beyond itself for the very good reason that it represents the system of all systems. This is to say that a mythical system cannot be subordinated to aims other than *its own*: it cannot be used as a means to reach *other* aims. Myth can never be a 'method' for writing poems. To have used it as foundation for *The Waste Land* makes this poem a milestone in our century's culture: but it places it already *outside literature*. More exactly: *The Waste Land* is a cultural milestone precisely because it is no longer literature.

It is now possible to connect the problems dealt with in the last two sections. Mass culture's perennially uncertain and interminable semantics integrates with its fundamentally mytho-aesthetic character. The loss of all referential aim and the progressive assimilation of heterogenous codes allow and foster an approximate and nebulous perception, which, in turn, encourages the development of a code that becomes ever poorer and, to use Eliot's word, 'autotelic'. Mass culture therefore shows how art's destiny in bourgeois civilization was to be very different from that envisaged by Schiller: '*Utility* is the great idol of the age, to which all powers must do service and all talents swear allegiance. In these clumsy scales the spiritual service of Art has no weight. . . The very spirit of philosophical inquiry seizes one province after another from the imagination, and the frontiers of Art are contracted as the boundaries of science are enlarged.'[46] It is all too evident that things took a completely different course: the proliferation of gadgets has made it almost impossible to establish what is 'useful' and what is not, even in the field of everyday objects, let alone in the case of symbolic practices; and as to the relationship between science and art, there is no doubt that scientific progress, far from restricting art's field of action, has, rather, allowed its disproportionate expansion.

This is no apocalyptic situation: quite the contrary. It is clear that an elusive and contemplative mythology is far preferable to that much more compact, sparkling, and effusive myth which, in the thirties, spread itself across the plains of Europe. Contemporary mythology's elective residence is civil society – the sphere, as Baudrillard has written, of consumption and 'everyday life'. Thus it aims at drastically limiting the pretensions of the state with its ethico-political imperatives – as demonstrated by the fact that Western societies have become virtually incapable of performing that most exemplary of acts of state, 'duty' *par excellence*: winning a war. For good or for evil, this is the state of affairs: the spreading of the mytho-aesthetic dimension has made our culture *inoffensive* as perhaps it had never been before.[47]

Of course, 'inoffensive' does not mean 'useless'. But here is a usefulness with a different function from that usually attributed to culture. To paraphrase an old proverb backwards, in our civilization, culture is not used to orient our lives – for good or for evil: rather, we live in order to consume culture. And this consumption is no longer useful to assure a 'consensus' centring on the values capable of directing the individual's behaviour in those fields which we consider fundamental – political life and, especially, work – but rather to empty those fields of all symbolic value: to reduce them to mere *means* lacking all intrinsic value. The frantic vogue-driven curiosity which dominates within the system of mass culture is symmetrical and complementary to the bored and slightly obtuse indifference nourished with regard to work and politics. In the first pages of *La Société de consommation*, Baudrillard observes with precision and irony that the contemporary Western world – which has built an imposing symbolic network around the consumption of commodities – looks at the *production* of the latter in the same way as the Melanesian tribe that, to explain the origin of objects, invented the Cargo Myth. That is, production is to a great extent considered a sort of miracle whose fruits are to be enjoyed – for as long as they exist – without asking too many questions.

This is a disquieting state of affairs, and may seem the exact opposite of the hopes and aspirations of the pioneers of bourgeois society. Yet a more careful examination shows that, on a crucial point, the contemporary situation is rooted precisely in the original intertwining of Protestantism and capitalism. 'In fact, the *summum bonum* of this ethic', writes Weber, 'the earning of more and more money, combined with the strict avoidance of all spontaneous enjoyment of life, is above all completely devoid of any eudaemonistic, not to say hedonistic, admixture. It is thought of so purely as an end in itself, that from the point of view of the happiness of, or utility to, the single individual, it appears entirely transcendental and absolutely irrational.'[48] Transcendental and irrational: these two adjectives reveal the meaning of the *Beruf* analysed by Weber. Work, in its capitalist form, would be irrational if it had to furnish *terrestrial* happiness to man: if, that is, its meaning consisted in the realization of specific cultural values *within the world*. But it is rational – implacably so – if the place in which it acquires meaning is not this world *but the next*, then the orderly lining up of figures – the Puritan doesn't produce objects, but abstract quantities – in the double-entry account becomes a magic mirror where everyone's destiny and *certitudo salutis* is inscribed.[49] God had become inscrutable and hostile, and work abstract and therefore potentially unlimited: and their conjunction produced extraordinary and upsetting consequences, especially after the Reverend John Wesley, at the dawning of the industrial revolution, took it upon himself to spread the new principles among those whose lives – for many decades – were to consist *only* of work. Work thus became the essential nucleus of human existence, but only to the extent that it transferred all its meaning, all its symbolic value, from this life to the next. Thus the warmth emanating from the language of numbers was like the light from the moon: it could suffice, it could exist, only as long as the invisible other-worldly sun reflected itself on it. But the sun also dies, and one day the West, which had long since forgotten hell, no longer believed in heaven. At the same time, millions of people decided that twelve or fourteen hours work per day were really too many. Reduced to an ever smaller *part* of human life, and no longer animated by obscure hopes of salvation, bourgeois work appeared then, for the first time, in its true, and truly modest, light. The extraordinary fascination of Marx and Freud's work is due to the fact that both – although in very different and, to some extent, irreconcilable, ways – attempted to invest work with a rigorously *terrestrial* meaning: in this light, the theory of the conscious and collective reappropriation of work and the theory of sublimation are the two final, proud *illusions* Western culture has produced about itself.

Matters took a different course indeed. The twentieth century has not produced a new culture of work *within* work: it has widened the gap between work and culture. In the West, no one any longer believes that work – like politics, about which much the same could be said – can *give a significance* to the world. Those values for which everyone considers life worth living are by now sought *elsewhere*: work and politics are tolerated – and no more than tolerated – only in so far as they permit entrance into this elsewhere which has lost all relationship to them.

I believe this situation has no precedents in history. It is difficult to say how long a society that nourishes this opinion of itself can survive, and even more difficult to hypothesize what ever it might become. And although I realize that the poetry of Thomas Stearns Eliot must appear, at this point, terribly remote, one must admit that we are doing our best to ensure that the last two lines of *The Hollow Men* – themselves now a banalized property of mass culture – will in the end prove prophetic: 'This is the way the world ends/Not with a bang but a whimper.'

Notes

The Soul and the Harpy

1. Kenneth Burke, *A Rhetoric of Motives*, New York 1950, p. 23.
2. Giulio Preti, *Retorica e logica*, Turin 1968, pp. 157 and 163–4.
3. Antoine Arnaud and Pierre Nicole, *La logique ou l'art de penser*, 1662–83, third part, chapter 20.
4. Preti, pp. 150–1. On the epideictic genre precursor of 'literature' see also Heinrich Lausberg, *Elemente der literarischen Rhetorik*, Munich 1949, paragraphs 14–16: 'The discourse of re-use is a speech held in typical situations (solemn, celebratory) . . . Every society of a certain strength and intensity has three discourses of re-use, which are social instruments for the conscious maintenance of a full and continuous social order . . . speeches established in order to evoke, repeatably, socially important acts of collective consciousness. These texts correspond to what, in societies with a freer social order, presents itself as "literature" and "poetry".' On the steadily strengthening connection between rhetoric and literature see also Vasile Florescu, *La retorica nel suo sviluppo storico*, Bologna 1971.
5. Arnaud and Nicole, first part, chapter 14. See also Michel Le Guern, *Sémantique de la métaphore et de la métonymie*, Paris 1973, p. 75: 'Metaphor . . . is one of the most effective ways of conveying an emotion. Nearly all metaphors express a value judgement because the associated image they introduce arouses an affective reaction . . . The most common function of metaphor is to express a sentiment which it wants one to share: it is here that its most important motive is to be sought.'
6. Max Black, *Models and Metaphors*, Ithaca 1962, pp. 39–40.
7. Chaim Perelman and Lucie Olbrechts-Tyteca, *La nouvelle rhétorique. Traité de l'argumentation*, Paris 1958, p. 543.
8. Lausberg, paragraph 2.
9. Jacques Le Goff, 'Les mentalités: une histoire ambiguë', in Jacques Le Goff and Pierre Nora, eds., *Faire de l'histoire*, Paris 1974, pp.
10. See above all the essays 'Semantik der kühnen Metapher', *Deutsche Vierteljahrsschrift für Literaturwissenschaft und Geistesgeschichte*, no. 3, 1963, and 'Semantik der Metapher', *Folia Linguistica*, no. 1, 1967.
11. 'Der Begriff des Kunstwollens', *Zeitschrift für Ästhetik und allgemeine Kunstwissenschaft*, XIV (1920), 4, p. 339. The italics are mine.
12. Panofsky in fact talks here about a 'conflict . . . between a forming power

and a material to be overcome', a formula which does not seem to allude to a contrast between different *forms* but to the more usual dialectic of form and content. Elsewhere, however, he makes it clear that the form-content opposition has no historical relevance whatsoever: 'the pair of concepts "form-content" does not designate in the least, as do the other two ["objectivistic-subjectivistic" and "realistic-idealistic"], an opposition between two principles of figuration which can define a stylistic difference between diverse phenomena, but rather the limits of two spheres which are [logically] distinguished within one and the same artistic phenomenon' ('Über das Verhältnis der Kunstgeschichte zur Kunsttheorie', *Zeitschrift für Ästhetik und allgemeine Kunstwissenschaft*, XVIII, 1925, note 19).

13. Georg Lukács, *Il dramma moderno* (originally published in Hungarian in 1911), Milan 1967, pp. 8, 9, 11.

14. Georg Lukács, *Osservazioni sulla teoria della storia letteraria* (originally published in Hungarian in 1910) in *Sulla povertà di spirito. Scritti 1907–1918*, Bologna 1981, pp. 59, 69–71.

15. Ibid., pp. 87, 90–

16. Not for nothing do Lukács's first doubts about the solidity of the connection between aesthetic form and historical existence arise, as early as the *Observations*, in the course of a discussion of the 'wearing out' of a style. This phenomenon indicates the 'fundamentally conservative nature of the public' and the 'impoverishment' of formal energies, and Lukács intends to eliminate it from his analysis for precisely these reasons.

17. Jean Starobinski, *1789. Les emblèmes de la raison*, Paris 1973, p. 5.

18. See on this the splendid first chapter of Peter Szondi, *Einführing in die literarische Hermeneutik*, Frankfurt 1975.

19. Basically one will have to ask what relation obtains between classifications founded upon 'literary genres' and those referring to 'style-period' concepts. One will need to establish whether expressions such as 'naturalist novel' or 'neoclassical sonnet' are conceptual hybrids which ought to be done away with or valid hermeneutic tools, and – if they are the latter – what respective weight the adjective and the noun carry; and so forth.

20. Raymond Williams – in *Marxism and Literature* and in the interviews collected in *Politics and Letters* – has put forward a hypothesis whose *pars destruens* is similar to this. However, if I have understood his intentions correctly, Williams's main aim is to break down the barriers between 'creative' communication (what for the last two centuries has been termed 'literature') and communication which is 'non-creative' or not considered creative. Although he does not deny the possibility of proceeding to a new theoretical partitioning at a subsequent stage, he seems to be far more concerned with rejecting the old boundaries and setting up a continuum of texts to be subsumed under the general concept of 'culture'. If this is the case, then the project outlined here could be seen as a possible 'second phase' of Williams's programme: the phase in which the boundaries are re-established, but this time paying no heed to the previous hierarchizing concepts.

21. Kant, *Critique of Judgement*, Oxford 1952, pp. 14–5.

22. Luciano Anceschi, 'Considerazioni sulla "Prima Introduzione" alla *Critica del Giudizio* di Kant', introductory essay to Kant, *Prima Introduzione*, Bari-Rome 1969, p. 15. The italics in the first phrase are mine.

23. Kant, pp. 37–8.

24. Friedrich Schiller, *On the Aesthetic Education of Man* (1793–4), Oxford 1967, p. 61.

25. Ibid., pp. 35, 37, 41, 43.

26. Hence the 'exemplifying' nature which is so characteristic of literary works, particularly works of narrative fiction: 'A typical element [of literary, i.e. rhetorical, discourse] is the interconnection between fact and value, knowledge and emotion. The fact is given in the concrete situation of human behaviour, where every element is laden with axiological meanings and every value is traditionally and habitually exemplified in determinate facts. Both the consideration of the fact in itself, abstracted from every emotional concomitant, and the consideration of pure value, as value in itself, isolate the discourse from the *doxa*, from the concrete everyday life of the "majority". The lack of emotion makes the discourse "arid". The lack of example makes it "abstract". In each case the discourse becomes unpersuasive, and thus uneffective as an instrument of pragmatic culture within a society.' (Preti, p. 174).

27. 'Compromise' does not of course mean an *equally* advantageous (or disadvantageous) deal for all the parties involved. As I try to explain in 'Kindergarten', it is perfectly possible for it to involve agonizing losses and grave imbalances. Its distinctive function is not to 'make everybody happy' but, precisely, to 'compromise': to create a broad area with uncertain boundaries where polarized values come into contact, cohabit, become hard to recognize and disentangle. Needless to add, this is a supremely anti-tragic configuration.

28. Paul Ricoeur, *Freud and Philosophy*, New Haven and London 1970, p. 7.

29. 'Art offers substitute satisfactions for the oldest and still most deeply felt cultural renunciations, and for that reason it serves as nothing else to reconcile a man to the sacrifices he has made on behalf of civilization.' ('The Future of an Illusion', 1927, in *Standard Edition of The Complete Psychological Works of Sigmund Freud*, London 1953–74, volume XXI, p. 14). Similarly, two years later, Freud defines art as 'illusions, which are recognized as such . . . expressly exempted from the demands of reality-testing and . . . set apart for the purpose of fulfilling wishes which were difficult to carry out . . . Beauty has no obvious use; nor is there any clear cultural necessity for it. Yet civilization could not do without it . . . Psychoanalysis, unfortunately, has scarcely anything to say about beauty either. All that seems certain is its derivation from the field of sexual feeling. The love of beauty seems a perfect example of an impulse inhibited in its aim.' ('Civilization and its Discontents', 1930, ibid., pp. 80, 82, 83).

30. Francesco Orlando, *Toward a Freudian Theory of Literature*, Baltimore/London 1978, p. 140.

31. Ibid., 'Analytical Part', especially pp. 8–10.

32. Ibid., p. 10.

33. 'One may . . . venture the hypothesis that a great part of the sense of guilt must normally remain unconscious, because the origin of conscience is intimately connected with the Oedipus complex, which belongs to the unconscious. If anyone were inclined to put forward the paradoxical proposition that the normal man is not only far more immoral than he believes but also far more moral than he knows, psychoanalysis, on whose findings the first half of the assertion rests, would have no objection to raise against the second half.' In a footnote he adds: 'human nature has a far greater extent, both for good and for evil, than it thinks it has – i.e. than its ego is aware of through conscious perception.' ('The Ego and the Id', 1923, in Freud, volume XIX, p. 52).

34. Orlando, p. 169.

35. Freud, 'The Ego and the Id', p. 56.

The Great Eclipse

1. Andrew Marvell, 'An Horatian Ode Upon Cromwell's Return from Ireland', *Poems of Andrew Marvell*, Hugh MacDonald, ed., Cambridge, Mass., 1952, 53–6.

2. 'The outbreak of war itself', writes Lawrence Stone, 'is relatively easy to explain; what is hard is to puzzle out why most of the established institutions of State and Church – Crown, Court, central administration, army, and episcopacy – collapsed so ignominiously two years before.' Recapitulating the four principal causes of the revolution, he adds: 'Last but not least was the growing crisis of confidence in the integrity and moral worth of the holders of high administrative office, whether courtiers or nobles or bishops or judges or even kings' (*Causes of the English Revolution: 1529-1642*, London 1972, pp. 48, 116). In his summary of the controversy among English historians of the revolution, Mario Tronti writes: 'Of so many interpretive approaches, the hypothesis of a power vacuum works best. Stone and Trevor-Roper are basically agreed on this point: one lays stress on the subjective crisis of the body of politicians who administered power and society, the other underscores the crisis of the objective structures of power in society. In either case, the origin of the revolution, rather than in the offensive of new social forces wanting change, lies in the crisis of the old forces, in the vacancy of their power, in the political space that after a long and slow erosion of the barriers raised to defend it, suddenly opened up' ('Hobbes e Cromwell', in *Stato e rivoluzione in Inghilterra*, Milan 1977, pp. 235–6). The same schema may be found in the attempts to reconstruct the cultural antecedents of the revolution. Here, for example, is Christopher Hill: 'The most striking feature . . . of the intellectual life of pre-revolutionary England is its confusion and ferment. . . .In retrospect Renaissance and Reformation, the discovery of America and the new astronomy, had been far more successful in undermining old assumptions and prejudices than in substituting new truths' (*Intellectual Origins of the English Revolution*, Oxford 1965, pp. 7–8).

3. See Carl Schmitt, *Die Diktatur*, Berlin 1968, pp. 25–8; Friedrich Meinecke, *Die Idee Der Staatsräson*, Munich and Berlin 1925, pp. 70–80; and Perry Anderson, *Lineages of the Absolutist State*, London 1974, pp. 49–51.

4. *The Modern World-System*, New York 1974, pp. 146–7.

5. *Hamlet oder Hekuba*, Dusseldorf and Cologne, p. 67.

6. *Either/Or*, Princeton 1971, vol. 1, pp. 141, 147.

7. The inexorable dialectic that conjoins the absolute sovereign and the tyrant is described by Marx in his reflections on Hegel's *Philosophy of Right*. 'Hegel says only that the *real*, i.e., the *individual*, *will* is the *power of the crown*. . . . Insofar as this moment of 'ultimate decision' or 'absolute self-determination' is separated from the 'universality' of the content and the particularity of counsel, it is the *real will* in the form of *caprice*. In other words, "*caprice* is the power of the crown", or "the power of the crown is caprice"' 'Critique of Hegel's Doctrine of the State', in *Early Writings*, New York 1975, p. 76. By a different route, Walter Benjamin reaches similar conclusions: 'In the baroque the tyrant and the martyr are but the two faces of the monarch. They are the necessarily extreme incarnations of the princely essence. As far as the tyrant is concerned, this is clear enough. The theory of sovereignty which takes as its example the special case in which dictatorial powers are unfolded, positively demands the completion of the image of the sovereign, as tyrant' *The Origin of German Tragic Drama*, London 1977, p. 69.

8. Thomas Sackville and Thomas Norton, *Gorboduc*, I, ii, 218–20. The text is taken from the first volume of *Drama of the English Renaissance*, Russell A. Fraser and Norman Rabkin, ed., 2 vols., New York 1976.

9. *Politische Theologie: Vier Kapitel zur Lehre von der Souveränität*, Munich 1934, p. 11.

10. 'When a concrete result is to be produced, the dictator must intervene in the causal sequence of events with concrete measures. He takes action . . . he exercises an executive power, in contrast to the simple passing of a resolution or delivering of a legal decision, the *deliberare et consultare* . . . In the dictatorship, therefore, the aim or end, freed of legal restrictions and determined only by the necessity of producing a concrete state of affairs, triumphs over other considerations' (Schmitt, *Die Diktatur*, pp. 11–12).

11. *The Governaunce of Kynges and Prynces* (The Pynson Edition, 1511). Reason for the Elizabethans was a term that bridged the two fields of knowledge and ethics. It was the faculty that allowed man to understand the universe as an organic whole regulated by laws that delimited the individual's sphere of action as well. Will was subordinated to it, just as the individual – as a particular will – was himself subject to the organism of which he was a part. The conflict between these two faculties can therefore become truly explosive with the appearance of an individual (such as the absolute sovereign) who is no longer subject to any law.

12. *The Boke Named The Governour* [1531], London 1907, p. 242.

13. William Baldwin, *The Mirror for Magistrates* [1559], Lily B. Campbell, ed., 1938, p. 111. The quotation is taken from the third line of 'Howe kyng Richarde the seconde was for his euyll goueraunce deposed from his seat, and miserably murdered in prison'.

14. Richard Hooker, *The Laws of Ecclesiastical Polity*, London 1888, Book I, p. 76.

15. *The Mirrour of Policie* (anonymous translation of Guillaume de la Perrière, *Le Miroir politique*), London 1598, B.

16. *Mirrour of Policie*, Eiiij retro.

17. See for example the passage from Thomas Starkey's *Dialogue between Cardinal Pole and Thomas Lupset* cited and discussed in E. M. W. Tillyard, *The Elizabethan World Picture*, London 1943, pp. 90–1.

18. *Shakespeare and the Nature of Man* (Lowell Lectures, 1942, 2nd ed., New York 1961).

19. *Classical and Christian Ideas of World Harmony: Prolegomena to an Interpretation of the Word 'Stimmung'*, Anna Granville Hatcher, ed., Baltimore 1963. The original version appeared in *Traditio* II (1944) and III (1945).

20. *The Elizabethan World Picture*, pp. 2, 5. Two passages from Shakespeare are frequently adduced in support of this conceptualization: Ulysses' speech on *degree* (at once supreme power and principle of inequality of station) in *Troilus and Cressida*, and Agrippa's apologue in *Coriolanus*. It is true in these cases, of course, that Shakespeare becomes the spokesman for the Elizabethan world picture; but both speeches prove to be totally ineffective: Agrippa fails to placate the plebeians, and Ulysses does not re-establish the principle of hierarchy in the Greek army. If these passages demonstrate anything, then, it is not the force of Elizabethan ideology in Shakespeare, but rather its weakness.

21. The relationship between Lear and his daughters anticipates the advice of a manual from the most abject years of English absolutism, *The Mirrour of Complements* (1635). In the speeches recommended for addressing a king, two points already evident in Shakespeare stand out. In the presence of the king, the supplicant forfeits all rights, and to prove it, makes the monarch the arbiter of his fate ('the greatest honour I can possibly attain, is to dye worthily in some action at your service'; 'a fit occasion to maintain [my most humble service] with the perill of my life and bloud' [pp. 2, 3]). He also forfeits his rights in the domain of language,

which he employs not to convince, but only to attest the social gap between sender and receiver ('Sir, if words were able to expresse the duty in which I holde myselfe obliged'; 'I should much forget myselfe, if I thought my vowes along sufficient to deserve the favour of your most princely grave' [pp. 1, 2]).

22. All quotations from Shakespeare's plays have been taken from *The Riverside Shakespeare*, G. Blakemore Evans, ed., 1974.

23. *Origin*, p. 70.

24. '[The] heroes [of Greek tragedians] seem to us always more superficial in their speeches than in their actions; the myth, we might say, never finds an adequate objective correlative in the spoken word. The structure of the scenes and the concrete images convey a deeper wisdom than the poet was able to put into words and concepts. (The same may be claimed for Shakespeare, whose Hamlet speaks more superficially than he acts. . .)' (Friedrich Nietzsche, *The Birth of Tragedy*, Garden City, NY, 1956, p. 103). Nietzsche's position, accepted also by Benjamin (*Origin*, pp. 108–9), requires two qualifications, even leaving aside his sybylline pronouncement on Hamlet. For one thing, the inadequacy of word to action of which he speaks does not apply only to the hero, but also to the dramatic structure as a whole, including all the other characters as well as the chorus. And second, what Nietzsche calls 'superficiality' and Benjamin 'silence' cannot be seen as an effect of the violence of mythic events (in which alone, therefore, the true kernel of the tragedy would reside), but as a constitutive element of tragic structure as such. I shall return to this shortly, but to broach the distinction involved with the most famous example, let us say that it is possible to treat even the myth of Oedipus in non-tragic form: what makes it tragic is only the specific form in which it is structured.

25. George Steiner, *The Death of Tragedy*, London 1961, p. 11. The same point is made in Lily B. Campbell, *Tudor Conceptions of History and Tragedy in 'A Mirror for Magistrates'*, Berkeley 1936, p. 17.

26. Anonymous, *Arden of Feversham*, Fraser and Rabkin, vol. 1, iii, 168.

27. Thomas Kyd, *The Spanish Tragedy,* Fraser and Rabkin, vol. 1, II, i, 92–3.

28. Elyot, *The Gouenour*, p. 41; Philip Sidney, *An Apologie for Poetrie* (1585?), London 1929, p. 45; George Puttenham, *The Arte of English Poesie* (1589), Kent, Ohio 1970, p. 49.

29. *Aesthetics*, tr. T. M. Knox, Oxford, 1975, p. 1210.

30. Thomas Heywood, 'The Author to his Booke', prefatory poem to *An Apology for Actors*, Richard H. Perkinson, ed., New York 1941, 1–4, 12.

31. C. B. Macpherson, *The Political Theory of Possessive Individualism: Hobbes to Locke*, Oxford 1962, p. 49.

32. Walter Ullmann, *The Individual and Society in the Middle Ages*, Baltimore 1966, pp. 40, 42, 44.

33. 'With the generalized commutation of dues into money rents, the cellular unity of political and economic oppression of the peasantry was gravely weakened, and threatened to become dissociated (the end of this road was "free labour" and the "wage contract"). The class power of the feudal lords was thus directly at stake with the gradual disappearance of serfdom. The result was a *displacement* of politico-legal coercion upwards towards a centralized, militarized summit – the Absolutist State. Diluted at village level, it became concentrated at "national" level. The result was a reinforced apparatus of royal power' (Anderson, *Lineages*, p. 19). Immanuel Wallerstein's judgement is similar: 'In the heyday of western feudalism, when the state was weakest, the landowner, the lord of the manor thrived. . . . Lords of the manor then would never welcome the strengthening of the

central machinery if they were not in a weakened condition in which they found it more difficult to resist the claims of central authority and more ready to welcome the benefits of imposed order. Such a situation was that posed by the economic difficulties of the fourteenth and fifteenth centuries, and the decline of seigniorial revenues' (*The Modern World-System*, p. 28). The new function of the sovereign as a hedge against social disintegration is faithfully reflected in the activities of legislation and coercion that Hooker assigns to God (*Laws*, pp. 64–8, 81). Even natural laws are conceived as 'the edicts of His law', so many means to avoid the universal dissolution that would ensue if individual elements of the cosmos went each its own way (p. 66).

34. Elyot (*The Gouernour*, p. 5) establishes a strict correspondence between *understanding* and *estate*: 'they whiche excelle other in this influence of understandynge . . . oughte to be set in a more highe place than the residue where they may se and also be sene; that by the beames of theyr excellent witte . . . other of inferiour understandynge may be directed to the way of vertue and commodious liuynge.'

35. 'The term "country" suggested that the men whom it designated should be regarded as persons of public spirit, unmoved by private interest, untainted by court influence and corruption, representing the highest good of their local communities and the nation in whose interests they, and they only, acted' (P. Zagorin, 'The Court and the Country', *English Historical Review* [1962], i. 309; cited in Lawrence Stone, *The Crises of the Aristocracy: 1558-1641*, Oxford 1965, p. 502).

36. John Marston, *The Malcontent*, M. L. Wine, ed., Lincoln, Nebraska, 1964, V, vi, 154–62.

X   37. James I, speech of 1609, collected in *The Political Works of James I*, Charles Howard McIlwain, ed., Cambridge, Mass., 1918, p. 308. Besides the theatre, the game of chess is the other great social metaphor of the Elizabethans, and it is easy to see why. In chess, each piece is defined by a certain number of unalterable possibilities of movement different from those of the others – each piece in short is bound to its station. Furthermore (as is clear in Middleton's great success, *A Game at Chess*), each side in chess – each 'realm' – has a supreme and indisputable leader in the figure of the king.

38. To my central claim that the political sphere of the state is essential to tragedy, Marlowe's plays would constitute a conspicuous qualification. I can only glance at the problem here and say that Barabas and Faustus, to take the best examples, are unique on the Elizabethan stage as exponents (if peculiar ones) of civil society: on one hand, the great accumulator of wealth, on the other the great intellectual. The tragic conflict arises from the fact that prosperity and greatness both depend nonetheless on a superior power, despotic in nature, that denies them full liberty and finally destroys them. It would not be farfetched to call *The Jew of Malta* and *Doctor Faustus* 'tragedies of the monopolist', given that they illuminate with notable rigour the nexus of fear and antagonism that links this historical figure to absolute power.

39. *Aesthetics*, pp. 1229–30.

40. Ibid., pp. 1195–97.

41. London 1964, p. 57.

42. *Aesthetics*, pp. 1159–60, 1168.

43. *Il dramma moderno*, Milan 1976, pp. 24–5, 26, 48.

44. Niccolò Machiavelli, *The Prince*, Harmondsworth 1961, pp. 65–6.

45. And just as Hooker cannot understand Machiavelli, so Macbeth will never understand what it was that impelled him to action. On the only occasion he even makes a suggestion, he loses himself in a metaphor that explains nothing: 'I have no

spur/To prick the sides of my intent, but only/Vaulting ambition, which o'erleaps itself,/And falls on th'other' (I, vii, 25–8). Not only does the metaphor, reductive of the act Macbeth is about to commit, reduce its agent to the mute, non-human status of a horse to be pricked, but also it does not even claim 'ambition' as a 'cause' of action, only at best a 'spur' to it. The act that initiates the tragedy never is assigned a knowable cause, and the obscure motivation here reappears in Lear's 'darker purpose', Cleopatra's inexplicable flight at Actium, the destructive pleasure of Iago, and, in a special sense, Hamlet's inaction.

The presence of an unknowable element seems essential to tragic structure, and taking up the conclusions of the preceding section, I would argue that such an element is always situated on the plane of actions, and that it is unknowable because this plane, whose fullest expression is the sovereign acting in his unlimited independence, is suddenly dominated by fallen nature, which also has its highest expression in the sphere of royalty, specifically in the figure of the tyrant. By definition devoid of laws, fallen nature is unknowable. It can be represented, in the sense of re-presented, but never comprehended in the Elizabethan acceptation of the word: never, that is, inserted in the great system of causes and effects that is the world as constructed by the divine lawgiver. If at the centre of tragic structure, then, we encounter a 'realistic' element like the Machiavellianism of Macbeth, this, instead of reinforcing the cognitive power of the period, rather brings into relief its unknowability, its full petrification. Tragedy takes for its object not cognition, but its impossibility.

46. By the fifth act, up until just before being killed, Hamlet no longer thinks of revenging himself or unmasking the usurper. He recalls his original project only when Laertes tells him that he has 'not half an hour's life' – not as part of some uncontrollable vital instinct (whether of ambition or revenge or whatever), but as a man henceforth dead.

47. It is perhaps not chance that the two expressions occur practically at the same juncture in the drama, when it is a matter of choosing once and for all the line of action to follow: Macbeth decides to remain in that 'blood' of which he has spoken a few lines earlier, Hamlet to prolong his uncle's 'sickly days'.

48. What the court sees in *The Murder of Gonzago* is that a nephew of the king (like Hamlet in respect to Claudius), dressed in black (again like Hamlet), kills the legitimate sovereign (such as it holds Claudius to be). Blind to Claudius's usurpation, it sees instead Hamlet brazenly threatening his uncle.

49. The treatise writers of the time lose no occasion to praise the studied rhetorical preparation over the spontaneous production of discourse. Thus, Elyot in *The Gouernour* (pp. 42–3): 'The utilitie that a noble man shall haue by redyng these oratours [Demosthenes and Cicero], is, that, whan he shall happe to reason in counsaile, or shall speke in a great audience, or to strange ambassadours of great princes, he shall nat be constrayned to spake wordes sodayne and disordered, but shal bestowe them aptly and in their places. Wherefore the moste noble emperour Octauius is highly commended, for that he neuer spake in the Senate, or to the people of Rome, but in a oration prepared and purposely made.'

50. Christopher Hill has provided an extraordinary analysis of this historical transistion in *Society and Puritanism in Pre-Revolutionary England*, New York 1964, pp. 382–419.

51. On Botero and Baccalini and their conception of the role of the prince, see Meinecke, *Staaträson*, pp. 81–112, and especially pp. 6–8.

52. What follows is largely based on the arguments of Jean Starobinski, 'Sur Corneille', (in *L'Oeil vivant*, Paris 1961); and Serge Doubrovsky, *Corneille et la dialectique du héros* (Paris 1963).

53. Leo Tolstoy, *Tolstoy on Shakespeare*, New York 1907, p. 53.

54. On this problem see Michel Foucault, *The Order of Things*, London 1970, chapters 1–3; and Jurij M. Lotman, 'Different Cultures, Different Codes', *Times Literary Supplement*, 1973, October 12, pp. 1213–5.

55. Marx, *Critique of Hegel's Doctrine of the State*, p. 81.

56. Sidney's 'defence' of poetry consists precisely in the claim made for its moral and cognitive character. Urged on almost every page, this claim is particularly clear in the argument in which the poet ('the peerelesse Poet') is declared superior from a cognitive point of view to both the philosopher and the historian because 'hee coupleth the generall notion with the particular example'. And since the 'final end' of learning is 'to knowe, and by knowing to lift vp the mind from the dungeon of the body, to the enjoying of his owne diuine essence', then 'the ending end of all earthly learning, being vertuous action, those skilles that most serue to bring forth that, haue a most iust title to bee Princes ouer all the rest' (*Apologie*, pp. 33, 29–30). Thus the circle is closed, and poetry is victoriously defended in the name of her 'force in teaching'.

57. It is said by such as professe the Mathematicall sciences, that all things stand by proportion, and that without it nothing could stand to be good or beautiful. The Doctors of our Theologie to the same effect, but in other termes, say: that God made the world by number, measure and weight ... Poeticall proportion ... holdeth of the Musical, because as we sayd before Poesie is a skill to speake and write harmonically' (Puttenham, *English Poesie*, pp. 78–9). To a large extent Puttenham's work is a systematic collection of prescription on how to obtain this poetical proportion, with particular attention to the symmetry of versification and to the 'decencie', or moderation, of figurative language.

58. *A Pleasant Discourse of Court and Wars*, London 1596, A iv.

59. *The Traitor*, John Stewart Carter, ed., Lincoln Nebraska, 1965, II, ii, 112–6.

60. John Webster, *The White Devil*, Fraser and Rabkin, vol. 2, I, ii, 358–9.

61. Pierre Corneille, *Le Cid*, in *Théâtre Complet*, Pierre Lièvre and Roger Caillois, ed., Paris 1966, I, ii, 23.

62. A strange affection, brother, when I think on't!/I wonder how thou cam'st by it. – Ev'n as easily/As man comes by destruction' (Thomas Middleton, *Women Beware Women*, Roma Gill, ed., London and Tonbridge 1968, II, i, 1–3).

63. John Ford, *'Tis a Pity She's a Whore*, Fraser and Rabkin, vol. 2, I, iii, 11.

64. Cyril Tourneur, *The Atheist's Tragedy*, Irving Ribner, ed., Cambridge, Mass., 1964, II, iii, 43–4, 65–6.

65. Cited in Lawrence Stone, *Crisis of the Aristocracy*, p. 27.

66. Cyril Tourneur, *The Revenger's Tragedy*, Fraser and Rabkin, vol. 2, III, v, 44.

67. John Webster, *The Duchess of Malfi*, Fraser and Rabkin, vol. 2, II, i, 62–5.

68. Benjamin, *Origin*, p. 166.

69. Puttenham, *English Poesie*, p. 197.

70. *Phenomenology of Spirit*, Oxford 1977, p. 116.

Dialectic of Fear

1. Mary Wollstonecraft Shelley, *Frankenstein* (1817), London 1977; John Polidori, *The Vampyre* (1819) in *Gothic Tales of Terror*, Baltimore 1973; Robert

Louis Stevenson, *The Strange Case of Dr Jekyll and Mr Hyde* (1885), London 1924; Bram Stoker, *Dracula* (1897), London 1974.

2. Marx, 'Economic and Philosophical Manuscripts' (1844), in *Early Writings*, Harmondsworth 1975, p. 322.

3. The 'classic' detective novel has a similar function. The crime casts suspicion over all the characters: their actions become equivocal, their ideals questionable, their aims mysterious. But once the culprit is found, the suspicion immediately evaporates and everyone is rehabilitated. 'A murderer has to be indicted because that is the only way to provide the rest of the cast with an acquittal wholly satisfying to reason. But the psychological purpose of the story is summed up in that acquittal. The detective myth exists not to provoke or endorse guilt but to dissipate it. The solution pronounces the general absolution.' Brigid Brophy, 'Detective Fiction: A Modern Myth', *Hudson Review* 1965, no. 1, p. 29. General absolution is nothing other than the instinctive approval of the general laws of society which proclaim their goodness and justice in the presence of the individual transgression, the exceptional criminal 'case'.

4. Marx, 'Economic and Philosophical Manuscripts'.

5. In Fisher's films, the vitality of the monster and the vampire is completely lost. They never begin with an offensive by the monster (who would be quite happy to stay at home), but with an error or an act of stupidity by 'man'. The invitation is transparently to refrain from wandering, to leave things as they are. The monster is no longer frightening in himself but because his zone of influence has been violated, because men have not kept to the agreement. It is a *welfare state* sort of terror, proper to an era of peaceful coexistence.

6. Mary Shelley's monster is an *assemblage of different corpses*. By presenting it as a single corpse (albeit gigantic and abnormal) restored to life, the film tradition greatly trivializes its social meaning.

7. '*Thus capital presupposes wage labour; wage labour presupposes capital. They reciprocally condition the existence of each other . . . capital and wage labour are two sides of one and the same relation*.' Marx, 'Wage Labour and Capital' (1849) in the one-volume *Selected Works*, London 1970, pp. 82–3.

8. Walter Benjamin, 'Zentralpark'.

9. Marx, 'Economic and Philosophical Manuscripts', pp. 325–6.

10. *Frankenstein* can be read as the inversion of *Robinson Crusoe*. In the eighteenth century, disobedience to the father is rewarded; a century later it is punished by death. The difference in the endings depends entirely on the relations that are set up between the son and labour-power. Friday is a negro ('race of devils') but Crusoe civilizes him, forces him to become a 'man', to speak English, believe in God, wear clothes, serve his master. The monster, on the other hand, is the man who becomes inhuman, who rejects God, betrays his master, abandons civilization and threatens to found a new race. The difference is reflected in the different narrative techniques: Crusoe *controls* the situation, and this enables him to be a universal narrating ego; Frankenstein, who has lost control of it, cannot even command the edifice of the novel.

11. It should also be noted that Mary Shelley is unable to construct a wholly successful image of the family. Walton's family, for instance, amounts to one married sister, who is the addressee of all his letters. It is as if the 'domestic affection' celebrated by the author began being obscured by the shadow of incest.

12. This clarifies another aspect of the fear aroused by the monster. As Kant had already written in the *Analytic of the Sublime*: 'An object is *monstrous* where by its size it defeats the end that forms its concept.' (*Critique of Judgement*, Oxford 1952, p. 100). The monster's size prevents it from fitting into the precise and limited

compartments of the pre-capitalist division of labour. The fact 'defeats its concept', in other words, its 'humanity', making it – precisely – a monster. It can only use its immense productive capacity at night, concealed, for mere survival. It would make a capitalist happy (and it practically goes so far as to say as much itself): but there are no capitalists in the novel.

13. Harker himself is forced to recognize this clear-headed bourgeois rationality in Dracula, after the latter has saved him from the purely destructive desire of his lovers: 'surely it is maddening to think that of all the foul things that lurk in this hateful place the Count is the least dreadful to me: that to him alone I can look for safety, even though this be only whilst I can *serve his purpose.*' (My italics). So *un*-cruel is Dracula that, once he has made use of Harker, he lets him go free without having harmed a hair on his head.

14. Before Dracula there had been another literary character who had lost his shadow: Peter Schlemihl. He had exchanged it for a purse full of money. But he soon realizes that money can only give him one thing: more money, still more money, all the money he wants (the purse is bottomless). But *only* money. The only desire Peter can satisfy is thus the abstract and immaterial desire for money. His mutilated and unnatural body denies him access to tangible, material, corporeal desires. So great a scandal is it that once the girl he loves (and who loves him) finds out, she refuses to marry him. Peter runs away in desparation: he can no longer love. (Just like Dracula: '"You yourself have never loved; you never love!" ... Then the Count turned ... and said in a soft whisper: – "Yes, I too can love; you yourselves can tell it from the past. Is it not so? ..."') Chamisso's story is a fable (*The Marvellous Story of Peter Schlemihl*); published in 1813, the same period as *Frankenstein*, it too revolves around the conflict between the spread of capitalism (Peter) and feudal social structures (Mina and her village). As in *Frankenstein*, capitalism appears in it as a fortuitous episode, involving just one individual and lasting only a short time. But the underlying intuition has an extraordinary power; it stands on a par with the punishment of Midas, for whom gold prevented consumption.

15. Marx, *Capital* Volume I, Harmondsworth 1976, p. 342.

16. '... the Un-Dead are strong. [Dracula] have (*sic*) always the strength in his hand of twenty men; even we four who gave our strength to Miss Lucy it also is all to him' (p. 183). One cannot help recalling the words of Mephistopheles analysed by Marx: 'Six stallions, say, I can afford,/ Is not their strength my property?/ I tear along, a sporting lord,/ As if their legs belonged to me.' (quoted in 'Economic and Philosophical Manuscripts', p. 376).

17. Marx, *Capital* Volume 1, p. 741.

18. Marx, 'The Property of Philosophy' (1847) in Marx and Engels, *Collected Works*, Volume 6, London 1976, p. 195.

19. This is the case with all the minor characters in the novel. These (the stevedores and lawyers, sailors and estate agents, porters and accountants) are always more than satisfied with their dealings with Dracula, for the simple reason that Dracula pays well and in cash, or even facilitates the work. Dracula is one of them: an excellent master for wage-earners, an excellent partner for big businessmen. They understand one another so well, they are so useful to each other, that Dracula never behaves like a vampire with them: he does not need to suck their blood, he can buy it.

20. The finishing touch is Jonathan Harker's short 'Note', written seven years after the events have ended. Harker informs the reader that he and Mina have christened their son 'Quincey', and that 'His mother holds, I know, the secret belief that some of our brave friend's spirit has passed into him.' (p. 336). The American

outsider Morris is 'recycled' within the triumphant Victorian family, not without being made to undergo a final tacit humiliation (which would delight a linguist): his name – Quincy, as appears from the signature of the only note in his own handwriting – is transformed, by the addition of an 'e', into the much more English Quincey.

21. In Stoker's novel the function of Van Helsing describes a parabola: absent at the beginning, dominant at the centre, removed to the margins of the action at the end. His aid is indeed irreplaceable, but once she has obtained it, Britain can settle matters herself: it is indicative that he is only a spectator at the killing of Dracula. In this, yet again, Fisher's *Dracula* betrays the ideological intention of the original: the great final duel between Dracula and Van Helsing belongs to a very different system of oppositions from Stoker's, where there prevails the conflict between Good and Evil, Light and Darkness, Frugality and Luxury, Reason and Superstition (see David Pirie, *A Heritage of Horror. The English Gothic Cinema 1947–1972*, London 1973, p. 51 ff.).

22. The story of Lucy illuminates the interrelationship of the characters. In the opening chapters, no fewer than three of the main characters (Seward, Holmwood and Morris) enter into competition for her hand. In other words, Lucy objectively turns these men into *rivals*, she divides them, and this makes things easier for Dracula who, making them by contrast be friends again, prepares her downfall. The moral is that, when faced with the vampire, one must curb all individual appetites and interests. Poor Lucy, who acts solely on her desires and impulses (she is a woman who *chooses* her own husband, without mentioning it to her mother!) is first killed by Dracula and then, for safety's sake, run through the heart by her fiancé on what, going by the calendar, should have been their wedding night (and the whole episode, as we shall see, oozes sexual meanings).

23. Pirie, p. 84.

24. For Hegel too love originates from 'the surrender of the person to an individual of the opposite sex, the sacrifice of one's independent consciousness'. But then Hegel dialectically resolves and pacifies this self-negation from which love originates: 'this losing, in the other, one's consciousness of self ... this self-forgetfulness in which the lover ... finds the roots of his being in another, and yet in this other does entirely enjoy precisely himself.' (*Aesthetics*, 1820–29, Oxford 1975, pp. 562–3.)

25. Stendhal, *De L'Amour* (1822), Paris 1957, p. 118.

26. Marie Bonaparte, *The Life and Works of Edgar Allen Poe. A Psychoanalytic Interpretation*, London 1949, pp. 209–10.

27. Ibid., pp. 218–9.

28. 'Totem and Taboo' (1913) in Freud, Volume XIII, p. 61. See also the essay 'The "Uncanny"' (1919): 'Most likely our fear still implies the old belief that the dead man becomes the enemy of his survivor and seeks to carry him off to share his new life with him.' (Ibid., XVII, p. 242).

29. 'The "Uncanny"', p. 241.

30. Ibid., p. 249.

31. Mary Shelley claimed to have 'dreamt' the story of Frankenstein. And one of the passages that stands out in the text is Frankenstein's dream, which takes place immediately after the creation of the monster. At the moment when, in the dream, he is about to kiss Elizabeth, she changes into his mother's corpse. Frankenstein wakes to find the monster by his bed, in an unmistakable maternal pose: 'He held up the curtain of the bed; and his eyes ... were fixed on me ... a grin wrinkled his cheeks ... one hand was stretched out.' (p. 52). Other things about the monster suggest a reworking of the mother figure: the fact that he is a dead man who comes

back to life; his physical 'bigness'; his language, improbably more 'archaic' than Frankenstein's. The analogy, however, rests mostly on the *function* of the monster within the plot: he kills Elizabeth, punishing Frankenstein for having married her ✓ and thereby avenging his mother, killed by the scarlet fever she had caught from Elizabeth, with whom her son is now getting ready to 'betray' her. The situation recalls many of Poe's tales.

32. Think of Renfield, Seward's patient who is given considerable space in *Dracula*. Seward examines his case with the utmost care, draws on all the known psychiatric techniques, even forms new hypotheses, and calls Van Helsing for a second opinion: nothing – they draw a blank. Then, all of a sudden, the penny drops: Renfield is the servant of Dracula.

33. *Orlando*, pp. 138 and 140; my italics.

34. That a desire or a fear underlie the uncanny is entirely secondary for Freud. The terror is caused by the sudden re-emergence of something repressed: having established this, 'it must be a matter of indifference whether what is uncanny was itself originally frightening or whether it carried some *other* effect.' ('The "Uncanny"', p. 241). This ambivalent unconscious origin confers a peculiar function on the literature of terror. The distinction suggested by Freud in his study of jokes – 'Dreams serve predominantly for the avoidance of unpleasure, jokes for the attainment of pleasure' – and extended by Orlando to literature (which also functions for the attainment of pleasure, for the manifestation of a repressed desire), becomes highly uncertain. In the literature of terror the two functions – avoidance of unpleasure and attainment of pleasure – seem to balance each other perfectly. Indeed the one exists for the other: a terror novel that doesn't frighten doesn't give pleasure either. In this respect, and not just because of its contents, the literature of terror seems to be that whose workings approximate most closely to those of the dream: and like the dream it 'imposes' an obligatory context of enjoyment: alone, at night, in bed.

35. D. H. Lawrence, *Studies in Classic American Literature*, London 1924, chapter 6.

36. Tzvetan Todorov, *The Fantastic. A structural Approach to a Literary Genre*, Ithaca 1975, pp. 76–7.

37. The ideological aim of *Frankenstein* recalls that assigned by Kant to the sublime. 'If we are to estimate nature as dynamically sublime, it must be represented as a source of fear'. But Kant adds: '*One who is in a state of fear* [cannot] play the part of a judge of the sublime of nature ... [The sight of natural catastrophes], *provided our position is secure*, is all the more attractive for its fearfulness; and we readily call these objects sublime, because they raise the forces of the soul *above the height of vulgar commonplace* .... Sublimity, therefore, does not reside in any of the things in nature, but only in our own mind'. (Kant, pp. 109, 110, 114; my italics). Kant already indicates the two paths open to the literature of terror: the path of the 'sublime', which does not arouse fear but moral reflections, ✓ and is confined to educated readers; and the path of the 'terrible', which negates reflection and is reserved for the mass. 'In fact, without the development of moral ideas, that which, thanks to preparatory culture, we call sublime, merely strikes the untutored man as terrifying.' (Ibid, p. 115).

38. Roland Barthes, 'Structural Analysis of Narratives' in *Image-Music-Text*, London 1977, p. 119.

39. Barthes describes suspense thus: 'on the one hand, by keeping a sequence open (through emphatic procedures of delay and renewal), it reinforces the contact with the reader (the listener), has a manifestly phatic function; while on the other, it

offers the threat of an uncompleted sequence, of an open paradigm..., that is to say of a logical disturbance which is consumed with anxiety and pleasure (all the more so because it is always made right in the end). "Suspense", therefore, is a game with structure, designed to endanger and glorify it, constituting a veritable "thrilling" of intelligibility'. (Ibid., p. 119). Once we *realize* who Dracula is, once the logical disorder √ is smoothed over, Stoker's novel changes from a terror novel into an adventure novel: the action is entirely taken up with journeys, duels, chases, plans of battle.

40. Adorno has observed that the 'collective norms of individual behaviour', namely the super-ego, must *necesarily* be irrational: 'a "conscious" super-ego would lose precisely the authority for the sake of which its apologists cling to it.' T. W. Adorno, 'Sociology and Psychology II' (1955), *New Left Review*, 47 (1968), pp. 82, 83.

Homo palpitans

1. Based on the Italian translation in Massimo Cacciari, *Metropolis*, Roma 1973, p. 136.

2. Robert E. Park, Ernest W. Burgess, Roderick D. Mckenzie, *The City*, Chicago 1925, chapter 1, p. 3.

3. Erich Auerbach, *Mimesis: The Presentation of Reality in Western Literature*, Princeton 1953 (4th printing 1974), pp. 470, 472, 473.

4. Ibid., p. 473.

5. Balzac demonstrates this perfectly. Vautrin – the great criminal, the man of the submerged city, of the mysteries of Paris – contributes to the plot negligibly both in *Père Goriot* and in *Lost Illusions* (and when his role is enlarged, as in *A Harlot High and Low*, the effect is really boring). Although he often affirms that he wants to take the place of fate, Vautrin gives his best not in the production of the story (as is the rule with the other monsters) but in the *comment* on it (a role usually not bestowed upon his confrères): his observations are among the most memorable pages of Balzac's work.

6. 'Normal' embodies two different meanings which are perfectly symmetrical to those of 'unheard-of': whereas the latter refers to the 'rare' and the 'deplorable', normal indicates what is both 'widespread' and 'commendable'.

7. Benjamin picks up the Freudian statement that 'For a living organism, protection against stimuli is an almost more important function than the reception of stimuli' (*Beyond the Pleasure Principle*, section 4), and maintains that the fact that 'shock is thus cushioned, parried by consciousness, would lend the incident that occasions it the character of having been lived in the strict sense. If it were incorporated directly in the registry of conscious memory, it would sterilize this incident for poetic experience.' (in *Charles Baudelaire: A Lyric Poet in the Era of High Capitalism*, London 1973, pp. 115–6.) Baudelaire's poetry ('assigned to a mission') on the contrary attempts to effect 'the emancipation from experiences.' (Ibid., p. 116). Thus far, everything is clear, but only twenty lines later, one encounters the well-known statement that 'Baudelaire made it his business to parry the shocks' (p. 117): which takes us straight back to that 'experience' from which one had to 'emancipate' oneself. The rest of the essay is incapable of snapping this vicious circle (if anything, it duplicates it in the reflections on 'recollection' and 'experience' in

the tenth paragraph). Yet, to come across logical contradictions in the work of a critic as extraordinary as Benjamin is quite natural. Perfection belongs only to the Patron Saints – but not even to them: only to the alienated needs of their adulators.

8. Simmel, and later, Park, insisted on the essentially 'intellectual' or 'rational' character of the urban personality. This is not entirely apt. Certainly, lasting feelings weaken in the city, and even the most sacred customs, under the corrosive effects of an ever quicker transformation, find themselves cast off and exposed to rational and disenchanted criticism. Still – leaving strictly professional activity aside – it would appear that urban life is marked by an uninterrupted succession of sudden and short-lived emotional choices. The city dweller's typical sensation of never having enough time is itself a stimulus to choose impulsively and irrationally. That haste gives bad counsel is especially true in the city, as that exquisitely urban game, roulette, proves. As anyone knows, it is extremely easy to win at roulette: just wait for black to come up four or five times in a row and then play red, doubling at every loss. Except for suspect coincidences, within a few bets one wins, and if one repeats the system about ten times one earns about 25% on the necessary overall capital, which isn't at all bad. So why does one always lose at roulette? Because one wants to win too quickly, too hastily . . .

9. When the great nineteenth-century narrators (Pushkin, Stendhal, Balzac, Manzoni, Flaubert, Turgenev, Maupassant, and even Melville: all obviously in different ways) make use of the duel, it is always to deride or devalue it. Usually the wrong people fight, at the wrong time, and for the wrong reasons (Evgeny Onegin and Lucien de Rubempré are the extreme cases as they end up by fighting their only friends). The duel is a definitely inadequate type of event (or 'function') for resolving what is at stake in the plot. Its centrality is preserved only in one narrative genre, the spy novel in the broad sense. It is not accidental that in this genre an archaic – almost patrimonial – conception of the state and of the conflicts between states still reigns: D'Artagnan and James Bond limit themselves to 'acting out' (they are actors: that's why they are so fussy about their clothes) the real duel which occurs between Richelieu and the Duke of Buckingham, or between M and Dr. No.

10. In *Lost Illusions*, Lucien wants to become a journalist and therefore he goes straight to a newspaper to speak to the editor, but he can't even see him. Lucien manages in his intent only by joining forces with the equivocal Lousteau, seducing Coralie, and writing an article of a very peculiar kind. He can manage, that is, only by using devious ways and provoking a myriad of private interests, whose criss-crossing becomes ever more complex and precipitous, causing first Lucien's success and then his ruin. Besides, the 'straight line'/'tortuous line' opposition is one of the principal paradigms in Balzac's work.

11. In his essay 'The Metropolis and Mental Life' (in *On Individuality and Social Forms: Selected Writings*, Chicago 1971, p. 325), Georg Simmel wonders how the city dweller manages to resist 'the swift and continuous shift of external stimuli . . . the rapid telescoping of changing images . . . the unexpectedness of violent stimuli'. His answer is that the city dweller underrates all external stimuli and thus becomes indifferent to their phantasmagoria. Yet the real answer lies in his own words: to 'the *rapid* telescoping of changing images' one responds with *rapidity* – of the glance, but especially of life. Precisely because he knows that 'one life is not enough' to do and see everything he wants, the city dweller limits his expectations and makes a continuous and unconscious *selection* of them. Once more, urban space is divided and classified on the basis of a personal-temporal sequence.

12. Walter Benjamin, 'Paris – The Capital of the Nineteenth Century', in *Charles Baudelaire*, p. 174.

13. Simmel, p. 330.

14. I deal with this problem in 'The Long Goodbye: *Ulysses* and the End of Liberal Capitalism' and 'From *The Waste Land* to the Artificial Paradise', also included in this volume.

Clues

1. T. Todorov, 'The Place of Style in the Structure of the Text' in Seymour Chatman, ed., *Literary Style: a Symposium*, London 1971, p. 31.

2. Criticism of political economy or of philosophy or social history or whatever: it is all the same, and this also holds true for that other great source of functional hypotheses – psychoanalysis. Further: what was *Opera aperta* if not a *diffusion*, through literature, of some elements of modern scientific culture?

3. W. Hendricks, 'Methodology of Narrative Structural Analysis', *Semiotica*, VII, 2, 1973, pp. 166–7.

4. See Umberto Eco on the process of code-building in *A Theory of Semiotics*, London 1977, p. 91: 'At first glance it would seem that a theory of codes merely has to consider the sign-function in itself, for its combination with a context is a matter of sign production. But sign production is permitted by rules previously established by a code, for a code is usually conceived not only as a correlational rule but also as a set of combinational ones. . . . At this point it may seem necessary to conceive of a code as a double entity establishing on the one hand correspondences between an expression and a content and, on the other, a set of combinational rules.'

5. R. Jakobson, 'Due aspetti del linguaggio e due tipi di afasia' (1956), in *Fundamentals of Language*, 1956, pp. 55–82.

6. '"It seems, from what I gather, to be of those simple cases which are so extremely difficult."

"That sounds a little paradoxical."

"But it is profoundly true. Singularity is almost invariably a clew. The more featureless and commonplace a crime is, the more difficult is it to bring it home. . .
"'. ('The Boscombe Valley Mystery').

7. The mass success of detective fiction became irreversible in 1891 with Conan Doyle's first short stories in *Strand Magazine*. 'A Study in Scarlet', which came out four years earlier and was absolutely identical to the later stories, was almost a fiasco. Between these two dates there fell the year of Jack the Ripper, 1889, and a series of unsolved crimes, that is, crimes *without a subject*. Detective fiction must quell the fear that the criminal may remain unknown and therefore continue to circulate in society.

8. 'You have heard me remark that the strangest and most unique things are very often connected not with the larger but with the smaller crimes, and occasionally, indeed, where there is room for doubt whether any positive crime has been committed.' ('The Red-Headed League').

9. Werner Fuchs, *Todesbilder in der modernen Gesellschaft*, Frankfurt Main 1969.

10. Sigmund Freud, 'Beyond the Pleasure Principle', in James Strachey, ed., *The*

Standard Edition of the Complete Psychological Works of Sigmund Freud, vol. 18, London 1955, p. 36.

11. Ibid., p. 36.

12. Max Horkeimer and Theodor W. Adorno, *Dialectic of Enlightenment*, London 1973, pp. 226–8.

13. Max Weber, 'Critical Studies in the Logic of the Cultural Sciences', part II: 'Objective Possibility and Adequate Causation in Historical Explanation', in *The Methodology of the Social Sciences*, New York 1949, p. 169.

14. In the same way, every *superfluous* object – an ornamental bell-pull, a kite – proves to be an instrument of death. For this reason there is no room for love in detective fiction. Love – the overrating of the object ('she/he is not like the others') and the refusal to exchange it ('him/her or no one') – could indeed be indicted for gross contempt of the principle of equivalence. It is no wonder that true passion always ends up by playing into the hands of the criminal.

15. Claude Lévi-Strauss, 'Reflections on a Work by Vladimir Propp', in *Structural Anthropology 2*, Harmondsworth 1978, p. 135.

16. On this, see Umberto Eco, 'Il mito di Superman', in *Apocalittici e integrati* (1965), Milano 1974, p. 232 and *passim*.

17. The coincidence of the new and the never-changing referred to here was established by Benjamin in his writings on Baudelaire and considered homologous to the structure of commodities, where an ever new content (i.e., use value) is a mere support for the fixity and abstractness of the *form* of the commodities, that is, their exchange value. (See the introduction to *calibano* 2: *Il nuovo e il sempreuguale*, Rome 1978, on this and on its connection with Benjamin's theory of allegory.) Benjamin's solution, however, seems to me ever more unsatisfactory – even though it certainly explains *one* aspect of the problem. In fact, the 'never-changing' formulation, unlike exchange value, is not a truly abstract entity, i.e., lacking all determination; on the contrary: it is a combination endowed with meaning, and with a specific meaning, which is different according to whether one is dealing with detective fiction or science fiction or modern allegoric poetry. Benjamin, in effect, tells us what *links* a commodity to a text – not what *differentiates* them.

18. Max Weber, 'Science as a Vocation', H. H. Gerth and C. Wright Mills, eds., *From Max Weber: Essays in Sociology*, London 1970, p. 137.

19. T. S. Eliot, 'Tradition and the Individual Talent', in *The Sacred Wood*, London, 1960, pp. 53–4, 58.

20. On this, see Karl Polanyi, *Origins of Our Time: The Great Transformation* (1944), London 1945; and Michel Foucault, *Discipline and Punish: the Birth of the Prison* (1975), London 1977.

21. Max Weber, 'Objective Possibility . . .', p. 169.

22. Max Weber, '"Objectivity" in Social Science and Social Policy', in *The Methodology of the Social Sciences*, p. 57.

23. The only problem can consist in an unusual *combination* of them, which Poe very early saw as the only possible form of novelty. The same idea will crop up in numerous twentieth-century handbooks addressed to would-be mystery writers, where detective fiction is often compared to chess ('The Purloined Letter' opens with a discussion of games), which allows an infinite number of situations with a finite set of rules and pieces.

24. Eco, *Theory*, p. 224. To touch on a parallel currently in vogue: the true investigator, who has to *build* a previously *non-existent* code to explain the clues, is not Holmes but Freud.

25. Holmes always accuses Watson of being too 'literary' in his stories: 'Crime is common. Logic is rare. Therefore it is upon the logic rather than upon the crime that you should dwell. You have degraded what should have been a course of lectures into a series of tales' ('The Adventure of the Copper Beeches'). But when (in 'The Adventure of the Blanched Soldier') Holmes tries to tell the story himself, he can only reproduce exactly the same techniques employed by Watson: 'I am compelled to admit that, having taken my pen in my hand, I do begin to realize that the matter must be presented in such a way as may interest the reader.'

26. Hence, the great possibilities detective fiction offers to kitsch, that is, to the ostentatious deployment of prefabricated and superfluous 'literary effects', of which Raymond Chandler was master. His Marlowe continuously encapsulates, within the process of detection, digressions which, strictly speaking, have nothing to do with it (the thoughts on the fate of the beetle in *Farewell My Lovely*) and he never passes up the opportunity of a flashy metaphor ('he looked about as inconspicuous as a tarantula on a slice of angel food. . .'). That which has no value for detective fiction is passed off as *aesthetic value*: a nostalgic object which the work imperative and the readers' (and life's) vulgarity relegate to oblivion.

27. 'It [man's awareness of his existence] appears, on the one hand, as something which is *subjectively* justified in the social and historical situation, as something which can and should be understood, i.e. as "right". At the same time, *objectively*, it by-passes the essence of the evolution of society and fails to pinpoint it and express it adequately. That is to say, objectively, it appears as a "false consciousness".' (Georg Lukács, *History and Class Consciousness*, London 1971, p. 50).

28. 'If we view the relation between text and reader as a kind of self-regulating system . . . there is a constant "feedback" of "information" already received, so that he himself is bound to insert his own ideas into the process of communication. . . . The dynamic interaction between text and reader has the character of an event, which helps to create the impression that we are involved in something real. . .' (W. Iser, 'The Reality of Fiction: a Functionalist Approach to Literature', *New Literary History*, VII, 1, autumn 1975, pp. 19–20.)

29. Karl Marx, *Capital*, Volume 3, Harmondsworth 1981, pp. 956, 968 (my italics).

30. Nikolas Rose, 'Fetishism and Ideology: a Review of Theoretical Problems', in *Ideology and Consciousness*, no. 2, autumn 1977, p. 37.

31. Lucio Colletti, *From Rousseau to Lenin*, London 1972, pp. 234–5.

32. Georg Simmel, 'On the Concept and the Tragedy of Culture', in *The Conflict in Modern Culture and Other Essays*, New York 1968, pp. 35–6, 41–2.

Kindergarten

1. Edmondo De Amicis, *Cuore*, Milan 1886: references are to the authorized translation by G. S. Godkin, *Heart*, London 1895. Ferenc Molnár, *A Pál-utcai fiúk*, Budapest 1907: quotations here have been translated from *I ragazzi di via Pál*, Milan 1978, and page references are to that edition. The English title used is that of an out-of-print translation by Louis Rittenberg, New York 1927; Florence Montgomery, *Misunderstood*, London 1869. [Satisfactory translation of Moretti's term

letteratura commovente has proved very difficult. 'Tear-jerker' and 'weepie' are inappropriately perjorative, yet the literal 'moving literature' is neither specific enough nor emphatic enough to serve the purpose of the Italian phrase. The imperfect solution adopted here is to use the words *moving* and *moving literature*, with inverted commas. – Verso/NLB]

2. The return to a preliminary truth is underlined in the sentences which follow the 'moving' one: '"In yours, father? you've always got Miles in yours. You never take *me* in your arms." "I didn't ever think you would care to come, my little Humphrey." "Oh! but I often should, though; only I knew you would rather have him." "Oh, hush! hush! . . ."' (*Misunderstood*, p. 285). '[János Bóka] did not care if, for the first time in his life, he did not show himself to be calm in unfamiliar circumstances; he did not care if he felt like a child. He continued to cry . . .' (*The Paul Street Boys*, p. 183)

3. Humphrey is by now condemned to death and Ferruccio is actually dead. In Bóka's case, however, it is someone else who dies ('He too realized what everyone had understood but no-one had had the courage to say. He too saw his little soldier was fading away. He knew what end awaited him, and that the end was not far off. *The Paul Street Boys*, p. 183). Unlike *Heart* or *Misunderstood*, Molnárs novel has *two* protagonists, Nemecsek and Bóka. This structural feature (imitated by Segal in *Love Story*) makes it, as we shall see, the most interesting example of 'moving' literature.

4. J. M. Lotman, *The Structure of the Artistic Text*, Ann Arbor 1977, p. 267.

5. As Erwin Panofsky wrote in a famous essay also devoted to the problem of point of view: 'Perspective . . . may, to apply Ernst Cassirer's felicitously coined term to the history of art, be called one of those "symbolic forms" through which "a spiritual meaning is joined to a concrete sensuous sign and becomes intimately identified with this sign"'. And further on: 'The history of perspective may be understood with equal right as a triumph of the distancing and objectifying feeling for reality or as a triumph of the human will to power which negates distances; equally as a consolidation and systematization of the external world or as an extension of the sphere of the ego.' 'Die Perspektive als "symbolische Form"' in Fritz Saxl, ed., *Vorträge der Bibliothek Warburg 1924—25*, Leipzig-Berlin 1927, pp. 268 and 287.

6. This is what distinguishes 'moving' literature from tragedy. Tragedy also revolves round an implacable antagonism between actual behaviour and culturally recognized values. But in the course of the tragic action, the sphere of values, rather than being reasserted in a clear-cut way as in the endings we are examining here, becomes increasingly ambiguous and unrecognizable. This impedes the spontaneous and immediate emotional concord essential for making one cry. The best example is perhaps the frequently cruel and hypocritical Hamlet of the last two acts: how can one cry over his fate? Things are different in *Othello* and *King Lear*, but only as regards Desdemona and Cordelia. Othello and Lear, who inevitably draw most of the audience's attention, undergo metamorphoses comparable to Hamlet's. The only one of Shakespeare's plays which might conceivably be classified as a 'tear-jerker' is *Romeo and Juliet*, and it is perhaps no accident that critics have always felt ill at ease when they want to assign it to a specific 'genre'.

7. The problems we have touched on in the last four paragraphs are a long way from having found a satisfactory solution within literary theory, although they are evidently crucial ones. The day one decides to look again at the concept and the period of 'realism' in fiction – a task which critics in recent years have studiously avoided – then some advance might perhaps be made.

8. ' "Think of it, Ferruccio! Think of that wretched youth of this village, Vito Mozzoni, who is now in the city, playing the vagabond; who at twenty-four has already been twice in prison; he who has made his poor mother die of a broken heart, and made his father fly, in desperation and shame, to Switzerland. Think of that bad creature whose greeting your father would be ashamed to return, always wandering about with rascals worse than himself. . ." ' (*Heart*, p. 166).

9. This model of the transmission of values has backfired against *Heart* itself (there is justice in this world after all): who ever looks at it again, once they have escaped the five elementary grades? *Heart* is 'part of' school in Italy in an essential way, like break, the Christmas holidays and the unique fear of not knowing the lesson. Once one finishes school these things lose all meaning, and one is even amazed that they could ever have possessed any.

10. From now on I refer exclusively to Enrico Bottini's diary: the rhetorical system, and the cultural values, at work in the 'monthly stories' are far closer to those of *Misunderstood* or *The Paul Street Boys* than to the rest of *Heart*. I cannot explain why there should be this structural discontinuity in De Amicis's book. But there is no doubt at all that it is present. It is confirmed by the fact that Enrico's diary never contains one word of commentary on the 'monthly stories': almost as if he hadn't read them, or hadn't managed to understand them. [The narrative of *Heart* is in the form of a diary, divided into months, by the schoolboy Enrico Bottini. Each month he transcribes a story which the teacher tells the class. This is always an exemplary tale about a good boy or girl from one of the various regions of united Italy. The tale of Ferruccio, 'Romagnol Blood', is the monthly story for March. – Translator's note.]

11. Consider the only two deaths in the diary part of *Heart*: that of Garrone's mother (when Garrone is already 'a man') and that of Enrico's ex-teacher (when Enrico is past the first grade). Is it accidental that on each occasion the woman who dies is one whose son, or pupil, has 'grown up'? Is it not the case that the accusing finger is implicitly pointed at growing up as the cause of that death, since once a son has grown up, what is there left for a mother to do in a De Amicis novel? And who would ever want to grow up in the face of such a deadly interlocking of cause and effect?

12. This 'adult' behaviour is copied by the members of the Putty Club, a gang of boys with purely economic ends, assailed by continued, utterly petty rivalries. Molnár devotes a great deal of space to the dealings of the Club, probably in order to heighten the contrast between this kind of behaviour and the very different ideals governing the gang led by Boka. But it is worth remembering that when, at the end of the battle, the two rival gangs break up, the Putty Club reforms and the whole of the penultimate chapter (when Nemecsek is already dying) is taken up with its umpteenth meeting. As if to say: the real test, the real battle is not against the Botanical Gardens Gang and its general Ferenc Ács, but against these boy-adults, already so prosaic and, when the need arises, cruel. It should not be forgotten that Nemecsek's death is ultimately caused precisely by his desire to exculpate himself from the accusations of the Putty Club, which had scorned and humiliated him by mistaking what was really an act of heroism for a betrayal.

13. Walter Benjamin, 'Fate and Character' in *One-Way Street and Other Writings*, London 1979, p. 127. Almost identical considerations are to be found in *The Origin of German Tragic Drama*, London 1977.

14. Whether the civilization and culture of bourgeois Europe have actually been faithful to this ideal is a different matter altogether. It is quite clear that *Bildung* was always reserved for the few – the very few. If one looks at the history of the novel – which is generally considered the locus classicus of the development of this

ideal – there are excellent reasons for believing that it has been one long attempt to frustrate, rather than promote, the concept of *Bildung*. I shall touch on this again in the next section of this essay, but the problem clearly needs a much more extensive treatment.

15. T. W. Adorno, 'Sociology and Psychology II', p. 92.

16. Hegel, *Phenomenology of Spirit*, Oxford 1979, pp. 214–5 and 221.

17. Ibid., p. 226.

18. Hegel, *Aesthetics*, Oxford 1975, p. 567: 'But in romantic love everything turns on the fact that *this* man loves precisely *this* woman, and she him. The sole reason why it is just this man or this individual woman alone is grounded in the person's own private character, in the contingency of caprice.' What could be more 'merely intended' than the superiority of *that* person over *all others?*

19. Ibid., p. 559: 'the man of honour . . . fabricates capricious aims for himself, presents himself in a certain [assumed] character, and therefore binds himself in his own eyes and those of others to something which has neither obligatoriness nor necessity in itself. In that event it is not the thing itself but his subjective idea which puts difficulties and complications in his way because it becomes a point of honour to uphold the character he has assumed.' One cannot help seeing here the always *excessive*, disproportionate obstinacy of our little heroes.

20. *Phenomenology of Spirit*, pp. 234–5.

21. *Aesthetics*, p. 593.

22. Professor Giuseppe Petronio, in certain reflections on my essay on detective literature, has observed that to wheel on Marx, Jakobson or Lévi-Strauss in order to talk about Conan Doyle is quite idiotic (see the introduction to G. Petronio, *Letteratura di massa. Letteratura di consumo*, Bari 1979, pp. XVI–XVIII). Who knows what sort of face he will pull now on finding Hegel arm-in-arm with Nemecsek! It is obvious that one can easily find a lot of Hegel in Goethe and a lot of Goethe in Hegel: how could it be otherwise? But the great intellectual construction is not the one which always surfaces *only* in the masterpieces of other great intellectuals. It is that which seizes, channels and modifies the 'spririt of the age' over the *entire* scale of its manifestations, from the highest to the most negligible. I also realize that finding Hegel in Goethe is easy and 'safe', while finding him in Molnár is arduous and perhaps wrong. But unfortunately university teachers are paid to develop arguments too.

23. At the opposite pole from the character who stands firm to the last is evidently the type of the *traitor*, who is also, according to Julia Kristeva, the novelistic hero *par excellence* ('in the novel [unlike in the epic] the hero does not turn into a traitor, he *is* a traitor.' 'Narration et transformation', *Semiotica* I (1969) 4, p. 436.) *The Paul Street Boys* also contains the story of a traitor – Geréb – who subsequently repents, managing to redeem himself completely and finally winning back our sympathy. His story would be the ideal example with which to show the moral elasticity of the novelistic world and the advantages of compromise. But it is symptomatic that Molnár does not make Geréb the protagonist of the novel, and that his story is relegated to the margins of the plot, like a possible and acknowledged – but rejected – narrative model.

24. Sigmund Freud, 'Civilization and its Discontents' (1930) in Freud, Volume XXI, p. 81.

25. Michel Foucault, *Histoire de la folie à l'âge classique*, Paris 1961, pp. 549–50.

The Long Goodbye

1. 'The conflict of 1914–18 merely precipitated and immeasurably aggravated a crisis that it had not created. But the roots of the dilemma could not be discerned at the time; and the horrors and devastations of the Great War seemed to the survivors the obvious source of the obstacles to international organization that had so unexpectedly emerged. For suddenly neither the economic nor the political system of the world would function and the terrible injuries inflicted on the substance of the race by World War I appeared to offer an explanation. In reality the post-war obstacles to peace and stability derived from the same sources from which the Great War itself had sprung.' (Karl Polanyi, *Origins of Our Time: The Great Transformation*, London 1945, pp. 30–1).

2. Alberto Asor Rosa, 'Cultura e società di massa', in *Quaderni storici*, 20, 1972.

3. Stephen Heath, 'Ambiviolences', *Tel Quel*, 50, 1972.

4. Umberto Eco, *Le poetiche di Joyce*, 2nd edn., Turin 1966, pp. 91–2.

5. Lucio Colletti and Claudio Napoleoni, *Il futuro del capitalismo: crollo o sviluppo?*, Bari-Rome 1970, pp. 153–4 (A partial translation of Colletti's essay has been published under the title 'The Theory of the Collapse of Capitalism' in Ted Honderich, ed., *Social Ends and Political Means*, London 1976.)

6. Karl Marx, *Theories of Surplus Value*, New York 1952, p. 388.

7. Karl Marx, *Capital*, Volume 1, London 1957, p. 45. At this point it is necessary to refer to *Ulysses* – to the 'Circe' chapter in particular. Here Joyce translates 'the nebulous world of religion' (the chapter is also known as 'Walpurgisnacht') back into the everyday reality of the metropolis. All of a sudden, commodities emerge as the modern divinities: objects slip out of people's control and start to move, sing, and talk. Conversely, people fall prey to continuous metamorphoses that dominate and suffocate them to the extent that they lose all identity in this alienating merry-go-round, which is evidence of the precariousness of social and psychic roles.

8. E. J. Hobsbawm, *Industry and Empire*, Harmondsworth 1971, pp. 130–1, 151. Cf also Maurice Dobb, *Studies in the Development of Capitalism*, London 1946, pp. 313–4.

9. Cf. Rudolph Hilferding, *Finance Capital: A Study of the Latest Phase of Capitalist Development* (London 1981, p. 408, note 8): 'There can be no doubt that the different course of development taken by the banking system in England, which gives the banks far less influence over industry, is one cause of the greater difficulty of cartelization in England. . . Improvements in the organization of English industry, particularly the growth of combinations in recent years, are due to American and German competition. *English industry has been retarded by its monopoly on the world market. . .*' (italics mine).

10. Stuart J. Woolf, 'Le trasformazioni del mondo europeo 1880–1910', *Quaderni Storici*, 20, 1972.

11. Alick West, *Crisis and Criticism and selected Literary Essays*, London 1975, pp. 120–1.

12. *Ulysses*, Harmondsworth 1968, p. 567. All quotations are from this edition.

13. Mirsky's and Radek's texts are included in the anthology *James Joyce: The Critical Heritage*, vol. 2 (1928–41), Robert H. Deming, ed., London 1970, pp. 592, 625.

14. The best analysis of the overall significance of this phenomenon is Perry Anderson's 'Components of National Culture', *New Left Review*, 50, 1968. For the literary side of the question – which is also the most conspicuous – see Christopher

Caudwell, *Romance and Realism. A Study in English Bourgeois Literature*, Princeton 1970, and Terry Eagleton, *Exiles and Emigrés*, London 1970. It is also worth noting, however, that the immigrants directive function emerges even in the economic sphere (the political domain, which is traditionally 'closed', remains extraneous to the phenomenon and in obtaining this immunity, pays the price of provincialism). Cf. Hobsbawm, *Industry and Empire*, p. 169. 'The somnolence of the economy was already obvious in British society in the last decades before 1914. Already the rare dynamic entrepreneurs of Edwardian Britain were, more often than not, foreigners or minority groups (the increasingly important German-Jewish financiers who provided the excuse for much of the pervasive anti-semitism of the period, the Americans so important in the electrical industry, the Germans in chemicals, Quakers and late-flowering provincial dissenters like Lever, who exploited the new resources of the tropical empire).'

15. The choice enacted in *Ulysses*, of squeezing the time of the novel into one day, is truly radical. By doing so, Joyce is telling us that all days are the same: this devastates – to Lukác's dismay – historical and literary 'perspective' (which is one of the basic structural features of the novel as genre) and with it the idea of historical 'progress'. Such a choice was, however, possible only for someone who was so engrossed in the specificity of the English crisis as to be oblivious of the conspicuous phenomena of reorganization taking place elsewhere. A comparison of Joyce and Kafka is revealing here, and, if carried out systematically, would help us to understand many aspects of the link between literature, ideology, and society in our century.

As regards the problem at hand – 'time' in the novel – Kafka could justifiably be placed at the opposite pole from Joyce: his novels develop almost exclusively along the diachronic axis and have as their core an irremediable conflict (unthinkable in Joyce) between an isolated individual and impersonal apparatuses of power (the Bank–Court–Church triumvirate, unified finally in the Castle) which already belong to the world of twentieth-century capitalism. The outcome of Kafka's diachronic plots, needless to say, also devastates all consolatory 'perspectives'.

16. I believe it secondary that, in *The Waste Land*, myth is incapable of fulfilling this function completely and in the end shares history's anarchic futility: the point is that the poem stages a continual tension, a reiterated opposition between these two poles, so that religion – which closes *The Waste Land* and ushers in the Eliot of the following years – is called upon to resolve the same problems that faced the myth: it is indeed a sort of super-myth.

17. That it is a myth about a *King* is as important as its being a myth: it indicates that society can regenerate itself only by starting *from the summit*: it evidences the problem of this summit's *consciousness*, and hence underscores the essential function of a *dominant culture* and of literature as an example of formal and ordering ability: with this, one returns exactly to the specific function of myth.

18. Max Horkheimer and Theodor W. Adorno, *Dialectic of Enlightenment*, London 1973, pp. 43–4, 46, 61 (italics mine). Horkheimer's and Adorno's interpretation of Homer is certainly questionable, but what I am concerned with here is not the true historical meaning of the *Odyssey*, but rather the role the poem played in shaping Western imagination. (In this respect, I believe that the *Dialectic of Englightenment* offers us a faithful picture.)

19. *Science & Sociology*, vol 28, no. 1, winter 1964.

20. Ernst Cassirer, *Language and Myth*, New York 1946, pp. 33, 32 (italics mine).

21. Umberto Eco, *Le poetiche di Joyce*, p. 78 (italics mine).

22. Here too Kafka's narrative technique is at the opposite pole from Joyce's. In Kafka's novels, an equally radical destruction of individual freedom and unity proceeds from completely different causes. The reason no longer lies 'within' the individual and his inability to control his desires and ideal associations rationally – but 'outside' him, in his inevitable surrender to a practical and ideological authority which denies him any appeal to 'concrete' evidence. Kafka's narrative technique, therefore, does not express 'confusion', but, rather, a rigorous and abstract rationality.

23. Baran and Sweezy, p. 24.

24. Cassirer, p. 13.

25. Galvano Della Volpe, *Critique of Taste*, London 1978, p. 240.

26. Ernst R. Curtius, 'Technique and Thematic Development of James Joyce', in Deming, ed., p. 469.

27. The quotation, taken from Musil's journal, is included in Cesare Cases's introduction to *L'uomo senza qualità*, Torino 1972, pp. xviii–xix.

28. The difference between 'decadent' poetics and *Ulysses* can be summed up in the following formula: in the former a single signifier produces many signifieds, whereas in Joyce a single signified produces many signifiers. This reversal dissolves the demiurgic role of the author, who is placed on the same level as all other possible authors.

29. *Ulysses* is not, therefore, a work 'bristling with possibilities' and consequently 'open', as Eco would have it: the idea of 'possibility' that it communicates has lost all concreteness and objectivity (as Lukács very clearly saw in *The Meaning of Contemporary Realism*) and has become a subjective and merely formal phantasm. In *Ulysses*, in other words, everything is possible because everything is indifferent.

From *The Waste Land* to the Artificial Paradise

1. Perhaps the most famous example: 'When a poet's mind is perfectly equipped for work, it is constantly amalgamating disparate experience; the ordinary man's experience is chaotic, irregular, fragmentary. The latter falls in love, or reads Spinoza, and these two experiences have nothing to do with each other, or with the noise of the typewriter or the smell of cooking; in the mind of the poet these experiences are always forming new wholes.' ('The Metaphysical Poets' (1921), Frank Kermode, ed., *Selected Prose of T. S. Eliot*, London 1975, p. 64.)

2. More exactly: it forms the skeleton of the first three sections of the poem, justifiably the most famous and interesting. Alessandro Serpieri ('Il doppio registro del *Waste Land*', in *Hopkins – Eliot – Auden. Saggi sul parallelismo poetico*, Bologna 1969) has written a very convincing essay on *The Waste Land*'s structural discontinuity and the consequent shift from the mythical to the allegorical–didactic method.

3. 'Ulysses, Order, and Myth', *The Dial*, November 1923.

4. Georg Lukács, *The Theory of the Novel*, London 1978, pp. 46, 56.

5. 'On Sense and Reference', in Peter Geach and Max Black, eds., *Translations from the Philosophical Writings of Gottlob Frege*, Oxford 1952, p. 57.

6. Ibid., pp. 59–60.

7. Max Weber, '"Objectivity" in Social Science and Social Policy', in *The Methodology of the Social Sciences*, New York 1949, p. 57.

8. Ibid., p. 58.

9. This is, for example, the function of the principle of 'adequate causation': 'the *one-sided* analysis of cultural reality from specific "points of view" . . . is free from the charge of arbitrariness to the extent that it is successful iin producing insights into interconnections which have been shown to be valuable for the causal explanation of concrete historical events.' (Ibid., p. 71).

10. 'The Letter of Lord Chandos', in *Selected Prose*, London 1952, pp. 133–5.

11. R. M. Rilke, *The Duino Elegies*, New York 1972, I, lines 69–78.

12. 'L'impassibilité!' So opens Lukács's essay on Stefan George ('The New Solitude and Its Poetry', in *Soul and Form*, London 1974, p. 79). And later: 'The man of George's songs . . . is a lonely man detached from all social bonds. The content of each of his songs and that of their totality is something that one must understand, yet never can: that two human beings can never become one. . . . In George's poems there is virtually no complaint: it looks life straight in the eyes, calmly, with resignation perhaps, yet always courageously, always with its head held high. . . . A fine, strong, courageous farewell, after the fashion of noble souls, without complaint or lamentation, with broken heart yet with a firm tread, "composed" as the wonderful, all-comprising, truly Goethean expression has it.' (Ibid., pp. 87–90.)

13. Sigmund Freud, *Civilization and its Discontents*, in James Strachey with Anna Freud, ed., *The Standard Edition of the Complete Psychological Works of Sigmund Freud*, vol. 21 (1927–31), London 1961, p. 76.

14. 'Hamlet And His Problems', *The Sacred Wood* (1920), London 1967, p. 100, italics mine.

15. On this, see Terry Eagleton, *Exiles and Émigrés: Studies in Modern Literature*, London 1970, p. 140: 'In the early poems, the objective correlative, in a sense broader than the realizations of local imagery, is not achieved; or, to put it more exactly, the subject-matter of some of these early poems is itself the quest for the objective correlative.'

16. G. Ferraro, *Il linguaggio del mito*, Milano 1979, pp. 164–5.

17. Ibid., p. 22.

18. Claude Lévi-Strauss, *The Savage Mind*, London 1962, p. 223.

19. '. . . the universe is never charged with sufficient meaning and . . . the mind always has more meanings available than there are objects to which to relate them.' It is precisely this discrepancy between a world too 'poor' in meaning and a culture too 'rich' in inapplicable values that myth attempts to heal. (Claude Lévi-Strauss, *Structural Anthropology*, Harmondsworth 1972, p. 184.)

20. *The Savage Mind*, p. 22.

21. Ibid., p. 21

22. The past as an immense heap of materials to use at will: from this point of view *The Waste Land* is the literary translation of one of the great nineteenth-century cultural institutions: the museum. The work of art preserved in the museum, like Eliot's 'quotations', is always the product of a decontextualization: to be brought to the museum, it must be torn from its original setting. (To put it more prosaically, it must be stolen: and Eliot's remark – 'immature poets imitate; mature poets steal' – could well have been Lord Elgin's motto.) In compensation, however, the museum piece is subtracted from the devastating effects of time and all expedients are used to make it virtually immortal: in the same way, their arrangement within the mythic structure confers on *The Waste Land*'s thefts a metatemporal validity.

23. *The Savage Mind*, pp. 232, 234. Claude Lefort expresses similar concepts in an essay of 1952 ('Sociétés sans histoire et historicité', in *Les formes de l'histoire*,

Paris 1978, p. 39): primitive societies also find themselves in the position of having to confront 'events', but they do not possess a culture capable of ascribing them value. 'Event' and 'meaning' emerge thus as unreconcilable entities: 'Whatever the impact of the event on society and culture or the diffusion of its effects may be, it does not put a dialectics of change into operation. It is not a bearer of meaning; people seem intent on assimilating it, on favouring the compromise between the imperatives of adaptation and the desire for preservation and in no way give into the appeal of the *new*.'

24. Oswald Spengler, *The Decline of the West*, London 1926, p. 96.

25. Ibid., p. 112. Spengler's 'Culture' (*Kultur*), while having a long and specifically German tradition behind it, coincides on the essential points with Eliot's 'Myth'.

26. Lucien Febvre, 'De Spengler à Toynbee. Quelques philosophies opportunistes de l'histoire', *Revue de Metaphysique et de Morale*, Paris 1936, pp. 579, 578.

27. *Structural Anthropology*, p. 211.

28. Theodor W. Adorno, 'The Stars Down to Earth: The Los Angeles Times Astrology Column: A Study in Secondary Superstition', *Jahrbuch für Amerikastudien*, Heidelberg 1957, Band 2, p. 27.

29. Cléanth Brooks, *Modern Poetry and the Tradition*, New York 1965, p. 167.

30. 'The pre-bourgeois order does not yet know psychology, the over-socialized society knows it no longer. . . . The social power-structure hardly needs the mediating agencies of ego and individuality any longer. . . The truly contemporary types are those whose actions are motivated neither by an ego nor, strictly speaking, unconsciously, but mirror objective trends like an automaton. Together they enact a senseless ritual to the beat of a compulsively repetitive rhythm and become emotionally impoverished. . .' (T. W. Adorno, 'Sociology and Psychology – II', *New Left Review*, 47, January–February 1968, p. 95.)

31. This, incidentally, brings it close to the first great manifestations of mass literature. The world of detective fiction is also populated only with stereotypes, pure and simple bearers of a social role: and he who does not make do with what he is inevitably ends up as a criminal. On this point, and others still, it would be illuminating – though it is unfortunately impossible here – to compare Eliot's and Wagner's work systematically: the *Tetralogy* was the first attempt to found the most advanced European culture on a mythical structure.

32. There are only two exceptions: lines 359–65 and 422–33. The first is a passage of dubious usefulness (motivated, according to Eliot, by what happened during one of the Antarctic expeditions); the second is an echo of the compositive method used in the first three sections, by now completely tempered by the prevailing allegorical-didactic register.

33. This term was already quite outmoded in Eliot's times; he probably used it – as in the case of 'significance' – because the word allowed him to rejoin meanings which, with the passing of time and the specialization of language, had grown apart from each other: 'real person', 'literary character', 'actor', 'social role'.

34. Max Horkheimer and Theodor W. Adorno, *Dialectic of Enlightenment*, London 1973, p. 31.

35. Clearly I do not mean that prohibitions and taboos no longer exist in mass culture. The point is, rather, that the forbidden is no longer the hidden source of cultural production, as was the case in the Freudian system, which, not accidentally, was founded on the concept on 'negation', whereby a cultural phenomenon can exist only in so far as it 'negates', that is, makes a forbidden desire acceptable. As

Marcuse rightly remarks in the first lines of *Eros and Civilization*, for Freud 'The methodical sacrifice of libido . . . *is* culture.' (London 1972, p. 23.)

Yet it seems to me that the dynamics involved have changed over the past decades and that the forbidden areas are ever more reduced to mere residues destined to corrosion by passing time: they may be perceived as obstacles, as painful or even intolerable limitations: but they no longer possess a *founding* role with respect to our cultural system. It is not therefore that taboos have disappeared, but that their *function* has changed.

36. '. . . the knowledge contained in a mythological concept is confused, made of yielding, shapeless associations. One must firmly stress this open character of the concept; it is not at all an abstract, purified essence; it is a formless, unstable, nebulous condensation . . . *quantitatively*, the concept is much poorer than the signifier, it often does nothing but re-present itself.' (Roland Barthes, 'Myth Today' in *Mythologies*, London 1972, pp. 119–20.) One must remember that, as the title of the essay says, Barthes is dealing with myth *today*: anthropological criticism has tended to overlook this specification.

37. Horkheimer and Adorno, p. 131.

38. Roland Barthes, 'Structure du fait divers', in *Essais critiques*, Paris 1964, pp. 196–7.

39. Jean Baudrillard, *La Société de consommation : ses myths, ses structures*, Paris 1970, pp. 39, 113.

40. Ibid., pp. 80–1: 'The consumer experiences [the process of differentiation through consumption] as freedom, as an aim, as a choice of his distinctive behaviour, he does not experience it as a compulsion towards differentiation and obedience to a code. To differentiate oneself is always at the same time to establish the order of differences which is, from the start, the reality of the total society and which inevitably overcomes the individual. . . . It is, however, this *compulsion of relativity* which determines, in the measure in which it is referred to it, that the differential inscription *will never end*. It can only give reason to the fundamental character of consumption, its unlimited character – which is an inexplicable dimension for any theory of needs and satisfactions. . . The distinctive sign is always *both* positive *and* negative – precisely this makes it refer to other signs constantly and causes an ultimate dissatisfaction in the consumer.'

41. Frege, pp. 62–3.

42. A reconstruction of this process within English culture can be found in Luciano Anceschi's essays collected in *Da Bacone a Kant*, Bologna 1972.

43. Herbert Marcuse, *One Dimensional Man*, London 1972, p. 82.

44. Baudrillard, pp. 191, 197.

45. An indirect proof of this state of affairs can be found in Eliot's theoretical writings. A careful reading demonstrates that it is almost impossible to speak of Eliot's 'aesthetic', if by aesthetic one means the delimitation of a strictly autonomous sphere. From his first essays, Eliot was already interested in art not for its distinctive features and, therefore, its limits, but for its capacity for *fusion*: because it seems to him the ideal means for knocking down boundaries between various cultural areas and reuniting them. All his most famous remarks clearly move in this direction: art must be all-inclusive, it must lead to the formation of 'integral wholes', it must reunite sense and intellect . . .

46. The quotation is from the second letter in *On The Aesthetic Education of Man*, London 1954, p. 26.

47. Many objections have been raised to the last two sentences. Since what is done cannot simply be undone, I have left them as they were, although I now feel

that the phrasing was slightly misleading and the whole idea expressed in a far too elliptical way. What I meant – and still maintain – is that the 'dominant culture' – the most pervasive value-system of Western societies – is fundamentally extraneous and hostile to war. War has lost the significance it had in nineteenth-century Europe (let alone in previous social formations). This makes traditional wars – based on long-term conscription, which is the 'democratic' way of forming an army – more and more difficult, if not simply inconceivable. Western societies have therefore probably become incapable of waging and winning wars *as societies*: as collective bodies engaged in a general mobilization and bound together by a set of common principles, like post-revolutionary France at the end of the eighteenth century. Yet I now realize that I grossly overlooked those developments of military technology which have made the model of 'democratic war' obsolete. Contemporary wars are fought – and might be – by a body of select professional soldiers, or by a team of nuclear experts. Hence they no longer need a 'belligerent' value-system and a compact society to back them up. By pushing the argument further, we encounter the paradox that wars can now take place *precisely because* the dominant culture feels extraneous or hostile to everything that concerns the State. The 'paradise of liberties' does in fact work both ways: it frees 'everyday life' and, at the same time, leaves the State much freer to act through separate bodies on which little or no public control can be exerted. This situation was elegantly summed up one hundred and fifty years ago by Alexis de Tocqueville: 'Democratic Nations are Naturally Desirous of Peace – Democratic Armies, of War.'

48. Max Weber, *The Protestant Ethic and the Spirit of Capitalism*, London 1965, p. 53.

49. Ibid., p. 80: '. . . the valuation of the fulfilment of duty in worldly affairs as the highest form which the moral activity of the individual could assume. . . . inevitably gave everyday worldly activity a religious significance, and . . . first created the conception of a calling in this sense.'

Index

8969--